Controlling Corruption

BY THE SAME AUTHOR

Choosing Elites

Data Analysis for Development

Elitism and Meritocracy in Developing Countries

Tropical Gangsters

CONTROLLING CORRUPTION

Robert Klitgaard

UNIVERSITY OF CALIFORNIA PRESS
Berkeley | Los Angeles | London

University of California Press
Berkeley and Los Angeles, California

University of California Press, Ltd.
London, England

First Paperback Printing 1991

Library of Congress Cataloging-in-Publication Data

Klitgaard, Robert E.
Controlling Corruption.

Includes index.
1. Corruption (in politics) 2. Corruption (in politics)—Developing countries—Case studies. I. Title.
JF1525.C66K45 1987 350.9'94 86-14656
ISBN 978-0-520-07408-8 (alk. paper)

Printed in the United States of America

11 10 09 08
9 8 7 6 5

The paper used in this publication is both acid-free and totally chlorine-free (TCF). It meets the minimum requirements of ANSI/NISO Z39.48-1992 (R 1997) (*Permanence of Paper*). ♾

For TOM SCHELLING

In my own thinking they have never been separate. Motivation for the purer theory came almost exclusively from preoccupation with (and fascination with) "applied" problems; and the clarification of theoretical ideas was absolutely dependent on an identification of live examples.

Thomas C. Schelling, *The Strategy of Conflict*

Contents

Preface to the Paperback Edition

The first thing that needs to be said is that corruption is a sensitive subject.

In my experience with policymakers and students from many countries, the topic tends to evoke a particular pattern of reactions. First there is evasion. Then excuses. And finally, with luck, useful analysis.

Evasion. You encounter almost a reflex. "Nothing can be done about corruption," someone tells you flatly. "Corruption is everywhere in the world and has existed throughout history. You have it in America, in Japan, not just here in X. And if the people on top are corrupt, if the whole system is corrupt, as they are here, it's hopeless." An article from Guatemala illustrates this alarmingly widespread view. It begins: "When in a society the shameless triumph; when the abuser is admired; when principles end and only opportunism prevails; when the insolent rule and the people tolerate it; when everything becomes corrupt but the majority is quiet because their slice is waiting. . . ." After a series of such laments, the author concludes: "When so many 'whens' unite, perhaps it is time to hide oneself, time to suspend the battle; time to stop being a Quixote; it is time to review our activities, reevaluate those around us, and return to ourselves."[1]

Excuses. Next you hear that nothing *should* be done about corruption. This reaction has been prevalent among social scientists. "Bribes are a form of gift-giving consistent with local mores," an anthropologist tells you. Someone with an economic bent notes a similarity between a bribe and a market price when a market is not allowed; and isn't that "efficient"? A political scientist points out that in unjust settings corrupt payments may be the only means of making one's wishes known; thus, corruption may be an important avenue of political participation. Some social scientists aver that bribes cannot be distinguished from transactions, that to try to do so is to import Western or one's own normative assumptions. A bribe, a fee for service, a gift: analytically, it is said, they are the same.[2] So—all these views concur—we should not talk too much about corruption or, if we do, should not condemn it. There are many excuses for not tackling the problem of corruption.

Analysis. But the next reaction is more encouraging. Once the subject is broached and taken seriously, the same people who evaded the issue and offered excuses for the phenomenon prove able to analyze concrete situations and devise useful solutions.

This book is designed to help readers analyze corrupt behavior and decide what to do about it. It asks them to set aside a certain cynicism they may have developed on this topic and to read with an open mind.

Corruption is one of the foremost problems in the developing world, and it is receiving much greater attention as we reach the last decade of the century. As poor countries slide into deeper economic trouble, the economic and social devastation that widespread corruption causes cannot be evaded or excused. Around the globe corruption is increasingly a central issue in popular uprisings and election campaigns. In the past two years international aid organizations such as the World Bank, the U.S. Agency for International Development, la Cooperation Française, and the United Nations Development Programme have launched seminars and programs concerned with corruption and what to do about it.

But policy analysis has lagged. True, scholarly work shows how rent seeking and "directly unproductive profit-seeking activities" can be harmful by distorting incentives.[3] Recent research on influence activities in organizations reveals other sources of distortion.[4] And new empirical work documents, despite the social scientists' excuses, that corruption in fact does harm.[5]

Yet too little is said about how to reduce corruption. Typical is a recent article, which contains models of corrupt behavior and its spread. At the end of the article, the author says: "Understanding the microeconomic basis of corruption is the aim of this paper, not suggesting ways of fighting it. Yet a few remarks about the general lines of attack seem to be in order." The statement is followed by a paragraph of vague, schematic, and therefore unhelpful advice.[6]

This book tries to take the practical problem seriously. It presents both *analytical tools* and *case studies* that I hope will kindle enthusiasm and creativity.

Definitions and Ultimate Causes

I will not spend much time on definitions. Corruption exists when an individual illicitly puts personal interests above those of the people and ideals he or she is pledged to serve. It comes in many forms and can range from trivial to monumental. Corruption can involve the misuse of policy instruments—tariffs and credit, irrigation systems and housing policies, the enforcement of laws and rules regarding public safety, the observance of contracts, and the repayment of loans—or of simple procedures. It can occur in the private sector or in the public one—and often occurs in both simultaneously. It can be rare or widespread; in some developing countries, corruption has become systemic.

Corruption can involve promises, threats, or both; can be initiated by a public servant or an interested client; can entail acts of omission or commission; can involve illicit or licit services; can be inside or outside the public organization. The boundaries of corruption are hard to define and depend on local laws and customs. The first task of policy analysis is to disaggregate the types of corrupt and illicit behaviors in the situation at hand and look at concrete examples.[7] I do this by examining five cases of corruption and reform.

I will not spend much time on what might be called the ultimate causes of corruption. An extreme example of the opposite predilection is a recent book by the Nicaraguan accountant Francisco Ramírez Torres. After observing at length that corruption is caused by the family, the school, attitudes toward work, the enterprise, the nation, and the international situation, the author arrives at the level of the individual transgressor. Here the causes of corruption include excessive consumption of alcohol, extramarital activities, speculative losses, excessive gambling, "causes related to vanity," administrative disorganization, resentment inside the business, frustration on the job, "the thirst for illicit enrichment," and five others.[8]

For practical purposes I have found it useful to bracket these undoubtedly important concerns and focus instead on other questions. Even with the imperfect people and societies and international orders we now encounter, what can we do to reduce, if never eliminate, corruption? What can we learn from the experience of other countries?

Consider this excerpt from a fascinating article by the economist Thomas C. Schelling:

> An organization, business or other, is a system of information, rules for decision, and incentives; its performance is different from the individual performances of the people in it. An organization can be negligent without any individual's being negligent. To expect an organization to reflect the qualities of the individuals who work for it or to impute to the individuals the qualities one sees in the organization is to commit what logicians call the 'fallacy of composition.' Fallacy isn't error, of course, but it can be treacherous.[9]

Schelling is addressing the subject of the social responsibility of business, but his insight applies to the topic of this book as well. Too often it is assumed that organizations or entire governments are corrupt simply because people are immoral; and, it is concluded, nothing can be done to curb corruption short of generations of moral education. But let us avoid the fallacy of composition. Let us ask instead how organizations and countries might change their "systems of information, rules for decisions, and incentives" in order to reduce corruption.

Economic Metaphors

In approaching this question, this book employs economic metaphors at two levels. First, it considers the economic calculations of a public *agent*—for example, a tax collector, a prosecutor, a procurement officer. The economic metaphor says that the agent faced with a bribe makes a calculation, trading off the potential personal benefits of accepting the bribe and undertaking a corrupt act against the potential personal costs of doing so. (A similar analysis can be made of the person offering the bribe.) The practical point of the metaphor is this: the agent's potential benefits and costs can be affected by public policy and management.

The policymaker or manager has to make calculations as well. In this book I suppose for the sake of analysis that *the reader* is the *principal* or policymaker—surely, therefore, acting in the public interest.

The principal faces another tradeoff: between the social benefits of reducing the agent's corrupt activity and the social costs of taking various steps to obtain that reduction. The combination of these two metaphors is the *principal-agent-client model* discussed in Chapter 3.

I have found economic metaphors useful in working with policymakers in developing countries. It enables them to confront the topic of corruption without becoming ensnarled in moralisms and local sensitivities. The economic metaphors and the framework are novel for many policymakers and students; they are also antiseptic, "safe." (Contrast an approach based on Islamic ethics or Roman law or professionalism.) In the first instance, corruption becomes just another problem to be analyzed with the tools of public policy and management.

The purpose of using economic reasoning is not to create a formal optimizing model with inevitably highly restrictive assumptions. Rather, I seek in Chapter 3 a heuristic framework that can help policymakers think more creatively about ways to control corruption.

Real Examples

The book uses case studies to explore and elaborate this framework for policymakers. With sensitive subjects like corruption, it is good to begin with the concrete. This is why the book introduces the Philippines case in Chapter 2 before exploring models of corrupt behavior and possible cures.

Many readers familiar with other developing countries will recognize the difficult problems that confronted Justice Plana. Positions in the Philippines Bureau of Internal Revenue were auctioned internally because corruption made them so lucrative. Officials took bribes for reducing taxpayers' obligations. Speed money and embezzlement, to name two quite different forms of corruption, were widespread. Tax officials sometimes extorted tribute from taxpayers. Systematic corruption reached the top ranks of the organization, even the unit whose job it was to investigate misdeeds. Filipino culture is said to encourage all of this—for example, Stanley Karnow ascribes corruption in the Philippines to the *compradazgo* system, a ritual network of relatives and adopted relatives that commands the loyalty of Filipinos more than any formal institution, and to the cultural trait of *utang na loob*, "the debt of gratitude."[10] The country's president was himself known to be corrupt. Under these circumstances, many readers—and many policymakers—might despair that Justice Plana could do little or nothing.

Luckily, Justice Plana concluded otherwise. As Chapters 2 and 3 describe, he launched an exemplary campaign against corruption. His example should help dispel the idea that nothing can be done about corruption. And by linking this case with the economic analysis mentioned above, I hope that the reader will gain a deeper understanding of both.

The book's other cases span areas (police, customs agencies, procurement, the delivery of services), types of illicit behavior (bribery, extortion, speed money, kickbacks, collusion, and fraud), and countries. Cases of judicial or high-level political corruption are, alas, not included. Chapter 7 goes beyond the design of anti-corruption measures to strategies for implementing them—metaphorically, not just what medicine the patient should take but how to induce him or her to take it.

The final chapter reviews some of the major findings and provides suggestions for future research on corruption. It will become clear that I consider this book a first and heuristic step, greatly in need of further theoretical and empirical work. The final chapter also presents some thoughts about the implications of the approach of this book for the field of "development administration" and more generally for the study of developing countries.

I hope the book illustrates a way of thinking about policy analysis. Faced with a topic like corruption, the first task is to disaggregate the types of corruption, their scope and seriousness, the beneficiaries and the losers. One approaches a sensitive subject by highlighting not the moral failures of individuals but the structural failures of information and incentives. One uses a simplifying theory to obtain not an optimizing model under restrictive assumptions but a heuristic framework that enables problem solvers to address the complex problem of corruption in their varied and unique circumstances. Finally, one tries to illuminate both the utility and limitations of the framework by looking at real examples.

Acknowledgments

Many people have favored me with their help and encouragement. Seema Hafeez, Kamran Aslam Khan, Paul Khoo, Deborah Matthews,

Jacinto Solís, Frank Wong, and especially Ana Teresa Gutiérrez San Martín provided excellent research assistance. Leonor Magtolis-Briones, Ledivina Cariño, and Raul de Guzman aided my research on the Philippines case. George Martin's monograph on Korea served as starting point for the analysis in Chapter 6. On one or another portion of the book, I received the comments and suggestions of Edward Banfield, Ledivina Cariño, Robert Coulam, Mia de Kuijper, Shantayanan Devarajan, Jameson Doig, Laurence Dougharty, David Ellwood, Olivia Golden, Philip Heymann, Ira Jackson, Derek Leebaert, Nathaniel Leff, Herman Leonard, Marc Lindenberg, George Martin, John D. Montgomery, Joseph Nye, Dwight Perkins, Susan Rose-Ackerman, Bengt Sandberg, Gregory Treverton, Raymond Vernon, Michael Wallace, Geralyn White, and Richard Zeckhauser. I am grateful to Graham Allison of the Kennedy School of Government, Bruce Bushey of the Ford Foundation in Rio de Janeiro, and Marc Lindenberg of the Instituto Centroamericano de Administración de Empresas in Costa Rica. A grant from the Russell Sage Foundation provided the freedom to complete this book; I am particularly grateful to Marshall Robinson. The Japanese Corporate Associates Program of the Kennedy School of Government also helped support the final stages of the writing. The Spanish edition (*Controlando la Corrupción* [La Paz: Editorial Quipus, 1990]) was made possible by the support of the Hanns Seidel Foundation. Special thanks to Thomas C. Schelling and Richard Zeckhauser for help when it was really needed.

The usual caveat absolving these colleagues and institutions from further responsibility is, of course, in order.

To anyone interested in the subject of this book, I recommend John T. Noonan's *Bribes*.[11] It is a learned account of what might be called the evolution of bribery from ancient times to the present. Noonan shows how different societies and cultures have distinguished, with varying degrees of subtlety and practical effect, "bribes" from "transactions." Noonan emphasizes the ethical, even religious, aspects of corruption that I exclude. Only indirectly does he deal with this book's question of practical policies to reduce corruption. We both agree that, "next to tyranny, corruption is the great disease of government. Skillful surgeons need more than a single way of curing the disease" (p. 700).

Robert Klitgaard
La Paz, Bolivia
30 November 1990

Notes

1. Marta Altolaguirre, "Cuando Sucede . . . ," *La Prensa* (Guatemala City), 22 February 1990 (my translation).

2. The classic statement is Marcel Mauss, *The Gift: Forms and Functions of Exchange in Archaic Societies,* trans. Ian Cunnison (New York: W. W. Norton, 1967 [1925]). For differing views, see Colin Camerer, "Gifts as Economic Signals and Social Symbols," *American Journal of Sociology* 94, Supplement (1988), and Robert Klitgaard, "On Tributes," in *The Strategy of Choice,* ed. Richard J. Zeckhauser (Cambridge: MIT Press, 1991).

3. For example, Susan Rose-Ackerman, *Corruption: A Study in Political Economy* (New York: Academic Press, 1978); T. N. Srinavasan, "Neoclassical Political Economy, the State and Economic Development," *Asian Development Review* 3 (1985): 38–58; and Robert P. Inman, "Markets, Government, and the 'New' Political Economy," in *Handbook of Public Economics,* Vol. 2, ed. Alan J. Auerbach and Martin Feldstein (Amsterdam: North-Holland, 1987).

4. For example, Paul Milgrom and John Roberts, "An Economic Approach to Influence Activities in Organizations," *American Journal of Sociology* 94, Supplement (1988): S154–S179; Milgrom, "Employment Contracts, Influence Activities, and Efficient Organization Design," *Journal of Political Economy* 96 (Jan.–Feb. 1988): 42–60.

5. See Chapter 2. Additional references include United Nations, *Corruption in Government,* TCD/SEM. 90/2. INT-89-R56. (New York: United Nations Department of Technical Co-operation for Development, 1990); Marcela Márquez, Carmen Antony, José Antonio Pérez, and Aida S. de Palacios, *La Corrupción Administrativa en Panamá* (Panama City: Instituto de Criminologia, University of Panama, 1984).

6. Harendra Kanti Dey, "The Genesis and Spread of Economic Corruption: A Microtheoretic Interpretation," *World Development* 17 (April 1989): 510.

7. For an interesting differentiation of forms of corruption—or "the politics of the gut"—in Africa, see Jean-François Bayart, *L'État en Afrique: La Politique du Ventre* (Paris: Fayard, 1989): 87–138.

8. *Los Delitos Económicos en los Negocios* (Managua: Talleres de Don Bosco, 1990), 22–26, 40–50.

9. Thomas C. Schelling, "Command and Control," in *Social Responsibility and the Business Predicament,* ed. James W. McKie (Washington: The Brookings Institution, 1974): 83–84.

10. Stanley Karnow, *In Our Image: America's Empire in the Philippines* (New York: Random House, 1989).

11. Berkeley: University of California Press, 1987.

1 | Introduction

"What worries me more than anything among our problems," said Nigerian President Shehu Shagari in 1982, "is that of moral decadence in our country. There is the problem of bribery, corruption, lack of dedication to duty, dishonesty, and all such vices."

He was right to worry. About a year later his civilian government was toppled in a military coup, which the generals justified by the need to control corruption. This topic dominated the new regime's policies, as foretold in its first press conference in early 1984: "It is necessary to reiterate that this new Administration will not tolerate fraud, corruption, squandermania, abuse of public office for self or group, or other such vices that characterized the administration of the past four years."[1]

The Shagari regime had tried. It had proclaimed an "ethical revolution" to combat corruption. The government had included a code of conduct for public servants in the 1979 constitution, and it had established a Code of Conduct Bureau to enforce the "prescribed behaviors." The leadership had even appointed a cabinet Minister of National Guidance to provide moral leadership against corruption. Yet according to popular accounts, Nigeria had grown even more corrupted, leaving its citizens more alienated from the government and its economy more vulnerable to official venality.

In recent years a remarkable feature of many governmental changes of command has been the promise to do something about the corruption of the previous regime. This is even so when one's predecessor is an intimate ally. In his first speech upon assuming the leadership of the

1. *Africa Now*, November 1982, 55; *The Guardian*, 19 January 1984. I am indebted to Stephen Riley of North Staffordshire Polytechnic for these citations.

Congress Party after his mother's assassination in late 1984, Rajiv Gandhi put government officials in India on notice that the corrupt and dishonest would no longer be tolerated. His overwhelmingly successful election campaign was partially based on promises to fight corruption. In a change of command a leader may even criticize one's own regime. At the inauguration of his successor in 1982, Mexican President José López Portillo decried corruption and the lamentable fact that Mexican citizens illicitly "have taken more money out of Mexico in the past two years than imperialists ever exploited during the entire history of our country."[2] The new Mexican president, Miguel de la Madrid, had built his campaign on the need to combat corruption, and among his first acts in office were the promulgation of a new code of conduct for public officials and the creation of a new agency to fight corruption. This phenomenon is not confined to the developing nations. Upon assuming office, leaders ranging from the late Soviet Chairman Andropov to Massachusetts Governor Dukakis called for new measures against corruption.

But what should such measures include? If in Nigeria "ethical revolutions," bureaucratic purges, codes of conduct, and a Ministry of National Guidance were not sufficient, what should or could be done? As policymakers speak out about the evils of corruption, how should they think about designing and implementing measures to control it?

This book is addressed to government officials, especially in developing countries, who are searching for answers to such questions. With such an intended audience, a cynic might respond, the book will not sell many copies. The prevalence and persistence of corruption are discouraging, for they imply that many policymakers and politicians do not want to control corruption. They may use illicit activities to maintain themselves in power, even at the expense of the nation's development, as has been argued in a careful study of Morocco.[3] Of course, corruption has

2. For further details about allegations of corruption during the administration of President López Portillo, see my *Corruption in Mexico* (Cambridge, Mass.: Kennedy School of Government, Harvard University, 1983). According to Jack Anderson, the Central Intelligence Agency estimates that López Portillo himself took between $1 and $3 billion out of Mexico during his six years in office (Jack Anderson, "Mexico's Riches Were Devoured by Ex-President," *Washington Post*, 18 June 1984, p. B-12).

3. John Waterbury, "Endemic and Planned Corruption in a Monarchical System," *World Politics* (July 1973): 533–55; reprinted in *Bureaucratic Corruption in Sub-Saharan Africa: Toward a Search for Causes and Consequences*, ed. Monday U. Ekpo (Washington, D.C.: University Press of America, 1979), 355–80.

self-serving aspects to those in power, not only as a means for lining one's pockets but as a mechanism for political dealing, forging linkages, and even inducing political participation, as we shall discuss in the next chapter. There are even occasions where corrupt acts may improve economic or organizational efficiency.

That corruption benefits at least some of those in power makes it a difficult problem to tackle. Nonetheless, many leaders and public managers in developing countries want to do better at controlling fraud, bribery, extortion, embezzlement, tax evasion, kickbacks, and other forms of illicit and corrupt behavior. Some of these concerned leaders are top legislators and chief executives. Others hold responsible positions in police forces, customs agencies, tax bureaus, ministries that distribute goods and services, and regulatory agencies. These people see corruption as threatening their agency's mission and the broader goals of national development. They are not naive: they recognize that corruption can never be completely eradicated, and they do not suppose that corruption has a simple cure, as polio has a vaccine. Still these officials would like to reduce many forms of corruption, and their hope is shared by most ordinary citizens in the developing world.

What exactly is the "corruption" they wish to control? It depends. What is corrupt in one society may not be in another. When historian J. S. Furnivall examined why, according to British standards, colonial Burma was so "corrupt," he concluded that in many cases the Burmese were simply following their customary norms of correct conduct.[4] Some of the activities most praised in capitalist economies—private investment, trading and retrading, accumulating resources—may be called "corrupt" in a communist system.[5]

What is lawful, and therefore what is unlawful, depends on the country and culture in question. While this valid insight should not be lost, it must not short-circuit our search for effective anticorruption policies. As a matter of fact, the majority of countries and cultures decry most instances of bribery, fraud, extortion, embezzlement, and most

4. J. S. Furnivall, *Colonial Policy and Practice: A Comparative Study of Burma and Netherlands India* (Cambridge, England: Cambridge University Press, 1948).

5. Several examples are cited in J. M. Montias and Susan Rose-Ackerman, "Corruption in a Soviet-type Economy: Theoretical Considerations," in *Economic Welfare and the Economics of Soviet Socialism: Essays in Honor of Abram Bergson*, ed. Steven Rosefielde (Cambridge, England: Cambridge University Press, 1981), 53–83.

forms of kickbacks on public contracts. Over a wide range of "corrupt" activities, there is little argument that they are wrong and socially harmful.

This point becomes clearer when we get down to specific cases. The following examples display some of the kinds of corruption faced by officials in developing countries. Despite the inevitable peculiarities of their specific contexts, these examples reveal general problems and—as I will try to show in later chapters—general lessons about controlling corruption:

□ *Tax departments.* Place yourself in the Philippines in 1975. Imagine that you have just been appointed to head the Bureau of Internal Revenue (BIR), which is notorious for corruption. Among your major problems is *arreglo*, the practice by which tax examiners take bribes to reduce what taxpayers owe the government.

> The opportunity for collusion presents itself in the review of both income and expenditures. . . . For example, a taxpayer reports a gross income of P100,000 [pesos] but did not report P500,000 which could be gains from capital asset transactions. Extraneous income for activities not directly related to the business or regular activity of a taxpayer cannot be traced easily. However, an enterprising examiner usually has other sources of information. He can conduct investigations and research to get documentary evidence of the unreported income. He accumulates this evidence and confronts the taxpayer. The negotiations begin. If all goes well, the agent may refrain from reporting the discovery of understated income for an "arreglo."[6]

You also find that positions within the BIR are being bought and sold; there is embezzlement; fraudulent tax stamps are being issued; and some tax examiners are extorting money from innocent taxpayers unwilling to complain through a costly process of litigation. Moreover, you are working in a national regime noted for its corruption and cronyism. How would you think about designing and implementing countermeasures? In Chapters 2 and 3 we discuss how one particularly able tax commissioner fought corruption in the Philippines Bureau of Internal Revenue.

□ *Police.* Put yourself in Hong Kong in the early 1970s. Corruption,

6. Leonor Magtolis-Briones, "Negative Bureaucratic Behavior and Development: The Bureau of Internal Revenue" (Paper prepared for the Seminar on Bureaucratic Behavior and Development, College of Public Administration, University of the Philippines, Manila, 3 October 1977).

especially in the police force, has grown so widespread that the new governor appoints a commission to recommend what could be done. The commission finds evidence of deeply rooted, systematic corruption.

> The worst forms are what is described by the Anti-Corruption Office as "syndicated" corruption, that is to say a whole group of officers involved in the collection and distribution of money. For example, it is said that groups of police officers are involved in the collection of payments from pak pai drivers, the keepers of gambling schools and other vice establishments. Frequently the "collection" is far more than corruption in the true sense. It is plain extortion accompanied by veiled threats of violence at the hands of triad gangsters. The "collections" seldom take the form of direct payments to any numbers of the corrupt group of officers. Almost invariably there is the middleman. He is referred to euphemistically as "the caterer." He receives the money: and in some cases, it is said that vast sums are involved.[7]

Many observers believed the Chinese culture in Hong Kong, with its tradition of using public position for private gains and its widespread practices of "gift-giving" and "commissions," provided a fertile ground for corruption. If you were the governor of Hong Kong, what would you do to get police corruption under control? The governor's answer and the ensuing success story of fighting corruption are the subjects of Chapter 4.

□ *Customs agencies.* In many countries customs bureaus are filled with corruption. Illegal imports are permitted in exchange for a bribe. Legal imports are taxed at lower-than-legal rates, again for a bribe. If you were in charge of a customs bureau, how would you think about reducing such activities? Chapter 5 examines Singapore's successful policies for overcoming corruption in its Customs and Excise Department.

□ *Procurement.* Imagine you are a top official in the U.S. Army procurement agency working in Korea in the mid-1970s. You are responsible for hundreds of local procurement contracts every year. You have evidence that Korean contractors are colluding on their bids, leading to exorbitant prices. You have discovered evidence that contractors are bribing your own employees in exchange for altering your agency's supposedly independent cost estimates. What would you do about these problems? The story of the U.S. Army's efforts to overcome corruption in procurement is analyzed in Chapter 6.

7. Excerpt from *Second Report of the Commission of Enquiry Under Sir Alastair Blair-Kerr*, Hong Kong, 1973.

□ *Food distribution.* You have just assumed command of the regional office of the government agency for distribution of wheat and sugar in a poor province threatened by rebel forces. Your organization is full of corruption. Some officers accept kickbacks from local farmers in exchange for letting the farmers sell half of their wheat on the black market. Other officers steal wheat from your government warehouses; still others substitute bad wheat for good, selling the good for personal profit. Your officers are illicitly issuing ration cards to such an extent that there are almost twice as many cards in circulation as there are eligible citizens. How do you begin to address these problems? The true story of an officer we shall call Rafiq Shabir, in a province we shall call Ruritania, is told in Chapter 7.

The literature on international development is surprisingly silent about such problems. One seldom encounters a practically oriented examination of anticorruption policies. Yet corruption is an issue of first-order importance. Illicit practices are widespread in the developing countries. Obviously it is difficult to generalize, but corruption by public officials probably constitutes one of the three or four most harmful problems facing Third World governments. The harm is hard to measure; as we shall see, it is economic as well as political, moral as well as material. Typical is one Asian country's survey that found graft and corruption to be the major cause of "low respect" for government and the second greatest "national problem."[8] Equally typical, if less statistically precise, are remarks like the following, which were spoken by a poor farmer in Bangladesh who had been victimized by a corrupt permit system of sugar procurement:

> To most of the farmers, getting a permit in time is something like getting the moon from the sky, because of the fact that the issuance of permits in a fair way is beyond their imagination. But why? The answer is known to all. Nepotism, trickery, and bribery have become contagious diseases. Stinking, offensive, and loathesome things have become a commonplace influence at the [procurement] center.[9]

8. Harvey Averch et al., *The Matrix of Policy in the Philippines* (Princeton: Princeton University Press, 1971).

9. Reported in Bernard Schaffer, "Access: A Theory of Corruption and Bureaucracy" (Paper presented at the International Political Science Association, Research Committee on Political Finance and Political Corruption, Oxford, England, March 1984), 19.

Box 1 Corruption Through History

One reason why corruption is understudied as a policy issue may be the nagging sense that there is nothing to be done about it. After all, corruption is as old as government itself. Writing some 2300 years ago, the Brahman Prime Minister of Chandragupta listed "at least forty ways" of embezzling money from the government. In ancient China, officials were given an extra allowance called *Yang-lien*, meaning "nourish incorruptness." Apparently such nourishment often failed to achieve that purpose. Writing in the fourteenth century, Abdul Rahman Ibn Khaldun said that "the root cause of corruption" was "the passion for luxurious living within the ruling group. It was to meet the expenditure on luxury that the ruling group resorted to corrupt dealing." Plato talked about bribery in *The Laws*: "The servants of the nation are to render their services without any taking of presents. . . . To form your judgment and then abide by it is no easy task, and 'tis a man's surest course to give loyal obedience to the law which commands, 'Do no service for a present.'"

Like illness, corruption will always be with us. But as this sad fact does not keep us from attempting to reduce disease, neither should it paralyze efforts to reduce corruption. Corruption involves questions of degree. Countries and agencies have more and less corruption, and various kinds of illicit behavior are more and less harmful. We can do better in controlling corruption.

India: Robert C. Tilman, "Emergence of Black-Market Bureaucracy: Administration, Development, and Corruption in The New States," in *Bureaucratic Corruption in Sub-Saharan Africa: Toward a Search for Causes and Consequences*, ed. Monday U. Ekpo (Washington, D.C.: University Press of America, 1979), 352; China and Ibn Khaldun: Syed Hussein Alatas, *The Sociology of Corruption: The Nature, Function, Causes, and Prevention of Corruption* (Singapore: Times Books, 1980), 9, 77; Plato: Plato, *The Laws*, ed. Edith Hamilton and Huntington Cairns (New York: Pantheon, 1961), bk. 12, sec. d.

Corruption is devouring the economies and polities of many Third World nations. And yet students of development policy tend to ignore it.

That I must immediately restate that such problems are not confined to the developing countries is itself revealing. Corruption in the poor nations has often attracted the wrong sort of Western attention—at the

Box 2 **Are Some Peoples More Corrupt Than Others?**

When Europeans "discovered" the new world of Asia, Africa, and America, one of their typical reactions was to point out apparent venality and lawlessness. This was not always the case: Leibniz, for example, believed that "the barbarians surpass us . . . even so far as the soul itself is concerned. . . . A wicked European is worse than a savage. He puts the finishing touches on evil." But even in more recent times writers have argued that non-Western cultures or peoples are more prone to the venal pursuit of private gain, even at the expense of public duty, despite what seem to be strict, traditional codes of behavior. Max Weber wrote:

> The universal reign of absolute unscrupulousness in the pursuit of selfish interests by the making of money has been a specific characteristic of precisely those countries whose bourgeois-capitalistic development, measured according to Occidental standards, has remained backward. . . . Absolute and conscious ruthlessness in acquisition has often stood in the closest connection with the strict conformity to tradition.

Weber is reluctant to attribute causation, but he is "inclined to think the importance of biological heredity very great." A distinguished contemporary author has argued that, in Latin America, corruption tends to be more prevalent in "the mulatto countries," those with significant proportions of blacks, but he attributes this not to race per se but the lower degree of social stratification in such countries.

To other observers, racial and cultural factors are not primary causes; they note that corruption has been prevalent at various times in all cultures. We might cite histories of the selling of offices in Europe, widespread corruption in Elizabethan England, or—as mentioned in the text—the present-day corruption scandals in Europe, Japan, and the United States. The real question for policymaking purposes is what to do about various forms of corrupt behavior, wherever they occur. When searching for answers, we should take cultural and other variables into account, while steadfastly resisting the temptations of cultural fatalism or insidious racialism.

New world: P. J. Marshall and Glyndwyr Williams, *The Great Map of Mankind: Perceptions of New Worlds in the Age of Enlightenment* (Cambridge, Mass.: Harvard University Press, 1983). Leibniz: *New Essays Concerning Human Understanding*, 1:20; cited in Leon Poliakov, *The Aryan Myth: A History of Racist* and *Nationalist Ideas in Europe* (New York: Basic Books, 1974), 146. Weber: Max Weber, *The Protestant Ethic and the Spirit of Capitalism* [1904–5], trans. Talcott Parsons (New York: Charles Scribner's Sons, 1958), 57, 58; the remark on heredity is from p. 31. Selling offices: K. Swart, *Sale of Public Office in the Seventeenth Century* (The Hague: Martinus Nijhoff, 1949). Elizabethan England: Joel Hurstfield, *Freedom, Corruption and Government in Elizabethan England* (Cambridge, Mass.: Harvard University Press, 1973). Mulatto countries: Samuel P. Huntington, "Modernization and Corruption," in *Bureaucratic Corruption in Sub-Saharan Africa: Toward a Search for Causes and Consequences*, ed. Monday U. Ekpo (Washington, D.C.: University Press of America, 1979), 318.

same time that for reasons approaching embarrassment, many serious students of development policy ignore corruption, or dismiss it with a cough and a rolling of the eyes. Early writers on "the backward nations" and colonies sometimes emphasized corruption as a sign of the moral weakness, even inferiority, of the "natives." These moralists included Western and colonialist authors, but they were not the only ones; the ethical condemnation of governmental corruption has a long pedigree in the Islamic world, China, India, and other civilizations. Though the West can claim no monopoly on the abhorrence of bribery, nepotism, and official venality, some Western authors did use allegations of corruption as a blunt instrument. In some cases they mistakenly classified as corrupt the manifestations of different mores and modes of socioeconomic organization; in other cases they used corruption as an excuse for colonial occupation. Later authors have condemned the parochial and self-serving perspective of such Western writers as emblematic of imperialist thinking. Therefore, partly to escape being labeled imperialists, many present-day scholars have simply avoided sensitive topics like corruption. Nobel prize-winning economist Gunnar Myrdal called this an example of "diplomacy in research." "The taboo on research on corruption is, indeed, one of the most flagrant examples of this general bias . . . [which] is basically to be explained in terms of a certain condescension on the part of Westerners."[10] Corruption expert Stanislav Andreski argued that "the conspiracy of silence on the part of the great

10. Gunnar Myrdal, "Corruption as a Hindrance to Modernization in South Asia," in *Political Corruption: Readings in Comparative Analysis*, ed. Arnold J. Heidenheimer (New York: Holt, Rinehart & Winston, 1970), 230.

majority of European intellectuals, due to inverted racialism, prevents the dissemination of knowledge about this phenomenon."[11]

My interest is not in moral judgments about illicit activities, nor do I wish to argue that corruption is the province of particular cultures or regions. Not so many years ago, corruption flourished in the countries we now call "developed"–and, indeed, there is evidence that some forms of corrupt behavior are today on the rise in the most economically and politically "advanced" nations.[12] Corruption scandals in recent years have led to changes at the highest levels of the governments of Holland, West Germany, Great Britain, Israel, Japan, and the United States. In Massachusetts, a recent inquiry revealed that 76 percent of a sample of public buildings manifested at least one "structural defect" that could not have occurred without corrupt deals by building inspectors.[13]

But the situation is particularly worrisome in the developing countries–some of which, of course, have fewer incidents of corruption than some developed nations. As a group the developing countries are particularly vulnerable to the harms of governmental corruption. The public sector plays such a large and central role in the society, usually encompassing economic activities left to private firms in many nations of the industrialized West. Often there are few or no alternatives to the party or ruler in power. Thus, in the realms of both economics and politics the citizen afflicted by corruption may have few alternatives to which to turn. Poor countries are, of course, less able to afford a given level of corruption than richer countries; also, although data are necessarily sketchy on such questions and some experts may disagree, corrupt activities are more widespread–and more systematically embedded–in many governments of the developing world than in the West.

I will not spend much time on such issues of more or less and here or there, however, because they may lead us away from the neglected questions of policy upon which I wish to focus. As an analogy, consider a

11. Stanislav Andreski, "Kleptocracy as a System of Government in Africa," in Ekpo, *Bureaucratic Corruption*, 276.

12. See, for example, Simcha B. Werner, "New Directions in the Study of Administrative Corruption," *Public Administration Review* 43 (March–April 1983): 146–54, and the references therein.

13. Cited in Robert E. Richardson, " A Proactive Model for Detecting Political Corruption: As Applied to the Purchase of Goods and Services in Middlesex County, Massachusetts," unpublished paper, Harvard Law School, May 1983.

Box 3 **Bribery Is Universally Condemned**

Legal scholar John T. Noonan, Jr. shows that, while bribery is as old as government itself, this longevity is not because bribery is approved in some cultures. Among his conclusions is the following:

> *Bribery is universally shameful.* Not a country in the world which does not treat bribery as criminal on its lawbooks. There are some laws such as those on gambling that are constantly broken without any particular sense of shame attaching to the offense. Bribery law is not among them. In no country do bribetakers speak publicly of their bribes, or bribegivers announce the bribes they pay. No newspaper lists them. No one advertises that he can arrange a bribe. No one is honored precisely because he is a big briber or a big bribee. . . . Not merely the criminal law—for the transaction could have happened long ago and prosecution be barred by time—but an innate fear of being considered disgusting restrains briber and bribee from parading their exchange. Significantly, it is often the Westerner with ethnocentric prejudice who supposes that a modern Asian or African society does not regard the act of bribery as shameful in the way Westerners regard it. . . .
>
> Shame and hypocrisy in the use of language are vice's tribute to virtue. Shame may be culturally conditioned. Shame so strong and so general is acknowledgment that there is something objectionable in the conduct that goes beyond the impolite and the merely illegal. Shame does not conclusively establish but it points to the moral nature of the matter.

John T. Noonan, Jr., *Bribes* (New York: Macmillan, 1984), 702–3.

physician treating a particular patient or a public health officer responsible for a particular state. For their purposes, it is not immediately pertinent to know the worldwide incidence of heart disease, or whether heart disease is a greater health menace in one country or continent than another.

John T. Noonan's masterful work on bribery has demonstrated that corruption is at its heart an ethical problem—and has been so for recorded history. Nonetheless, I will limit myself in this book to prescription in a different sense. I will try to avoid moral judgments of particular countries or cultures or individuals. Political scientist James Q. Wilson once wrote, "The problem with corruption is that it tends to become the Problem of Corruption. Moral issues usually obscure practical issues, even where the moral question is a relatively small one and the practical matter is very great."[14] At least with regard to anticorruption policies in developing countries, I tend to share Wilson's warning. And so I will leave to Noonan and others the important work of analyzing the moral, philosophical, theological, and cultural sides of corrupt behavior. I wish instead to explore illicit activities as problems that can be incompletely but helpfully analyzed with the tools of the economist and the manager.

I will therefore bracket out many important questions and focus on others, with no illusions of providing a complete account. How should government officials design and implement appropriate anticorruption policies? How should they think about the costs of various kinds of corruption? In what ways can they assess the effectiveness and costs of various countermeasures? What lessons can be drawn from successful efforts to control corruption? And what might all this mean for the field of international development itself?

14. James Q. Wilson, "Corruption Is Not Always Scandalous," in *Theft of the City: Readings on Corruption in America*, ed. J. A. Gardiner and D. J. Olson (Bloomington: Indiana University Press, 1968), 29.

2 | Objectives

Where should an anticorruption campaign begin and how far should it go? In this chapter we will use a case study and a review of the social scientific literature to help us think about the objectives of anticorruption policies. We will put ourselves in the position of a newly named leader of a remarkably corrupt organization and watch how he assessed its problems and defined his objectives. We will also take an abstract economic look at corruption and argue that the optimal amount of corruption is not zero. We will then examine what social scientists have said about the costs and benefits of bureaucratic corruption, and we will attempt a new synthesis of the problem. That the concerns of our case study's protagonist are not really addressed by the social scientific literature is one of the chapter's indirect lessons.

CORRUPTION IN THE PHILIPPINES' TAX SYSTEM

In 1975, the Philippines' Bureau of Internal Revenue (BIR) was awash in corruption. Tax officials were buying and selling jobs and transfers in the bureau. BIR employees were collecting and embezzling tax money. Other tax officials were accepting bribes from taxpayers for lower assessments. Some BIR officials went so far as to extort money from taxpayers, threatening them with high assessments and the prospect of costly litigation unless the victims paid a bribe.

When Justice Efren Plana took charge of the BIR in September 1975, he encountered the following examples of malfeasance:

□ Cruz, a collection agent in an affluent section of Manila, was known for lavish living, including three cars, a large house, and continual parties. His free-spending habits so impressed his colleagues at the night law school he attended that one of his professors would tease a more senior BIR official in the class for his relative poverty. An audit ended Cruz's time in the fast lane. He was found to have given taxpayers receipts for 12 million pesos (P) in payments but to have submitted only P9 million to the government. By manipulating official records, he had pocketed the other P3 million.

□ Lauro, a junior revenue collector in Central Luzon province, submitted to the BIR forged receipts from a local branch of the Philippines National Bank (PNB). The receipts represented P200,000 more than he had actually deposited. Lauro was caught through a check of the PNB's records.

□ Bong was revenue collector in a timber-rich province on the island of Mindanao. He apparently colluded with the largest taxpayer (a timber company) and a local bank. The company would make tax payments, which were then cashed at the bank. Part of these payments—over P1 million in all—ended up in Bong's personal account. The company obtained official receipts for its payments. Bong was found to have requisitioned ten booklets of such receipts that were never reflected in his monthly reports of collections.

□ Reyes and Santos were investigators. Their job at the BIR was to carry out confidential studies of possible underpayment or nonpayment of taxes. In the case of a molasses company they found evidence of a P2 million underpayment. But instead of reporting this to the BIR, they asked the head of the molasses company for a P1 million bribe in exchange for their silence. The company president bargained them down, while simultaneously calling in the police. Reyes and Santos were arrested by police undercover agents who were present at their payoff at a Caloocan City restaurant.

The fruits of such corruption were not hidden. One BIR official told a researcher that to see Manila's most "extensive, expensive, and lavish assortment of cars," she need only visit the BIR's parking lot.[1]

1. Leonor Magtolis-Briones, "Negative Bureaucratic Behavior and Development: The Bureau of Internal Revenue" (Paper prepared for the seminar on Bureaucratic Behavior and Development, Faculty of Public Administration, University of the Philippines, Manila, 3 October 1977), 34.

A Change of Command

The Philippines is a chain of some 7100 islands containing, in 1985, about 53 million people. Ferdinand Marcos became president in 1965. Marcos declared martial law in 1972, under which he introduced the concept of a "New Society" marked by more concern for the poor and more concern for discipline. This declaration had some success, particularly in eliminating the Philippines' notorious private armies. But when corruption had not abated in 1975, the president grew dissatisfied.

Few expected the dramatic purge he announced on 21 September 1975. At a celebration of the third anniversary of martial law, Marcos lashed into widespread corruption within his own government: "Have we earned the right to continue to demand . . . continued trust and confidence in us? Unless we can confidently answer these questions, we dare not proceed. . . . Now is the time to cut off the infected parts of society from active public life, before they endanger the entire body politic."[2]

Marcos summarily fired 2000 government officials whose activities had been questioned in a sweeping "performance audit." The officials included the secretary of public works and communications, the public works director, the entire board of transportation, the entire board of examiners, all commissioners of the civil service, and the commissioner for customs. Also sacked was the acting commissioner for audit; according to Marcos, "The conclusion is ineluctable that in a great number of cases, graft and corruption in the government has been possible only with the collusion, participation, if not at the instance, of personnel of the commission on audit."[3]

The commissioner of revenue was also replaced. A week later Marcos chose Justice Efren Plana for the job. In an interview in 1984, Plana recalled to me the suddenness of his appointment: "I was at the Court of Appeals on September 28, quietly doing my work. A phone call came from President Marcos. He said to come to Malacañang. I got there at one

2. Cited in Harvey Stockwin, "Overhauling the New Society," *Far Eastern Economic Review*, 3 October 1975, 13.

3. Ibid., 13

o'clock. We talked. He made his decision at two o'clock. And I was at the BIR before four o'clock. I went from Malacañang back to the Court of Appeals where I gathered up a few things, and then went to the BIR, where I met the Commissioner."

The bureau that Plana inherited was large, important, and battered. Numbering over 7000 people and responsible for collecting approximately two-fifths of the government's revenue, the BIR was the biggest of three revenue bureaus in the Ministry of Finance. (The other two were the Bureau of Customs and the Bureau of the Treasury.) The BIR was organized into nine divisions in the central office under the commissioner and seventeen regional offices spread across the archipelago. In 1975, direct taxes accounted for about 29 percent of government revenue, which was down from 42 percent in 1973. (Income tax, which made up 21 percent of government revenue, was down from 26 percent in 1973.)[4] About a quarter of the income taxes collected came through withholding taxes.

Positions at the BIR, especially revenue collectors' jobs, were highly sought. But at the same time many employees were not proud to be with the bureau; some would tell people only that they worked for the Ministry of Finance. The severity of this tension at the BIR—being part of an organization that was at once lucrative and popularly condemned as corrupt—may have accounted for a remarkable collegiality among its members. In her 1977 study of the BIR, Professor Leonor Magtolis-Briones, an expert on corruption now with the Philippines' Commission on Audit, emphasized

> the unusual closeness of the employees, especially at the middle management level with each other. All respondents at the BIR have made mention of the strong ties of affection and close interpersonal relations that bind the BIR employees together. This is particularly true among employees of long standing in the agency. The tendency to protect and to cover up for each other exists. The answer of one official interviewed about the case of a

4. "Performance Analysis of the Tax System, 1970–1981," *Tax Monthly* 24 (May 1983), Annex B. Other direct taxes and their percentage of total government revenue in 1975 included contributions to social security (6 percent), transfer taxes (0.2 percent), and various smaller categories. Indirect taxes accounted for 71 percent of government revenues, including import taxes (27 percent of total revenues); taxes on licenses, businesses, and occupations (15 percent); "specific taxes" (13 percent); export taxes (10 percent); and several smaller categories.

dismissed employee is perhaps typical, "I cannot comment on this case. It is difficult to cut off the head of a member of the family."[5]

When Plana took over, the BIR family was under attack and had become demoralized and defensive. The attitude of *kami at sila* (us and them), already strong in the BIR, had been reinforced. As an outsider, Plana was certainly not perceived as one of "us."

Plana himself had a spotless name and a distinguished record of public service. The justice also enjoyed excellent connections within the corridors of power. When he worked as a director of the Board of Investment, the chairman of that board was Cesar Virata, who was in 1975 the minister of finance. Later Plana served for two years as the undersecretary of national defense, in effect the number-two job, in charge of administration and what he called "implementation." There he worked with his old schoolmate of the University of the Philippines, Secretary of Defense Juan Ponce Enrile. Subsequently Plana spent two years as a justice of the Court of Appeals, where he was when President Marcos telephoned in 1975.

Plana was a pleasant, somewhat retiring man, with thick glasses, an inexpressive face, and an appealing natural modesty. His powerful mind and managerial talents were combined with a demeanor that some called "detached" and "like a lone wolf." One of his admirers and colleagues at the BIR told me: "A commissioner has to go into the field. I urged Plana to be less ascetic in his personal style. I told him to put his arm around the people, get in the pictures with them, make them feel like he was one of them. This was hard for him, but he did it, and it worked."[6] But Plana did not come to the BIR to be one of the family: he wanted to collect taxes and clean up corruption.

First Steps to Assess Corruption

Plana's first task was to learn as much as he could about the Bureau of Internal Revenue and its problems. He informed himself in several ways.

After studying the organization chart and the relevant law, Plana consulted the BIR's top ranks, first as a group and then individually. "I had

5. Magtolis-Briones, "Negative Bureaucratic Behavior," 8.

6. Interview with a high-level BIR official who wishes not to be identified, 2 April 1984. I will not footnote other interview material used in this chapter.

a meeting with the eight department heads. More than anything else, I wanted to get a feel for the Bureau. I had heard that things were not so good. But you cannot just rush into an office as if you were a knight in shining armor and assume everyone is a crook. Then, you don't get cooperation."

He asked for written reports in which each department head summarized the functions of his department, outlined its main problems, and proposed solutions for those problems. He gave only a two-day deadline for these reports. "I was surprised," he said, "that quite a number of them did not mention corruption, although it clearly was a major problem in the bureau."

Next Plana talked to lots of people: officials within the BIR, businesspeople, citizens, and officials in other agencies. One of his aims was to find out where corruption seemed to be. Another was to discover which of his senior officials were known for incorruptibility. "I could find the honest ones by talking to many people," Plana said. "They agree on the ones who cannot be corrupted. People won't name the dishonest ones among the group—they would be called squealers."

Then Plana gave the incorruptible ones special assignments. He asked them for reports on various alleged problems within the bureau. For example, one senior officer prepared two studies. One study concerned the BIR's system for assigning people to jobs—jobs with considerable discretion had often been assigned corruptly. The other study dealt with tax investigation policy, which had been abused by agents who threatened taxpayers with higher charges unless they paid a bribe. These reports helped define the location and extent of corruption problems.

Finally, Plana brought in six young, "cleaner than clean" CPAs and put them to work with two of the incorruptible senior officers. Their assignment was to review tax cases. These investigators went through an unprecedented number of cases, sometimes selecting at random, sometimes looking into areas that seemed "suspicious." Their inquiry proved to be another source of information about where and how much corruption was taking place. It had other benefits, as Plana said later: "More than what they actually accomplished through these reviews was their impact on the other examiners of the possibility that their work would be subjected to review. They would work harder and better as a result."

Through these varied means, Plana discovered that corruption in the BIR came in many forms.

External Corruption

Payment for licit services. *Lagay*, or speed money, was used to move a tax matter more rapidly through the BIR bureaucracy. As is often the case with speed money, it had become widespread: for example, officials had begun to require a small sum to furnish a record or a clearance. Although the practice of demanding *lagay* was prevalent, it usually involved petty amounts of money.

Sometimes taxpayers were extorted simply to receive the treatment due them legally. Such extortion occurred in several ways. In one of the most notorious versions a tax assessor would slap an unrealistically high assessment on the taxpayer. The taxpayer could appeal, but that would take time and effort; furthermore, the taxpayer might not be sure what the "correct" tax really was. The tax assessor would extort a payment from the taxpayer to obtain a correct assessment. (The "licit service" here is exactly that honest assessment to which taxpayers are entitled, without paying.) This practice was less widespread than *lagay*, but it was not rare either.

Payment for illicit services. Taxpayers often bribed tax collectors in exchange for the illicit service of approving too low a tax. This practice was called *arreglo* (arrangement). Here large sums were involved: according to estimates, without *arreglos* the government might collect up to 50 percent more in income taxes.

In one version of *arreglo* the taxpayer would submit a return with too many deductions, understated income, or incorrect tax computation. If a tax examiner discovered these "errors," he would bring them to the taxpayer's attention. At this point *arreglo* frequently occurred. Typically, the taxpayer paid half of the extra taxes he owed and kept the other half. Of the half paid, perhaps two-thirds was a bribe to the tax examiner and the other third was paid where it should have been, to the government coffers.[7]

In another version of *arreglo* a BIR tax inspector who was investigating a major taxpayer might discover omitted income or some other source of underpaid taxes. But instead of bringing the charges against the taxpayer, the inspector would offer the illegal service of squelching the charges in exchange for a bribe.

7. The estimate is President Marcos's (*Bulletin Today*, 2 October 1979, 1, referring to the days before Justice Plana took over the BIR).

Extortion of bribes for refraining from doing harm to the client. Innocent taxpayers were sometimes victims. "An examiner can also extort money by taking advantage of the non-knowledge of BIR regulations by the taxpayer," Magtolis-Briones noted. "He can accuse the taxpayer of not paying taxes on even non-taxable incomes, e.g. pensions."[8] Behind such extortion, of course, was the tax official's threat of legal action against the client.

Internal Corruption

According to knowledgeable estimates, various forms of corruption internal to the organization led to a loss of 10 to 20 percent in tax revenues.

Embezzlement through falsification of records. Official receipts for tax payments received by BIR agents suffered from many kinds of manipulation and falsification. The cases of the collectors Cruz and Lauro, mentioned earlier, are examples. The basic idea was to report a falsely low amount to the bureau and to embezzle the rest. These practices were hard to uncover, but Plana learned they were widespread and involved millions of pesos.

Overprinting of labels and stamps. Some BIR agents arranged to print extra, unreported documentary strip stamps, auxiliary labels, and cigarette stamps. One spectacular instance involved 108 cash clerks and collection agents and over 3 million pesos in collections that never made it to the government's hands.

Personnel scams. Many stories surfaced about the selling of choice positions within the BIR. Few jobs had educational prerequisites. The bureau lacked a sense of profession. The personnel system had become at least partially corrupted through the use of cash, nepotism, and influence to get jobs.

Delaying of remittances. BIR agents would delay remitting the taxes paid through them, enjoying the illicit financial benefits of the "float." Relatively small losses were involved, however.

Corruption of the internal investigative systems. The Internal Security Division was responsible for monitoring the bureau's own employees.

8. Magtolis-Briones, "Negative Bureaucratic Behavior," 14.

But illicit payoffs were prevalent there, too. "The practice is to bribe officials in charge of investigating erring officials so they will sit on cases, delay investigation and better still, dismiss complaints."[9]

Justice Plana clearly had his hands full at the BIR. In addition, he was supposed to take on corruption in a society full of illicit activities. The extent of the corruption of President Marcos, his family, and his cronies may never be known. Some estimates of the amount of money Marcos took out of the Philippines run into the billions of dollars. Plana apparently took the BIR job counting on Marcos's sincerity in wanting to clean up the tax bureau. Perhaps in a time of economic crisis such as the Philippines underwent in the mid-1970s, even a corrupt president may want a better functioning, less corrupt tax system. (In 1985, well after Plana had left the BIR, stories circulated that Marcos's colleagues pilfered the tax system for revenue for his campaign.)

How should Justice Plana begin thinking about controlling corruption in the Bureau of Internal Revenue? What objectives should he have in mind?

THE COSTS AND BENEFITS OF CORRUPTION

What Is "Corruption"?

The Bureau of Internal Revenue contained a host of illicit practices that were grouped together under the general label of "corruption." The variety of such activities within this single organization may seem almost endless. But the disease of corruption includes many other strains and mutations, such as illegal political contributions, the sharing of confidential or secret information, police corruption of various kinds, kickbacks to procurement officers, fraud in quality control, and many others. We'll examine some of these subcategories in later chapters.

What do such phenomena have in common? One of the definitions of *corruption* in *Webster's Third New International Dictionary (Unabridged)* is "inducement (as of a political official) by means of improper considerations (as bribery) to commit a violation of duty." This broad definition encompasses most of the illicit activities Justice Plana found in the BIR. Other definitions of corruption have been offered. In the definitional

9. Ibid., 11.

domain we could clarify matters by going beyond the general concept "corruption" and creating a typology of illicit and corrupt behavior, defining each type with great care and a number of examples.

For our immediate purposes, however, we may find a different approach to the definitional problem more fruitful. Anticipating an economic framework that we will use later to analyze corrupt behavior of many kinds, we will try here to sketch some of the *key features* of corruption.

Let us posit a "principal," such as Justice Plana, and his "agent," such as a BIR officer. (For convenience we will henceforth apply the feminine pronoun to the agent.) She interacts on the principal's behalf with a "client," such as a taxpayer. We will make an unrealistic assumption to clarify matters: suppose the principal embodies the public interest—that is, he is a highly principled principal—and is in charge of a major public agency like the BIR or even of an entire government. Let us also assume for now that the agent, a civil servant, has a less scrupulous devotion to the public interest.

The agent is employed on the understanding that she is to act on the principal's behalf vis-à-vis the client. But the agent also has her own private interests, such as her bank account. In the pursuit of her official duties as agent, she may betray the principal's interests for the sake of her own—that is, she may be corrupt. What makes this an economic model is the following proposition: the agent will act corruptly when her likely net benefits from doing so outweigh the likely net costs.

For example, the agent may be tempted to embezzle tax receipts if she believes that the chances of being caught are nil. Or when the agent has discretion over the amount of the client's income defined as "taxable," she may be tempted to use that discretion illicitly to make an *arreglo* if the payoff is large and the risks small. Though these two instances of corrupt behavior differ in important ways, the common element is that the agent is betraying her role as a public servant for her own private interests.

Now let us push the economic reasoning one step further. Suppose that the principal knows that the agent may be tempted to do this. Then the principal's task vis-à-vis the agent is to induce her to undertake her duties to the optimal extent—to induce the optimal level of public-spirited effort *and* the optimal level of corrupt behavior. (We'll explain this latter, rather surprising concept of "optimal level of corrupt behavior" in a moment.)

Box 4 **On Definitions**

Max Weber argued that one should not begin with a definition but should derive the definition by looking at specific examples—which, however, would never be a final definition, but one tailored to the purposes at hand. A definition

> must be gradually put together out of the individual parts which are taken from historical reality to make it up. Thus the final and definitive concept cannot stand at the beginning of the investigation, but must come at the end. We must, in other words, work out in the course of the discussion, as its most important result, the best conceptual formulation. . . . Thus, if we try to determine the object, the analysis and historical explanation of which we are attempting, it cannot be in the form of a conceptual definition, but at least in the beginning only a provisional description.

The literature on corruption contains several useful definitions. A widely cited definition of "corruption" is:

> behavior which deviates from the formal duties of a public role because of private-regarding (personal, close family, private clique) pecuniary or status-gains; or violates rules against the exercise of certain types of private-regarding behavior.

Historically the concept has referred both to political and sexual behavior. Like the Latin word *corruptus*, "corrupt" invokes a range of images of evil; it designates that which destroys wholesomeness. There is a moral tone to the word.

Definitions are not static. Societies' understandings of what counts as "corrupt" evolve. Over time societies have been able to make finer distinctions between "bribe" and allowable "reciprocity" or "transaction"—and have been more able to make these distinctions practically effective. And at any time in a society we are likely to find at least four different definitions of a bribe: "that of the more advanced moralists; that of the law as written; that of the law as in any degree enforced; that of common practice."

Max Weber, *The Protestant Ethic and the Spirit of Capitalism* (1904–5), trans. Talcott Parsons (New York: Charles Scribner's Sons, 1958), 47, 48; definition: Joseph S. Nye, "Corruption and Political Development: A Cost-Benefit Analysis," *American Political Science Review* 51 (June 1967): 417–29; John T. Noonan, Jr., *Bribes* (Berkeley: University of California Press, 1987), xii, 320.

This model should also incorporate the giver of the bribe or the taxpayer who participates in the *arreglo*. This person, the "client," will corrupt the agent if he or she (the client) perceives that the likely net benefits from doing so outweigh the likely net costs. The principal also wishes to induce appropriate behavior by the client.

To achieve these ends, the principal can enact various policy measures. Later we will cluster them in five groups:

- Selecting agents for incorruptibility as well as technical competence
- Changing the rewards and penalties facing the agent and the client
- Increasing the likelihood that corrupt actions will be detected and punished
- Changing the organization's mission or administrative system so that the agent's discretion is reduced
- Altering the agent's attitudes toward corruption

Such policies are the subject of the next chapter, where we shall return to the case of the BIR and develop a more complete principal-agent-client model of corruption.

For now, we will take note of two features of this way of approaching corruption. First, this approach defines corruption in terms of the divergence between the principal's or the public's interests and those of the agent or civil servant: corruption occurs when an agent betrays the principal's interests in pursuit of her own. Second, this approach stresses that corruption is a matter of degree and trade-offs: the principal wants to induce the optimal degree of corruption.

The Optimal Degree of Corruption

Should Justice Plana try to remove *all* the corruption in the Bureau of Internal Revenue? Or at some point would the costs of removing corruption be so great as to outweigh the benefits thereby obtained?

Probably the latter. *The optimal level of corruption is not zero.* This idea has a certain shock value. After making such an argument in a lecture in 1979 at the Philippines' Commission on Audit, I was attacked by several questioners for implying that corruption should be condoned. But I did not mean that an ideal world would contain corruption, nor that if we could remake a society completely we would want any corruption.

The train of thought I was trying to induce is as follows. Suppose a certain kind of corruption causes harm to society; it creates "social costs." Suppose, too, that efforts to fight this corruption are costly. To minimize the combined costs to society, we must balance the two. We should certainly consider the reduction in social costs that we obtain by reducing corrupt acts, but we must also take into account the increase in social costs entailed by our very efforts to fight corruption. And this leads to the conclusion that, in most cases, the minimum cost solution overall will not have corruption equal to zero or anticorruption efforts equal to the maximum amount.

The point applies in many contexts. Take accounting in the public sector as an example. In a recent paper, economist Herman Leonard took a broad look at the adequacy of public accounting in the United States. He argued that many prevalent techniques and procedures were "built around the problem of preventing direct fraud" in the short run:

> In the early years of this century and before, direct diversion of public funds was common enough to generate powerful "good government" movements. These political movements, with the aid of a developing professional society of accountants, formulated and adopted rudimentary control systems to track public funds. Illegal diversion of funds was a critical problem, so the systems had a "green eyeshade" orientation; they embodied rules for controls and checks that ensured that the appropriate authority existed and had been exercised before disbursement could take place. Not incidentally, they also created an audit trail so that culprits could be identified after the fact if funds were spent fraudulently.[10]

These early efforts, which met an important need, were fairly successful in the United States. Today, updated with technologies and organizations, public accounting practices are reasonably effective at preventing fraud. But Leonard also notes a drawback from the emphasis on corruption. The orientation toward short-run fraud has led public sector accountants to overlook serious long-run problems, such as valuing public assets and debts, and managing public pensions. His fascinating paper argues for a reorientation of public accounting. The details of his argument and recommendations are not the point here. Rather I wish to emphasize Leonard's point that, even in the relatively

10. Herman B. Leonard, "Measuring and Reporting the Financial Condition of Public Organizations," in *Research in Governmental and Non-Profit Accounting*, Vol. 1 (Greenwich, Conn.: JAI Press, 1985), 120–21.

Box 5 A Schematic Description of the Optimal Amount of Corruption

Imagine a function that relates the marginal social cost of a unit of corrupt activity to the total amount of that corrupt activity present in the society or organization. The very first unit of corruption may carry little social cost. But as corruption gets worse and worse—as the total amount of the corrupt activity grows larger—each additional unit may have ever greater social costs. For example, the costs might grow in such terms as breaking down norms of behavior, creating greater inefficiencies, worsening the distributions of income and power, and so forth. The result might be captured in the upward-sloping line in Figure 1.

Now imagine the marginal social cost of *reducing* corruption. If there were only a few instances of corrupt behavior, they might be very costly to detect. On the other hand, if corruption were widespread, detection might be easier, and taking steps that reduced corruption by one unit might be relatively cheap. We might, then, hypothesize a declining marginal cost curve for reducing corruption. This curve is also shown in Figure 1.

Figure 1 **The Optimal Amount of Corruption**

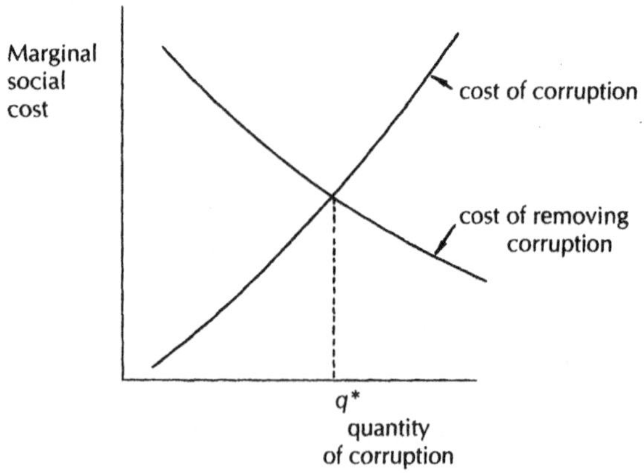

The intersection of these two curves indicates the least-cost *combination* of corrupt activities and efforts to reduce corruption. This point identifies in the situation at hand the optimal amount of corruption (labeled q^* in Figure 1).

The exact shapes of the curves are not crucial to the qualitative point. Corruption might display constant marginal social costs, and a different curve for the marginal social cost of reducing corruption might hold. For most combinations of such curves, the optimal amount of anticorruption efforts will not be infinite, and the optimal amount of corruption will not be zero.

narrow domain of public accounting, *a preoccupation with corruption can be costly*—not only in terms of the funds spent to control corruption, but in the deflection of attention and organizational competence away from other important matters.

Reducing corruption is only one of many objectives that a public official, politician, or legislator will (or should) have. For example, a tax commissioner cares about the effective collection of taxes. Energy and resources devoted to reducing corruption within a tax agency may lead to a more efficient tax-collecting organization. But anticorruption efforts may also be pushed too far, engendering large budget outlays, red tape, and poor morale. At *some* point, even if corruption is reduced by ever greater efforts, the direct costs of those efforts may be large, and the tax agency's performance could suffer enormously. At some point short of the eradication of corruption, these direct and indirect costs may be "too large."

This perspective is a helpful starting point for considering our objectives in controlling corruption. Corruption is not the only thing we care about. We also care about the costs of reducing corruption, which may be both direct (in terms of expenditures and staff) and indirect (in terms of hampering the organization's other objectives). Therefore, the design of anticorruption policies must be quite clear about how and how much various kinds of corrupt and illicit activities hurt our organization and the society.

Is Corruption Worth Fighting at All?

A prior question must be answered. Are we sure corruption is a bad thing for society or our organization? Indeed, in the context of developing nations, is it possible that, on balance, corruption might be healthful rather than harmful?

These questions may appear fatuous to Filipinos trying to retrieve the billions taken out of their country by the deposed Ferdinand Marcos or to Haitians who want to recover the $100 million to $700 million stashed abroad by the deposed "Baby Doc" Duvalier. Such questions may simply anger public managers who crack their heads daily on problems of illicit behavior. Likewise, contemplating the kinds of corruption Justice Plana found in the Bureau of Internal Revenue, we may have felt certain that such misbehavior caused social harm. And yet, it turns out that much of the social scientific literature on our topic consists of a debate over whether in general corruption helps or hinders "development."

This debate has distorted research on corruption. As they have debated the tonic and toxic effects of corruption on development—and fought fierce battles on definitional grounds—social scientists have paid virtually no attention to practical questions concerning how to control corruption.

In a recent literature review in the World Bank's Management and Development series, the authors spent all their energy to justify this conclusion: "Corruption has a deleterious, often devastating, effect on administrative performance and economic and political development."[11] The authors said nothing about how to manage such unwelcome phenomena; none of the monograph's eighty-six footnotes referred to strategies for fighting corruption. In its focus on whether or not corruption as a whole is "harmful," and its omission of policy analysis, the World Bank report is typical of studies of corruption in developing countries. There is something characteristic even in its awkward lurch in the final paragraph, when almost as an afterthought the authors state that "governments may increasingly wish to consider possible measures to counteract this scourge" and then simply list, without examples or supporting arguments, four vague, general, and therefore unhelpful "possible measures."[12]

11. David J. Gould and José A. Amaro-Reyes, "The Effects of Corruption on Administrative Performance: Illustrations from Developing Countries," Staff Working Paper no. 580, Management and Development Series no. 7 (Washington, D.C.: The World Bank, 1983), abstract; see also p. 34.

12. Ibid., pp. 34–35.

No wonder, then, that policymakers like Dr. Goh Keh Swee, the Deputy Prime Minister of Singapore, are puzzled. "Corruption as well as ineffective organs of public administration, can have an immediate impact on the economic growth of Third World countries," he said in a lecture in London in 1983. "It escapes my understanding why their importance has been ignored not only in the academic literature but also in the conduct of affairs."[13]

This puzzlement may turn to annoyance when policymakers read academic studies with titles like "What Is the Problem About Corruption?" and "Economic Development Through Bureaucratic Corruption." One minister from a developing country found the suggestion that corruption could be helpful an offensive one:

> I think it is monstrous for these well-intentioned and largely misguided scholars to suggest corruption as a practical and efficient instrument for rapid development in Asia and Africa. Once upon a time, Westerners tried to subjugate Asia . . . by selling opium. The current defense of Kleptocracy is a new kind of opium by some Western intellectuals, devised to perpetuate Asian backwardness and degradation. I think the only people . . . pleased with the contribution of these scholars are the Asian Kleptocrats.[14]

How could any scholar have said or implied that corruption was good for developing countries? How could the academic debate have stalled in such a way?

The answers are complex. First, the academic world has a penchant for description and explanation, rather than prescription and policy relevance. A useful analogy may be the profusion of academic research and debate on the question "Is smoking harmful?" contrasted with the neglect of practical matters such as "How can people be helped to stop smoking?"[15]

13. Goh Keh Swee, Harry Johnson Memorial Lecture, London, June 1983; cited in Bernard Schaffer, "Access: A Theory of Corruption and Bureaucracy" (Paper presented at the International Political Science Association, Research Committee on Political Finance and Political Corruption, Oxford, England, March 1984), 8.

14. S. Rajaratnam, Minister of Foreign Affairs and Labour in Singapore, in a speech given in 1968; reproduced in *Political Corruption: Readings in Comparative Analysis*, ed. Arnold J. Heidenheimer (New York: Holt, Rinehart & Winston, 1970), 54.

15. I am, therefore, pleased to insert a plug for the Institute for the Study of Smoking Behavior and Policy, founded in 1984 at Harvard's Kennedy School of Government by Thomas C. Schelling, which tackles questions of the latter kind. Perhaps corruption, too, requires the approach of a professional school in addition to the perspectives of academic social scientists.

Second, data are not usually available. Researchers find it difficult to study corruption empirically because the parties involved have every reason to keep data hidden and governments are reluctant to allow foreigners or even their own citizens to work on such sensitive questions. Consequently, academic debates over the tonic and toxic properties of corruption "tend to rely too much upon anecdotes, hypothetical cases, and speculative linkages between corruption and future social outcomes."[16] In such circumstances, debates are likely to remain inconclusive.

Another factor is the inevitably normative nature of the topic. The two sides of the academic debate have by now received labels: the "moralists" are pitted against the "revisionists." The former are accused of importing inappropriate, value-laden assumptions into their analyses. On the other hand, according to corruption expert Ledivina Cariño of the University of the Philippines, the revisionists' "careful balancing of good and bad effects seems to be a recognition that everyone knows corruption is not really beneficial but positive effects must be discovered so that one does not condemn a country completely. Compare the outrage of American scholars against Nixon's indiscretions and their near-approval of more blatantly corrupt regimes in countries where they have worked."[17] That values as well as facts drive the debate may help explain both its existence and persistence.

Three Reminders About the Utility of Corruption

Many professors have argued that corruption can play a positively useful role in developing countries. (This statement has a similar shock value to the idea that the optimal level of corruption is not zero. But it goes further: it is not just that fighting corruption may be so costly as not to be worthwhile, but that corruption itself may create economic, political, or managerial benefits.) I find it worthwhile to stylize three categories of

16. Michael Johnston, "The Systematic Consequences of Corruption: A Reassessment" (Paper presented at the International Political Science Association, Research Committee on Political Finance and Political Corruption, Oxford, England, March 1984), 2.

17. Ledivina V. Cariño, "Tonic or Toxic: The Effects of Graft and Corruption," in *Bureaucratic Corruption in Asia: Causes, Consequences, and Controls*, ed. Cariño (Quezon City, The Philippines: JMC Press, 1986), 168.

arguments that corruption *may*, on occasion, be socially beneficial. I call them the economist's reminder, the political scientist's reminder, and the manager's reminder.

The economist's reminder. Corrupt payments introduce a kind of market mechanism. In a system where goods and services are allocated by queue, politics, random selection, or "merit," corruption may instead allocate goods according to willingness and ability to pay. Corruption may thereby put goods and services in the hands of people who value them the most, who can use them most effectively. In some sense, then, after the corrupt act those goods and services are more "efficiently" allocated in the economic sense.

Business school professor Nathaniel Leff summarized:

> Corruption may introduce an element of competition into what is otherwise a comfortably monopolistic industry. . . . At the same time, the propensity for investment and economic innovation may be higher outside the government than within it. . . . Because payment of the highest bribes is one of the principal criteria for allocation, the ability to muster revenue, either from reserves or from current operations, is put at a premium. In the long run, both of these sources are heavily dependent on efficiency in production. Hence, a tendency toward competition and efficiency is introduced into the system.[18]

The economist's reminder has two aspects. First, a prediction: market forces are hard to avoid. When the market is not used to distribute goods and services, corruption will creep in as a kind of illicit market substitute. Second, an evaluation: when corruption does occur, it may lead to an allocation of goods according to willingness and ability to pay. This development, in turn, may be economically efficient—perhaps, therefore, socially useful.

The political scientist's reminder. Corrupt payments, appointments, and policies may have political benefits. Politicians may use corruption to foster the political integration of various tribes, regions, elites, or parties, which may in turn lead to political harmony in the face of fragmented political authority, disunity, and hostility. Analytically, one

18. Nathaniel H. Leff, "Economic Development through Bureaucratic Corruption," in *Bureaucratic Corruption in Sub-Saharan Africa: Toward a Search for Causes and Consequences*, ed. Monday U. Ekpo (Washington, D.C.: University Press of America, 1979), 329, 330, 333.

may classify some kinds of corruption together with "logrolling" arrangements and preferential quotas for various regions, ethnic groups, or parties. Although such devices usually spread public benefits in ways that strictly speaking are opposed to allocation by "merit" or "maximum social benefit," they may have political benefits. Quite apart from the evident benefits to the politically corrupt politician, then, the polity as a whole may be "better off" because of corruption.

Political scientists sometimes cite the experience of the United States, where corruption helped "political machines" in cities to deliver not only the vote but also public services, and where such corruption was eventually superseded by "good government." Corruption's emergence in the developing countries, it is hypothesized, may have similar benefits—and a similar benign prognosis. Corruption is sometimes seen as a mechanism of "political participation" and influence, particularly by ethnic minorities and foreign corporations: "In most underdeveloped countries, interest groups are weak, and political parties rarely permit the participation of elements outside the contending cliques. Consequently, graft may be the only institution allowing other interests to achieve articulation and representation in the political process."[19] Consequently, despite its apparent social costs, corruption may have important political benefits.

The manager's reminder. Corruption may have uses within an organization. If bureaucratic rules are constraining, the organization may sometimes benefit by the employees' corrupt circumvention of the rules. A limited amount of employee theft, embezzlement, misreporting of expenses, kickbacks, "speed money," and so forth may be tacitly allowed by top management, on the one hand, because controlling these illicit activities would be prohibitively expensive and, on the other hand, because such illicit sources of income may in the long run substitute for higher wages. A slush fund within an organization may function as a contingency fund, which top management may flexibly if illicitly allocate to further the organization's ends.

For example, the Food for Work program in Bangladesh in the late 1970s had strict rules concerning the allocation of donated wheat. Wheat could not be employed to compensate landowners for the use of their

19. Ibid., 328. Two sentences later, Leff refers specifically to ethnic minorities and foreign businesses.

property for flood embankments. Because the program's principal objective was to relieve local unemployment, wheat could not be given to labor contractors for the employment of migrant labor. Many of the project supervisors' expenses, such as transportation, meals, and lodging, could not be reimbursed by the program itself. And yet, in practice some wheat was used by many effective Food-for-Work managers for just these purposes. Political economist Judith Tendler concluded that these examples of corruption served the organization's mission:

> In all three cases of improper wheat use, the misappropriations can be seen as having furthered the execution of projects—rather than as having lined someone's pocket—by getting around constraining program regulations. In the case of the small land purchase, the flood embankment would have had to detour from the riverside if the small farmer's plot could not be used. In the case of labor contractors, it would have been difficult for the project committee to find local labor at FFW wage rates because the project was in a low-unemployment region. . . . In all these cases the diversion of wheat was public and agreed upon as worthwhile at the local level.[20]

These three "reminders" have some common features. First, they refer to the benefits from specific corrupt acts, not from systematic corruption pervading many or most decisions. Second, the putative benefits depend upon the assumption that the corruption transgresses a wrong or inefficient economic policy, overcomes limitations in an imperfect political system, or gets around imperfections in organizational rules. In short, *if the prevailing system is bad, then corruption may be good.* Our earlier equation of the principal's interest and the public interest may, alas, be too optimistic an assumption.

As Leff pointed out:

> The critique of bureaucratic corruption often seems to have in mind a picture in which the government and civil service are working intelligently and actively to promote economic development, only to be thwarted by the efforts of grafters. Once the validity of this interpretation is disputed, the effects of corruption must also be reevaluated. This is the case if the government consists of a traditional elite which is indifferent if not hostile to development, or a revolutionary group of intellectuals and politicians, who are primarily interested in other goals.[21]

20. Judith Tendler, *Rural Works Programs in Bangladesh: Community, Technology, and Graft* (Report for the Transportation Department of the World Bank, mimeo, June 1979), 22–23.

21. Leff, "Economic Development," 330.

In the words of political scientist Samuel Huntington: "In terms of economic growth the only thing worse than a society with a rigid, overcentralized, dishonest bureaucracy is one with a rigid, overcentralized, honest bureaucracy."[22]

As an example, consider economist Malcolm Gillis's assessment of Indonesia. Under President Sukarno's "Guided Economy," "whatever vestiges of the market mechanism that remained in 1958 were to be replaced by government planning, implemented by bureaucratic judgments. . . . The economy resisted complete collapse" . . . [only because] "farmers and businessmen circumvented the pervasive web of administrative controls through barter, smuggling, and black markets."[23] These controls, Gillis implied, were "hostile to development"; thus their evasion, even if through corruption, was a positive step.

Of course, the policies and rules circumvented through corruption are not always myopic and misguided. In the Philippines case, neither the corrupt evasion of taxes nor the embezzling of tax money to finance the high living of some BIR functionaries was in the country's interest. Moreover, the economic controls and "interference" decried by economists may be implemented for reasons of economic efficiency. Governments often (though certainly not always) intervene in the economy precisely in circumstances where markets cannot be counted on to distribute goods and services efficiently because of externalities, indivisibilities, collective goods, and other market failures.[24] In such cases corruption may simply reintroduce the market failure, harming the economy. A similar conclusion holds for the corrupt transgression of accepted political mechanisms or organizational procedures. The result may well be harmful to political stability and political integration and to an organization's effectiveness.

As regards the objectives of anticorruption policies, therefore, a key

22. Samuel P. Huntington, "Modernization and Development," in *Bureaucratic Corruption*, ed. Ekpo, 321.

23. Malcolm Gillis, "Episodes in Indonesian Economic Growth," in *World Economic Growth*, ed. Arnold C. Harberger (San Francisco: ICS Press, 1984), 241.

24. There is a vast literature in welfare economics analyzing the failure or absence of market efficiency. A useful application to public policy is Francis M. Bator, *The Question of Government Spending: Public Needs and Private Wants* (New York: Harper, 1959). The fact that the untrammeled market cannot, in many circumstances, be guaranteed to result in economic efficiency does not, of course, imply that if the government interferes the results will be any better.

issue concerns the social and organizational utility of the rules and policies being transgressed. Corrupt payments are themselves not socially productive; they do not add to the sum total of goods and services available to the society. But if such payments remove or mitigate inefficient policies, then despite their unproductive essence, they may lead to greater efficiency and thereby to a greater abundance of goods and services. On the other hand, suppose that corruption distorts otherwise efficient public policies. Then the result is doubly harmful: the corrupt payments are socially unproductive, and they result in socially inefficient policies.[25] Only when corruption circumvents already existing "distortions" can it be economically, politically, or organizationally useful.

Corruption may help in one way and hurt in others. The corrupt circumvention of public rules, for example, may lead to a sort of economic efficiency but at the cost of the other objectives the rules sought in the first place. An example can be found in the Tanzanian government's creation of marketing cooperatives "with a view to counteracting the largely Asian-dominated private trade in agricultural produce." This "equity objective," however, led to a less efficient marketing system. And corruption was a perhaps predictable consequence: "By the mid-1970s, however, it was evident that neither the extensive corruption nor the increased political manipulation of cooperatives by the rural elite could be avoided."[26] The cooperatives were disbanded in 1976. Corruption may have "corrected" some of the economic "distortions" introduced by the marketing cooperatives, but they accomplished this correction at the cost of subverting some of the cooperatives' social and political objectives (with which one may or may not agree).

Blanket statements about the helpfulness or harmfulness of "corruption" in general will not, therefore, aid us in assessing the effects of particular instances we may encounter. On the other hand, given the prevalence in academic circles of apologists for corruption, perhaps it is

25. One economist puts it this way: "The diversion of resources from directly productive to directly unproductive activities, when undertaken in the context of initially distorted situations, is fundamentally different from such diversion occurring in the context of initially distortion-free situations." (Jagdish N. Bhagwati, "Directly Unproductive, Profit-seeking (DUP) Activities," *Journal of Political Economy* 90 [October 1982], 994.)

26. Uma Lele, "Tanzania: Phoenix or Icarus?" in *World Economic Growth*, ed. Harberger, 185–86.

worthwhile to analyze the emerging negative consensus of scholarly studies on that question.

Corruption Is Usually Harmful

As the evidence mounts about corruption in developing countries, it seems clear that the harmful effects of corruption greatly outweigh the (occasional) social benefits. I have cited such a conclusion in a recent World Bank-sponsored review; much of the supporting evidence that is included there will not be reproduced here. But we will review a few particularly useful studies that help put in perspective the "reminders" that corruption may be useful.

In 1967, political scientist Joseph Nye published a schematic cost-benefit analysis of corruption. He distinguished three outcomes: effects on economic development, national integration, and governmental capacity. He then arrayed types of corruption along several scales:

- Level of government officials – top or bottom
- Political conditions in the country – favorable or unfavorable
- Inducements used in corrupt transactions – modern (that is, money) or traditional (that is, status)
- Extent of "deviation from the formal duties of a public role" induced by the corruption – extensive or marginal

Nye noted that he could add to his typology additional variables, such as the corruption's scale, visibility, "income effects," and so on. He also observed that within his categories further subdivisions might be desirable (for example, distinguishing between politicians and civil servants).

Nye then systematically estimated the likely benefits and costs from his various categories of corruption. His conclusion was that corruption is usually harmful: "We can refine the general statements about corruption and political development to read 'it is possible that the costs of corruption in less developed countries will exceed its benefits except for top level corruption involving modern inducements and marginal deviations and except where corruption provides the only solution to an important obstacle to development.'"[27]

27. Joseph S. Nye, "Corruption and Political Development: A Cost-Benefit Analysis," *American Political Science Review* 61 (June 1967), 427.

Nye's conclusion has been extended and elaborated in a host of empirical studies of corruption. For example, a thorough study of corruption in Morocco was sensitive to our three "reminders." But it found that corruption, far from helping Morocco, was undermining its economy, political system, and organizational efficiency.

> In conclusion: corruption in the Moroccan system does little to entrepreneurial efficiency and capital formation.
>
> [The civil servant] is being bribed to perform his normal duties rather than to cut red tape.
>
> In sum, [rather than encouraging access] corruption in Morocco may have contributed to the stratification of resources within a particularistic bourgeois elite.
>
> There is a general level of cynicism running throughout. . . . An atmosphere of every man for himself and every clan for itself emerges that precludes large-scale coalition-building or politicking in the bureaucracy.
>
> In this system, corruption serves only one "positive" function – that of the survival of the regime.[28]

Another study showed that corruption in Ghana had intensified ethnic conflict, ruined the efficiency of municipal government and federal agencies, crippled merit systems of hiring and promotion, generated "an atmosphere of distrust which pervades all levels of administration," and undermined the philosophy of African socialism.[29] An article on corruption in Uganda concluded: "'Good government' preceded and succumbed to corruption in Kampala, rather than following and supplanting corruption as it has done in many but not all American cities."[30] A review of corruption in Korea rejected the validity of the economist's reminder: "None of our case studies show that the money raised through corruption was directly and productively invested."[31]

Since the mid-1970s the College of Public Administration of the University of the Philippines has sponsored a dozen research projects on

28. John Waterbury, "Endemic and Planned Corruption in a Monarchical Regime," in *Bureaucratic Corruption*, ed. Ekpo, 366, 368, 370, 375.

29. Herbert M. Werlin, "The Consequences of Corruption: The Ghanaian Experience," in *Bureaucratic Corruption*, ed. Ekpo, 247–60. The phrase cited is from p. 253.

30. J. David Greenstone, "Corruption and Self-Interest in Kampala and Nairobi: A Comment on Local Politics in East Africa," in *Bureaucratic Corruption*, ed. Ekpo, 272.

31. Sintaek, Kang, "Conclusions and Recommendations" (Paper prepared for the Fourth Working Meeting on Bureaucratic Behavior and Development, Hong Kong, August 1978); cited in Cariño, "Tonic or Toxic," 189.

corruption in that country, including detailed organizational analyses and case studies. A summary of this work stated:

> Graft and corruption has strongly affected development efforts negatively, belying the so-called "revisionist hypothesis" prevalent in the West which considers corruption as either a necessary step in the development process or a means of speeding it up. Instead [our research] found that corruption leads to the favoring of inefficient producers, the unfair and inequitable distribution of scarce public resources, and the leakage of revenue from government coffers to private hands. Less directly but no less perniciously, corruption leads to loss of confidence in government.[32]

The most comprehensive empirical work was sponsored by the Canadian foreign aid agency in the late 1970s. Numerous studies were carried out in Hong Kong, Korea, Malaysia, Nepal, the Philippines, Singapore, and Thailand. Repeatedly, the case studies documented socially harmful effects from corrupt activities, and the positive effects summarized in our reminders were seldom encountered. A magisterial summary of this research has recently been produced. Among its conclusions:

> Does corruption help an agency in reaching its stated goals? The answer appears almost perfectly negative, except in one case [where corruption enabled the police to bribe informants]. . . . A major negative effect . . . is its role in displacing goals, as employees pursue their own pecuniary interests rather than the objectives of the organization. Energies of the staff are then spent in pursuit of their corrupt business interests, leaving behind what is their expected primary work. . . .
>
> Our conclusion then is: corruption is toxic, with very few exceptions. We wish we had more positive findings since we are faced with the problem of its strength and pervasiveness in most of the countries we studied.[33]

Analyzing the Effects of Corruption

Such findings may begin to set to rest the academic debate on the general harmfulness of corruption, but because they are stated at such a general level, they are not much help in thinking about anticorruption

32. Ledivina V. Cariño and Josie H. de Leon, *Final Report for the Study of Graft and Corruption, Red Tape and Inefficiency in Government* (Report for the President's Center for Special Studies, Manila, mimeo, 1983), 2.

33. Cariño, "Tonic or Toxic," 178, 194.

policies. Can we discern any clues from this literature concerning the kinds of corruption that are likely to be more harmful or less harmful in particular circumstances?

Let us consider the effects of corruption in four categories: efficiency, equitable distribution, incentives, and politics.

Efficiency. Earlier we examined the economist's reminder that corruption may sometimes lead to a more efficient allocation of resources. A classic instance is when people "bid" through bribes for a scarce license or permit. Revisionists used elementary economic reasoning to argue that a bidding system, even if illicit, would allocate the scarce good to the people whose willingness and ability to pay were highest, which would be efficient in the economic sense. But what if the scarce good is a license to practice medicine or a safety permit for a building? In such cases the highest bidder will not be the most efficient, nor will the bidding system result in economic improvement.

Or take the simple model of a queue for a public service. Would not a corrupt auction for places in line be more efficient than first come, first serve? The revisionists have said yes, and they have a point. But it is not necessarily so, according to political economist Susan Rose-Ackerman in her ground-breaking analysis of corrupt markets. "Even a legal price system," she proved, "cannot realistically be used to produce efficiency if all applicants are obliged to line up in a single queue."[34] A corrupt price system adds further sources of inefficiency: distortions due to the fear of penalties, monopolistic officials not making efficient choices, and the possibility that officials may slow down their pace of work to extract bigger bribes. Rose-Ackerman concluded, "Those economists who look favorably upon corruption generally have a limited point of view, a narrow definition of goodness and an oversimplified model of the corrupt marketplace."[35]

Corruption has efficiency costs in terms of the waste and misallocation that often accompany it. For example, a typical finding is that because of corrupt procurement policies, governments in developing countries pay from 20 to 100 percent more than the price they would pay under noncorrupt conditions. This has been documented in careful

34. Susan Rose-Ackerman, *Corruption: A Study in Political Economy* (New York: Academic Press, 1978), chap. 5. The quote is from p. 95.

35. Ibid., 9.

studies of Thailand, Indonesia, and India.[36] In Chapter 6, we will see the same thing in Korea. During the Sahelian drought in the early 1970s, President Tomabalbaye of Chad and his wife "were apparently involved in various kickback schemes (transport, resale, labor kickbacks, etc.) whose effect was to permit them to make a handsome profit on the assistance proferred from abroad. . . . Aid donors found themselves paying exorbitant commissions just to bring relief supplies to Njamena."[37] Now these extra payments are in a sense not "lost" to society, just as your car is not lost to society if it is stolen by a thief. But resources that should have been allocated to a public purpose are not so allocated, even though the corrupt private parties have gained.

Corruption may lead to other inefficiencies. If bribes lead to unsafe buildings, unqualified government employees, or police negligence, "public bads" may be produced. According to sociologist Robert Wade, corruption in Indian Soil Conservation departments has led government officers not to enforce the policy of "contour bunding," which is the careful construction of shallow ridges to prevent erosion during the rainy season. The result has been disastrous.

> Top soil is India's most precious resource; each inch of top soil takes roughly 1,000 years to form. Contour bunding is one of the main techniques for conserving it. . . . Without these conditions, rainwater will cut through unimpacted ridges at the weakest point, and gullies will begin to form.
>
> This is in fact what often happens, because the Soil Conservation departments commonly fail to impact or grass the newly constructed ridges, or to provide a structure for taking water from upper to lower terraces. The rate of soil erosion from an area treated in this way has been reported as some 10 times greater than from adjacent areas [where contour bunding is correctly implemented]. The costs are as follows: (1) permanent loss of production from the land on which the programme is situated; (2) semi-permanent loss of production from the alluvial fans lower down on which

36. Thinapan Nakata, "Corruption in the Thai Bureaucracy: Who Gets What, How and Why in Its Public Expenditures," *Thai Journal of Public Administration* 18 (January 1978): 102–28; Clive Gray, "Civil Service Compensation in Indonesia," *Bulletin of Indonesian Economic Studies* 15 (March 1979): 85–113; and Robert Wade, "The System of Administrative and Political Corruption: Canal Irrigation in India," *Journal of Development Studies* 18, 3 (April 1982): 287–328.

37. Ekpo, "Preface," *Bureaucratic Corruption*, vi. The president was toppled in a coup in 1975.

the sediment is deposited; (3) increased sedimentation in lower down rivers causing greater flood risk and reservoir siltation.[38]

Wade explicitly blames most of these deficiencies on the corrupt practices of Soil Conservation officers.

A third sort of inefficiency occurs when, because of corruption, top government officials skew public policies to benefit themselves and a small number of cronies. Public administration professor Victoria A. Bautista persuasively documented such "policy corruption" in the Philippines under Ferdinand Marcos.[39]

Equitable Distribution. A second category of consequences of corruption is to redistribute resources. Most studies show that the rich and privileged benefit from corrupt schemes at the expense of the poor, the rural, and the disadvantaged. Sometimes military or police powers are translated corruptly into economic gains to the disbenefit of those without such powers. "'The art of the possible' was Napoleon's definition of politics," noted a leading Uruguayan economist. "An observer of the Uruguayan scene might prefer to say that it is *the fine art of transferring real resources from the general public to the ruler's political friends*."[40]

Incentives. Possibilities for corruption create nefarious incentives throughout the society. Economists have analyzed the unproductive incentives found in a "rent-seeking society," where citizens and officials strive to achieve "monopoly rents," often doing so through bribes. For example, take "speed money." It may seem efficient to allow citizens to pay public servants for faster-than-normal service. One may think of it as a tip or an overtime wage. But the possibility of attaining such "rents" for their services has in many cases led government officials to extort payments for the providing of any service at all. In this fashion illicit tips and speed money tend to evolve into required payments and then into

38. Robert Wade, "The Market for Public Office: Why the Indian State Is Not Better at Development," Discussion Paper DP 194 (Sussex, England: Institute of Development Studies, July 1984), 34–35; emphasis in original.

39. Victoria A. Bautista, "Public-Interest Perspective: A Neglected Dimension in the Study of Corruption" (Unpublished paper, College of Public Administration, University of the Philippines, August 1983), 6–14.

40. Ramón Díaz, "Uruguay's Erratic Growth," in *World Economic Growth*, ed. Harberger, 394; emphasis in original.

extortionary fees, resulting in inefficiency. This phenomenon has been amply documented.[41]

This leads to a key point. Whereas an occasional act of corruption may be efficient, corruption once systematized and deeply ingrained never is. If, as Huntington wrote, "a traditional society may be improved–or at least modernized–by a little corruption," it is also true, he continued, that "a society in which corruption is already pervasive, however, is unlikely to be improved by more corruption."[42] Nor is such a society likely to be an economically efficient or politically well-functioning one.

At some point in a spiral of increasing corruption, even honest citizens may need to be corrupt to get by. As in Joseph Heller's novel *Catch-22*, if someone asks rhetorically, "But what if everyone did that?" the answer is "Then I'd be a damn fool not to." This sad distortion of incentives has also been documented in several developing nations. According to one Commission of Inquiry Report in Ghana, systematic corruption in the granting of import licenses meant that "against their will, decent importers were compelled to accept the improper methods of obtaining licenses as the only means of survival."[43] In the same country a local journalist noted that "when it is only the dishonest and corrupt contractors who get contracts by offering bribes, even honest contractors will follow suit, not because they are themselves corrupt, but because they want to remain in business."[44] In Zaire, the country's Catholic bishops in 1978 decried a society that had reached a point where "the individual has no choice left but to seek a solution in active corruption in order to defend his rights."[45]

Corruption adversely affects incentives in other ways. Its existence may enhance people's uncertainties about the likely benefits of their productive activities. This in turn may create incentives for inefficient risk-avoiding behavior. Government agencies and private citizens take

41. Salim Rashid, "Public Utilities in Egalitarian LDC's," *Kyklos* 34, fasc. 3 (1981): 448–60; Cariño, "Tonic or Toxic," 178–79; Waterbury, "Endemic and Planned Corruption," 368.

42. Huntington, "Modernization and Corruption," 321.

43. Cited in Ekpo, "Preface," *Bureaucratic Corruption*, xiii.

44. Cited in Herbert W. Werlin, "The Roots of Corruption–The Ghanaian Enquiry," in *Bureaucratic Corruption*, ed. Ekpo, 395.

45. Cited in Gould and Amaro-Reyes, "Effects of Corruption," 12.

Box 6 **Rent Seeking and Corruption**

A monopolist can charge a price higher than the price that would prevail in a competitive market. The extra earnings thereby obtained are called "monopoly rents." When the structure of the economy or the government allows monopolies to exist, a number of people may strive to gain that monopoly. The winner gets the monopoly; the losers do not. The resources the losers expended to get the monopoly usually create no goods and services but are in economist Jagdish Bhagwati's term "directly unproductive." As a result, rent-seeking behavior is socially unproductive in most cases.

By the very nature of many public sector activities, the government will have monopoly powers over the disbursements of certain goods and services, such as police protection, irrigation, export permits, admissions to a public university, tax assessments, and so forth. Thus, officials with discretion over such disbursements will be tempted to corruptly charge monopoly rents. Doing so will create inefficiencies, as citizens pay "too high" a price for these goods and services.

Rent *seeking* may also take place, creating a further social loss. Government officials may vie to capture positions of monopolistic disbursement, spending their time and energies not on productive behavior but in the unproductive pursuit of rents. Or officials may divert their jobs in such a way as to gain monopoly power over clients. The prospect of corrupt earnings, then, can create unproductive, rent-seeking incentives throughout government.

See Anne O. Krueger, "The Political Economy of the Rent-Seeking Society," *American Economic Review* 64 (June 1974): 291–303; James M. Buchanan et al., eds., *Toward a Theory of the Rent-Seeking Society* (College Station: Texas A & M Press, 1980); Jagdish N. Bhagwati, "Directly Unproductive, Profit-Seeking (DUP) Activities," *Journal of Political Economy* 90 (October 1982): 988–1002; and Arye L. Hillman and Eliakim Katz, "Risk-Averse Rent Seekers and the Social Cost of Monopoly Power," *Economic Journal* 94 (March 1984): 104–10.

preventive or evasive actions, which in themselves are socially unproductive. Corruption in a certain market may even induce people to get out of that business altogether. This apparently occurred in Zaire, where farmers growing cash crops faced increasingly corrupt markets for their produce, and as a consequence many returned to the inefficient but secure subsistence farming of their forebears.[46]

In short, when corruption becomes a decided possibility, the incentives of both officials and citizens are twisted toward socially unproductive, though personally lucrative, activities. Officials spend an increasing amount of their time looking for ways to secure bribes and extort payments, rather than exerting themselves in fulfillment of their public duties. Citizens, too, invest their energies in the pursuit of illicit favors, augmenting their incomes not through productive activity but through bribery, dishonesty, and collusion.

Politics. Earlier in this chapter we discussed the political scientist's reminder that corruption may sometimes benefit the polity. But many negative effects may result as well. Observers often claim that corruption leads to political alienation and instability. In Chapter 1, I noted that promises to fight corruption are politically popular; this response derives from widespread popular disaffection with illicit activities in the public sector. Popular opinion may give corruption too much credit as a source of the nation's difficulties. For example, consider the following dramatic outpouring by a top official in Mexico, where the economic crisis of the early 1980s was widely attributed to governmental corruption:

> Our country's powerful and diversified public sector, with more than 700 enterprises or entities, represents the largest constructor of works and the biggest buyer of every product, from pencils to turbines. A public service of more than a million and a half workers, with systems of administration and control that are obsolete, clumsy, and often useless, fomented corruption instead of preventing it, thereby provoking the economic collapse we have lived through; and the famous wave of growth on which we rode also collapsed like so much sea foam.[47]

Although perhaps exaggerated here, this perception is shared by many Mexicans. In Mexican villages one could see in 1983 this new slogan of the Communist Party painted on walls, alongside a hammer and sickle: "Contra la Corrupción, Somos la Oposición" (Against corruption, we are the opposition). And this was so even though Miguel de la Madrid's new government had initiated in 1982 a highly publicized drive against corruption.

46. David J. Gould, *Bureaucratic Corruption and Underdevelopment in the Third World: The Case of Zaire* (New York: Pergamon Press, 1980).

47. Enrique del Val Blanco, "Nuevo Marco de Referencia en el Combate a la Corrupción," in Robert Klitgaard et al., *Prevención de la Corrupción en el Sector Público: Un Enfoque Internacional* (Mexico City: INAP Praxis, 1984), 28; my translation.

Box 7 Corruption and Cynicism

Inside the developing countries, if not in the literature on development, corruption is widely discussed and debated. It is perhaps overestimated by the common man and woman as a source of their problems. The very attitude that corruption is widespread can breed cynicism and apathy.

One authority describes a common phenomenon:

> Mistrust becomes cynicism. And this, in my view, is the inevitable result for both public and internal reactions to mistrust and venality. Ordinary citizens in and out of government are led to expect that most public service is not a right but a scarce commodity whose supply and price are controlled by market forces and the entrepreneurial activities of officials. Even when real merit is rewarded, even when a public servant has done excellent service, in private conversation people denigrate these virtues and pass rumors, or tell jokes about illegitimacies, nepotism and other covert practices that they "know" or they have "heard" about in connection with this person's career. In checking these one finds suggestive evidence for a few, but generally no real evidence to support most, at least at the level of public knowledge.
>
> The belief helps to support the reality. Cynicism allows for the ordinary recruit into the public service to be ready for inefficiency and malfeasance.

Another expert cites similar phenomena in Ghana:

> Since many of the levy collectors in rural areas managed to own houses and farms while supposedly earning just a few cedis a month, it is understandable why "many a farmer refuses to pay his levy because of what he sees in his village." . . . How could the government admonish people to tighten their belts . . . when "members of the new Ghanaian aristocracy and their hangers-on, who tell them to do this, are fast developing pot bellies and paunches and their wives and sweethearts double chins in direct proportion to the rate at which people tighten their belts?"

Some evidence associates corruption with political instability. Political scientist Michael Nacht found that "corruption" was a significant independent predictor of "regime changes" in developing countries, even after statistically controlling for a host of other factors.[48] It is probably fair

48. Michael Nacht, "Internal Change and Regime Stability," in *Third World Conflict and International Security* (London: International Institute for Strategic Studies, Summer 1981).

TABLE 1 THE COSTS OF CORRUPTION

Efficiency	Wastes resources
	Creates "public bads"
	Distorts policy
Distribution	Reallocates resources to the rich and powerful, those with military or police power, or those with monopoly power
Incentives	Distorts energies of officials and citizens toward the socially unproductive seeking of corrupt rents
	Creates risks, induces unproductive preventive measures, distorts investments away from areas with high corruption
Politics	Breeds popular alienation and cynicism
	Creates regime instability

to say that widespread corruption leads to popular disillusionment with government, although the correlation, if we could measure it precisely, would not be perfect.

How might we summarize this discussion of the positive and negative effects of corruption? Table 1 outlines some of the important dimensions. In addition, policymakers should keep in mind the following ten propositions as they consider how far to go in persecuting various forms of corrupt behavior.

1. Corruption in general is harmful to economic, political, and organizational development. But all forms of corruption are not created equal. Some forms are more harmful than others. The differences are not just in terms of extent, which of course is important, but of the nature of the corruption and the circumstances in which it occurs.

2. Corruption involving the reallocation of strictly "private goods" may cause little harm to economic efficiency. Private goods are those goods such that one person's possession or consumption of them does not affect other people. Bribery may reallocate private goods and services in an economically efficient way. For instance, ticket scalping to soccer matches may not cause us to be concerned about "illicit" payments. On

the other hand, sometimes the private goods serve basic human needs; as regards such "merit goods" as access to donated food grains, we may mind a great deal if they are allocated corruptly. We need to consider the equitable distribution of the private goods as well as economic efficiency.

3. If corruption circumvents an inefficient or unjust policy, it may lead to social benefits. These putative benefits should, however, be weighed against losses measured in terms of the policy's original purposes.

4. Corruption generates negative externalities ("public bads"). It breaks down trust, confidence, and the rule of law. The social costs of particular corrupt acts can be particularly high when they create safety and environmental hazards, undermine merit systems, or otherwise threaten a broad public interest.

5. Corruption is particularly harmful when it distorts incentives. The combination of monopoly power and discretion—so often involved in the public sector—invites various forms of "rent-seeking" or "directly unproductive profit-seeking activities." As corruption spreads, officials and citizens waste their potentially productive energies on the pursuit of corrupt rents. The limiting case is when corruption becomes so systematized that ordinary citizens have to be corrupt to get by.

6. Corruption is sometimes a means for achieving political ends. But it can also generate great political costs. It may be a mechanism for buying political loyalty, which may occasionally lead to a sort of integration and participation. On the other hand, when this device is widely used, it leads to popular alienation and political instability.

7. Extortion is a particularly debilitating form of corruption. Extortion tends to outrage the citizen-victim. And the more corruption adversely and directly affects the general public, the more likely is public disaffection to grow.

8. Corruption may serve organizational interests, especially when it subverts unnecessary bureaucratic red tape. More commonly, though, corruption in organizations has disastrous effects on merit systems, the marshalling and allocation of resources, and the pursuit of the organization's primary mission. The practice of illicit "tips" or "speed money" may seem harmless or even efficient, but it often evolves into slowdowns, extortion, and the like.

9. It is important to notice who gains and who loses from corrupt

acts. This identification aids in identifying those forces likely to support and to oppose anticorruption programs.

10. Other things being equal, anticorruption efforts should be targeted toward the forms that cause the greatest damage. As we have noted, though, the damage can be of different kinds. In the following chapters we will see that other things are not usually equal. Anticorruption measures are not equally effective or equally costly. A good strategy, therefore, is to allocate anticorruption resources across various forms of corruption so that the marginal social costs of fighting each form of corruption are equated with the marginal social benefits of doing so.

JUSTICE PLANA'S OBJECTIVES

Upon assuming command of the BIR, Plana wisely realized that he should not blindly attack all forms of corruption. He began by finding out which forms were most serious – in terms of being widespread, involving the largest sums, and creating the greatest economic, political, and organizational damage. Then he had to consider his other objectives in the BIR. Fighting corruption was important, to be sure, especially in the context of President Marcos's purge; Plana had been brought in to clean up the BIR. But Plana recognized that fighting corruption could be pushed too far: an anticorruption campaign as his only initiative could render the bureau ineffective in its primary mission of collecting taxes.

"I had to prioritize the problems," Justice Plana told me in an interview in 1984. "One of the most important was the demoralization among personnel, which was closely related to their efficiency in tax collection."

Plana moved on this front immediately. He stressed a new system of measuring the effectiveness of BIR employees. They needed positive incentives.

> To the extent that they wouldn't put their heart into their work, or would pocket some of the money that should go to the government, then you don't get efficiency. So, we needed a system to reward efficiency. Before, inefficient people could get promotions through gifts. But even though I could not change pay scales, I could give them rewards through promotions and transfers.
>
> So, I installed a new system for evaluating performance. I got the people involved in designing the system, those who did the actual tax assessment and collection and some supervising examiners.

> Before, there was a personal evaluation by the supervisor, especially by the person who actually decided on the promotion. Now, instead of this I introduced a system based on the amount of assessments an examiner had made, how many of his assessments were upheld, the amounts actually collected – all depending on the extent and type of the examiner's jurisdiction.

Plana worked with his employees in this process; he wanted them to have a stake in the new system by which their performance would be judged. He developed a set of targets for each revenue district and each tax examiner. Plana himself took charge of approving major transfers within the bureau. He also implemented a small system of prizes. The best tax assessors would receive a cash award of P1000. There were also prizes for regional directors. Pay scales and job classifications could not be altered by the new commissioner: they were set in stone. But by taking control of promotions and transfers, implementing a new system of performance evaluation with the help of BIR employees, and giving a few prizes for top performers, Plana made an immediate impact. "In no time," he said later, "the examiners were asking for more assignments and were more conscious of their work."

It was in this context that Plana set out to reduce various forms of corruption within the BIR. Table 2 shows the kinds of corruption he had discovered and indicates their extent, the sums involved, whether taxpayers gain or lose, and other effects. Among these many problems, one stood out in Plana's mind.

"To me, it was evident. It was extortion. When you resort to intimidation, when you threaten the taxpayer with a fantastic assessment – that to me is the most serious form of corruption. This practice was fairly extensive and very pernicious."

Not least of the problems with extortion were its political effects. Notice that the other forms of external corruption involved complicit clients. When *arreglo* or *lagay* occurred, the individual clients involved benefited from the corruption. With *arreglo* the client received an illicit service to which he or she was not entitled – the lower tax payment. With *lagay*, in many cases the client received a licit service but faster than usual. (In some cases, though, *lagay* had degenerated into a standard payment for a service that should have been free.) But when extortion occurred, the client was directly victimized. If the client had no recourse, resentment and hostility would ensue; thus, this form of corruption, above all others, would lead to negative political consequences.

TABLE 2 A SUMMARY OF CORRUPTION WITHIN THE BUREAU OF INTERNAL REVENUE

	External Corruption
Lagay	Speed money and payments for supposedly free records and clearances. Extensive, small sums. Taxpayer involved gains, but overall taxpayers lose.
Extortion	Assessors threaten taxpayers with higher rates, preying on their ignorance or their unwillingness to subject their cases to costly litigation. Fairly extensive, and political dynamite. Taxpayers lose.
Arreglo	Assessors and taxpayers collude to reduce tax liabilities. Widespread, large sums. Taxpayer involved gains, but noncorrupt taxpayers lose and government loses millions in revenue.
	Internal Corruption
Embezzlement	Employees make off with funds collected. Widespread, especially in regions. Loses millions in revenue.
Fraud	Overprinting of tax stamps and labels. Not too widespread, not too costly.
Personnel scams	Choice positions within the BIR allocated for bribes. Systematized, widespread in regions. Contributes to the BIR's "culture" of corruption.
Delaying remittances	Tax collectors take the float on funds received. Fairly extensive, small losses.
Corruption of internal investigations	BIR's Internal Security Division rendered ineffective, exacerbating all the bureau's problems of corruption.

Plana also recognized that the BIR's culture of corruption—including its internal "market" for job assignments and the sometimes systematized sharing of bribes—had to be broken if progress was to be made. He saw his new performance evaluation system as one step in that direction. People could henceforth not deal for transfers or promotions. One's career success would be determined not by corrupt means and the amount of bribes received but by how effectively taxes were collected. Some of the incentives for corruption were thereby reduced.

Thus, Plana avoided many of the possible pitfalls in defining his anticorruption objectives. He saw that corruption was harmful but also that some varieties of corrupt behavior were more serious than others. He also recognized that when fighting corruption he had simultaneously to keep in mind the pursuit of the organization's other objectives.

With these points in mind, what policy alternatives should Plana consider for reducing corruption in the BIR? This question is the subject of the next chapter.

3 | Policy Measures

What policies should be considered as part of an anticorruption effort? In this chapter we continue with our Philippine case study and examine Justice Plana's masterful campaign to clean up the Bureau of Internal Revenue. Then we turn to more general analyses of the causes and cures for corruption. Various authors have emphasized cultural variables and economic structures (too much capitalism, too little capitalism). We will take a complementary tack, developing a principal-agent-client model based on microeconomic ideas of incentives and information. We enrich the simplest model with considerations of organizational structure and individual attitudes. From this we derive a framework for policy analysis, a heuristic outline of anticorruption measures. Its purpose is to help policymakers think creatively about the possible tools at their disposal. Finally, we will apply this framework to Plana's efforts in the Philippines and, in subsequent chapters, to other examples of anticorruption initiatives.

JUSTICE PLANA'S INITIATIVES

The new commissioner of the corruption-ridden Bureau of Internal Revenue later described his strategy as having three major components:

1. Establish a new performance evaluation system
2. Collect information about corruption
3. Punish corrupt high-level officials quickly

The first component, the *performance evaluation system*, was described at the end of the last chapter. This step would accomplish two things: it would boost morale and provide a positive orientation to the new commissioner's efforts. It also would help to control corruption by breaking the formerly corrupt system of transfers and promotions and by providing incentives for noncorrupt, efficient tax collection.

Information and the Probability of Detection

The second major component of Plana's strategy was to *collect information* about corruption. The goal here was not simply to find out which forms of illicit behavior were most severe but also to deter corruption. If BIR employees began to recognize that their corrupt activities would be detected (and punished), they would be less likely to undertake them.

Plana used several new sources of information. He brought in a new group of young CPAs and teamed them with a few irreproachable senior officials to review many tax cases, looking hard for signs of extortion and *arreglo*. As noted in the last chapter, Plana emphasized the deterrent effects of this step: "More than what they actually accomplished through these reviews was the impact on other examiners of the possibility that their work would be subjected to review. They would work harder and better as a result."[1]

Plana also used people from outside the BIR to provide him with information about corrupt activities. The most remarkable such step involved two teams of intelligence officers.

> One was a military group, and another was a civilian group. The military group I had known from my former days as Undersecretary of National Defense, under Defense Minister Ponce Enrile. There was a group of six officers that I could ask for help.
>
> The civilian group was from the National Intelligence Security Agency. The head of that used to be my subordinate in Defense.

Under Plana's direction these intelligence agents gathered both direct and indirect evidence about corruption. Some of these investigators were used as undercover agents. Plana placed some intelligence officers as tax examiners in "very suspicious groups," where they could learn firsthand about corrupt practices.

Other officers gathered indirect information about the life-styles of top

1. The quotations from Justice Plana come from an interview I conducted in Manila in March 1984. I will not footnote the rest of his remarks. Below I cite statements by current high BIR officials, which were based on interviews in the Philippines in March and April 1984; to preclude embarrassment or inconvenience, I avoid attributions.

BIR officials. Were these people living at levels beyond what seemed affordable on regular government salaries? The investigators obtained data on the finances of the bureau's 125 highest-ranking officers, from Revenue District Officers on up. Plana later said, "The intelligence people could identify about 30 percent of these top officials who on the basis of their properties seemed to have assets out of proportion to their visible incomes. I could look at these cases much harder."

In an interview in 1984, a senior officer of the BIR commented on this aspect of Plana's strategy: "Plana was an unknown here. He had only a few friends in the Bureau of Internal Revenue, so he needed to develop outside sources of information. He instituted the so-called intelligence network, which was met not only with disdain but scorn by many of the employees of the BIR. He used armed forces intelligence agents—covert agents, you know. But it worked!"

Plana also used sources of information inside the BIR. His Internal Security Division had to be completely revamped because of its complicity in past corruption. Three employees were removed, and all but two of the rest were reassigned. The BIR's Fiscal Control Division worked out a monitoring system to help identify potentially corrupt officers. They assembled a master list of approximately 2000 collection agents, and they gathered and tabulated several sources of information on each agent:

□ Evidence of delays in remittances, based on records from the Accounting Division

□ Evidence of remittances that could not be traced, based on both the reports of collection agents and BIR records

□ Evidence of divergences between remittance reports and the records of authorized respondents

Some of these data were not available, and other data were inaccurate, so these "red flags" did not automatically identify a corrupt official. If an employee had evidence of all three, however, he or she was subjected to an immediate audit. Having two out of three meant an audit when time permitted. During the first two years of this system's operation, all the employees thus identified for audit were found guilty of various offenses.

As the system developed, other information was added. The investigators identified more indirect indicators of possible corruption: "high living by collection agents (lavish consumption), gambling, frequenting night clubs, luxurious houses and accumulation of properties, maintaining *queridas*, membership in exclusive clubs."[2] Of course, such data were not always readily available to the Fiscal Control Division.

Penalizing the Corrupt

The third major component in Plana's anticorruption program was *quickly punishing some corrupt high-level officials.* "I wanted to set an example," Plana said, "because if people, especially the big ones, could commit extortion and graft and get away with it, the others would not be afraid to do it, because after all the Commissioner won't remove the big shots and maybe is not sincere."

He moved decisively. In a relatively short time thirty-four officials were dismissed, fifteen were required to resign, and thirty-nine were "reorganized out." Of those removed or demoted, eleven were regional directors, five were assistant regional directors, and nine were revenue district officers.[3]

Plana carefully cleared these moves with his minister and President Marcos. He later told me:

> We were able to get rid of the most notoriously corrupt. You will notice that the cleaning process was not limited to the lower levels. In fact, one of the deputy commissioners was removed, as were service chiefs, directors, and revenue district officers.
>
> To review all of them, it took more than a year. And the President backed me up.

Professor Leonor Magtolis-Briones, a longtime student of corruption and of the BIR, observed in 1977 that Plana's efforts achieved their desired effect on the rank and file. "The fact that those found guilty have been punished has had a tremendous psychological impact on the employees who are beginning to realize that perhaps the new Commissioner means business."[4]

2. Leonor Magtolis-Briones, "Negative Bureaucratic Behavior and Development: The Bureau of Internal Revenue" (Paper prepared for the Seminar on Bureaucratic Behavior and Development, College of Public Administration, University of the Philippines, 3 October 1977), 14.

3. Ibid., 28.

4. Ibid., 26.

Because they were beyond his jurisdiction, Plana could not raise the formal penalties for corruption. Indeed he found that it was often difficult to get a criminal conviction. The dismissal of an errant employee was frequently the most that he could accomplish. As a senior BIR officer explained in 1984:

> The penalties on paper are quite stiff. The funny thing is, though, that often they can't actually get an affidavit from the witnesses when it comes to trial. The friends and relatives of the accused person go to all the friends and relatives of the accusers, and they say, "Oh, you can't do this" or "Everyone is corrupt, why pick on this poor person?" or "How can you ruin this person?" And in most cases, when the situation comes to trial, the people who brought the charges are not willing to file the affidavits. Therefore, the punishments turn out to be weak.

Plana did obtain some criminal convictions. For example, Reyes and Santos, whose transgressions were mentioned at the outset of Chapter 2, were fired and convicted on criminal charges.[5] He also used other means of punishing the corrupt. For instance, realizing that publicity could raise the costs to transgressors, even if they could only be dismissed from the BIR, Plana furnished reporters with details on various cases. The sensational newspaper accounts that followed had a tremendous impact, especially in the Philippines where one's family name is almost sacred.[6]

5. Cruz was fired, and his criminal case was pending in late 1977; I have not been able to ascertain his fate. Lauro was dismissed from the service, and his case received wide coverage in the metropolitan dailies. The mysterious Bong was said to have died before his case came to court, but a government official who heard Professor Magtolis-Briones speak of Bong said Bong was alive and well. (Personal communication, Magtolis-Briones, March 1984.)

6. This attitude is well displayed in Plana's message to BIR employees on the occasion of the bureau's seventy-fifth anniversary:

> Perhaps I can best sum up my thoughts on the BIR's Diamond Jubilee by passing on to you a poem I picked up somewhere in one of my trips, in the hope that the idea it imparts will be enshrined in the heart of each and every one of us. It reads:

> You got it from your father,
> it was all he had to give.
> So it's yours to use and cherish
> for as long as you may live.
> If you lose the watch he gave you,
> it can always be replaced.
> But a black mark on your name,
> Son, can never be erased.
> It was clean the day you took it,

(Three of the corrupt BIR officials whose cases were publicized suffered heart attacks.) In this way Plana raised the *effective* penalties for corrupt behavior, even though he could not change the laws or the judicial process.

Other Anticorruption Measures

Plana later highlighted those three components as central: a new performance evaluation system, new sources of information, and quick punishment for some top, corrupt officials. But he used a number of other techniques in his effort to reduce corruption.

Professionalizing the BIR. Plana set higher professional standards. He tightened job requirements and initiated written examinations. He recruited high honors graduates from the elite University of the Philippines. Only CPAs or lawyers with eighteen units in accounting were considered for appointment to revenue examiner positions. He installed a tough antinepotism regulation that forbade the appointment of any relative of a BIR employee up to the sixth degree. And as noted earlier, he eliminated personnel scams by rationalizing promotions and transfers, which were referred to his office before enactment.

Identifying potentially corrupt taxpayers. The BIR instituted a "selective quality audit program," which was designed to identify taxpayers who were especially likely to have understated their incomes or overstated their deductions.

Toughening up control systems. The prevalence of so much internal corruption was a sign of weak accounting and control systems. Plana made several changes: an expanded system of tax payments through banks rather than revenue agents; confirmation letters to check taxpayers' payments; more spot checks and audits; closer supervision of collection agents by Revenue District Officers; use of a single tax receipt

---

and a worthy name to bear.
When he got it from his father,
there was no dishonor there.
So make sure you guard it dearly,
after all is said and done.
You'll be glad your name is spotless,
when you give it to your son.

(Letter from Plana to BIR employees, 1 August 1979)

instead of the former multiple copies; and various measures to halt the use of false official receipts and unauthorized tax stamps and seals.

Changing tax laws. Plana recommended many changes to the tax laws. Some were designed to raise more revenue, others to align the tax system with the country's developmental objectives. But of particular interest to us are his efforts to simplify the tax system and reduce the discretion of tax officials and taxpayers; both these measures were designed to reduce the possibilities for evasion and *arreglos*.

Tightening central supervision over the regions. Much of the BIR's corruption took place in the provinces. Many of the bureau's seventeen regional directors were at best incapable of managing effectively and at worst involved in corrupt relationships with tax examiners in the field. Plana tried to increase central control. Sometimes this was informal. One senior BIR official told me, "Plana had a day, each month, for the regional director. He would monitor him. It was not a social call. You would have to answer questions. 'Why did revenues drop last month?' or 'I heard that so-and-so inspector was gallivanting around. What is going on?'" Plana also used more formal procedures, such as reducing the discretion of tax examiners in the field. All cases involving amounts above P100,000 were referred to the central office.

Rotating agents. Field workers were periodically moved so as to avoid potentially corrupt personal relationships with taxpayers. Tax examiners were rotated every two years, and chiefs of provinces every three. In a single move Plana reshuffled 198 tax inspectors and fieldmen working under the Specific Tax Division.

Involving outside auditors. The Philippines Commission on Audit was brought in for the first time to oversee the remittance of tax revenues.

Changing attitudes toward corruption. Plana initiated "Reorientation Seminars," which were designed to inculcate the values of public service among BIR staff. One of his colleagues recalled: "There was also a total effort along the lines of moral reform. These included a lot of small things as well as big ones. For example, we initiated a Toastmaster's Club. We tried to get members to take time and turn them toward public and group activities. We revived the glee clubs and the athletic clubs. We even revived the religious organizations. There were daily masses held in the BIR building."

Moreover, Plana set a personal example. His honesty and incorruptibility became legendary, admired even by those most skeptical of

Marcos and his cronies. According to one knowledgeable observer, "He refused even the smallest gifts. When he would travel, he would refuse to have dinners bought for him."

This is an impressive array of initiatives. Interestingly, though, Plana did little to involve the public in his anticorruption efforts, which might have helped him gather evidence and improve taxpayer cooperation. He would occasionally tell the newspapers that his source of information was a tip from a taxpayer, even if in reality the source was his military intelligence group. Plana said that his actions were warmly received by the public. But there were no citizen's groups, hotlines, advisory boards, taxpayer committees, or other such measures.

The Results of Plana's Fight against Corruption

Plana made a deep impact on the BIR. When he left the bureau in 1980 to become deputy minister of finance—and shortly thereafter, a justice of the Supreme Court—he was widely praised for having stemmed the tide of corruption in the BIR. Even rabid opponents of the Marcos regime and critics of Marcos's own corruption recognized and admired Plana's achievements at the BIR.

It is difficult to measure such things, but from all accounts corruption had diminished greatly. *Lagay* and the internal selling of jobs were halted. Much of the embezzlement and fraud were eliminated. The BIR apparently reduced *arreglos* but did not eliminate them, especially in estate and corporate taxes. Reports of extortion and the harassment of taxpayers dropped sharply. Moreover, Plana had engendered a new sense of professionalism and pride within the BIR. When President Marcos spoke in 1979 of "the days when tax corruption was rife," he was referring to the time before Justice Plana took over.

These achievements took place in a country where other forms of corruption remained widespread. Martial law and Marcos's "New Society" had apparently made little difference in many domains. In a survey in Metro Manila in 1981, "graft and corruption" was the third most frequently cited "national concern which has worsened most since 1972," the year when martial law was declared. (The top two were inflation and crime.) Only 32 percent of the respondents thought the corruption problem nationwide had improved.[7] During and after Plana's time with the BIR the public widely believed that corruption in the Philippines went to the top of the political system. Since Marcos's fall from power and exile from the Philippines in early 1986, sources have estimated that he and his family took between $5 billion and $10 billion out of the country.

In this context it is not surprising that Plana's success was neither complete nor permanent. Indeed after his departure from the BIR in 1980, the ratio of taxes collected to the gross national product dropped, and the number of tax returns filed fell from a high of about 3 million in 1979 to about 2.6 million in 1981.[8] Stories of BIR corruption began to grow. In 1983, the new revenue commissioner noted that BIR officials were sometimes "harassing taxpayers through fantastic assessments of their tax liabilities"[9]—this was the form of corruption that Plana had found most repugnant. Several stories emerged about "suspected cover-ups involved from the bureau's intelligence and inspection service divisions."[10] Because the banks were increasingly called upon to vouchsafe tax payments, corruption scandals occurred there, too.[11] Corruption in the regional offices of the BIR was said to be on the rise again.

During my visit to Manila in 1984, I found hopeful signs but also reasons for new worries in the Bureau of Internal Revenue. Many top BIR officials were optimistic that policy changes would aid them in controlling corruption and tax evasion in the future. For instance, in 1982, the Philippines adopted a modified gross income tax—a sort of flat tax system—which was estimated to have raised revenues by 16 percent on a base of P2 billion.[12] This idea had been initiated under Plana and was pushed hard by him; one of its major advantages was its reduced

7. Felipe Miranda, "Metro Manila Survey on Government and Politics: Identification and Analysis of Potential Sources of Political Stress," A Final Report of the Social Weather Station Project (Manila: Development Academy of the Philippines, September 1981), 6.

8. "Performance Analysis of the Tax System, 1970–1981," *Tax Monthly* 24 (May 1983), 2.

9. "20 Top Revenue Men Face Charges," *Bulletin Today*, 16 May 1983, 1. He also noted that in the previous year 688 cases had been filed against BIR employees.

10. "'Tanod' Warns BIR Probers," *Bulletin Today*, 17 February 1983, 2; "BIR Forms Probe Team," *Bulletin Today*, 21 May 1983.

11. Jun Ramirez, "BIR Men, Bank Tie-up Exposed: Tax Money Used for Other Deals," *Bulletin Today*, 5 February 1984, 1.

12. This figure was cited by a top BIR official in an interview in April 1984.

susceptibility to *arreglos*. The officials also hoped that the Philippines' new public ombudsman—the Tanodbayan, founded in 1980—would gain further independence and influence, to become a helpful ally to top BIR officials in the continuing battle against corruption.[13] Within the BIR a new "sector operations office," with some 200 professional staff, concentrated on specific industries, trying to provide "independent" estimates of how much taxes should be paid. "This gives the BIR a lot more information on which to base audits or to use when confronting corporate taxpayers, in case there are negotiations," an official explained. In 1982 the bureau opened a taxpayer complaint office. The bureau also instituted new measures to induce nonfilers to file, to involve business groups in the detection of abuses, and to revamp the BIR's internal security forces.

But there were signs of trouble ahead, too. No one of Plana's acuity or widely acknowledged probity was at the reins of the BIR. (It might be said in criticism of Plana that he did not adequately prepare a successor.) And a particularly nasty form of corruption was on the rise. One middle-level regional official told me of ever greater political "interference" in tax collection at the regional level. Another mentioned stories of the Marcos machine directly seizing tax receipts in certain provinces. More accounts of such stealing occurred before the 1986 presidential elections. The *New York Times* reported, "There was also the judicious use of presidential influence to install Marcos relatives in the Bureau of Internal Revenue, where they were in a position to help family members evade taxes, investigators now say."[14] And some people have even maintained that Marcos financed much of his election campaign through high-level pilfering of BIR funds.

These abuses had never occurred under Justice Plana. Not only was there new leadership in the BIR, but also the times had changed: Marcos was in trouble and needed big money. Plana's accomplishments were not all permanent—as one of my students cracked, "For corruption, there is no Planacea"—but there were accomplishments, as even Marcos's foes

13. See, for example, Maria Concepcion de Alfiler, "Corruption Control Measures in the Philippines: 1979–1982" (Paper prepared for the President's Center for Special Studies [Manila: College of Public Administration, University of the Philippines, March 1983]).

14. *New York Times*, 30 March 1986, 12.

acknowledged. When we consider measures for controlling corruption, we can find much to study and admire in what Justice Plana did.

FROM CAUSES TO CURES

Justice Plana's choice of tools depended on his understanding of the conditions under which corruption will and will not thrive. What can we say about these conditions? Why is there corruption in the first place?

The literature on corruption in developing countries contains some broad answers. Let's call them "cultures favoring corruption," "too much capitalism," and "too little capitalism."

Cultures Favoring Corruption

"When we observe that corruption is more prevalent in South Asia than in the developed Western countries," wrote Gunnar Myrdal, "we are implying a difference in mores as to where, how, and when to make a personal gain."[15] In some cultures people (or perhaps just government officials) have such different values that corruption is less prosecuted, more accepted, perhaps even "part of the mores."

For example, one author attributes widespread corruption in Mexico partly to the greater importance there of personal relationships. If a friend asks you for a favor, you want to do it—even if you happen to be a government official and the favor is against the rules. "The prevalence in the society of personalism and *amistad*, primary loyalties being directed toward one's family and friends rather than toward government or administrative entity, has an important effect on the level of corruption. Mexicans treat one another as *persons*, with the result that formalized codes of behavior carry little weight in the society."[16] In other societies tribal and kinship loyalties may override an agent's obligations to his public duties, again creating a climate conducive to corruption.

> Thus, members of the African political elite corrupt themselves not only

15. Gunnar Myrdal, "Corruption as a Hindrance to Modernization in South Asia," in *Political Corruption: Readings in Comparative Analysis*, ed. Arnold J. Heidenheimer (New York: Holt, Rinehart & Winston, 1970), 237.

16. Martin Harvey Greenberg, *Bureaucracy and Development* (Lexington, Mass.: D. C. Heath, 1970), 70.

> for personal gain but also for their immediate families and for those who belong to the same kinship group or tribe that make up their clienteles. In fact, the distinction between personal and collective gain is academic. One has a strong obligation to one's group, but none to any others. The politics of tribalism, corruption, the sense of insecurity prevailing among members of the elite, and their mutual distrust exacerbate and reinforce each other.[17]

The custom of giving gifts is one of the "mores" that are said to lead to, or to be confused with, corruption. For example, in traditional Africa it is popular to give gifts to chiefs. Isn't a bribe to a public servant simply an extension of this practice? Indeed, might this not be corruption only to foreign eyes? Some Westerners have "explained" or excused African corruption in such a fashion.

Interestingly, many Africans disagree with this diagnosis, as historian Robert L. Tignor points out.

> Ironically, the Europeans I interviewed insisted that much of the corruption and bribery that took place was only traditional gift-giving . . . that what was called corruption was the result of the misapplication of European norms of good government to quite dissimilar societies. According to them, corruption existed only in the minds of moralizing Europeans.
>
> The African evidence is overwhelmingly to the contrary. Educated intellectuals attacked the chiefs, using European standards of upright bureaucracy. . . . The less well educated and the uneducated felt the chiefs to be violating traditional norms. . . .
>
> . . . On the whole, chiefs were seen as corrupt by whatever standard one employed.[18]

On the subject of gift giving leading to bribery, a Western political scientist reports African skepticism.

> A number of Ghanaian writers suggest that it is less important than situational or historical factors. Even in the traditional milieu there are clear-cut limitations on gift-giving and family obligations which preclude corruption. Moreover, the deliberate exploitation of traditional practices and the rational calculation of these benefits to be derived are completely alien to

17. Ken C. Kotecha, with Robert W. Adams, *African Politics: The Corruption of Power* (Washington, D. C.: University Press of America, 1981), 95.

18. Robert L. Tignor, "Colonial Chiefs in Chiefless Societies," in *Bureaucratic Corruption in Sub-Saharan Africa: Toward a Search for Causes and Consequences*, ed. Monday U. Ekpo (Washington, D.C.: University Press of America, 1979), 200.

customary social relations. In this regard, Ghanaians realize that a gift to a chief means one thing; a gift to a civil servant, another.[19]

Corruption has sometimes been attributed to the continuation of the exploitative patronage system found in traditional societies. "It has often been observed," wrote political scientist and Africanist John Waterbury, "that the search for protection from nature, violence, and the exactions of arbitrary and predatory governments was a constant theme of social life in so-called traditional societies." In the corrupt governments encountered in many countries today, "the poor of the Third World may have exchanged one kind of vulnerability for another."[20]

For a variety of cultural and historical reasons, then, societies differ in their mores, customs, and standards of behavior. These differences, in turn, may account for the differing degrees and kinds of corruption found across countries. On the other hand, as noted in Chapter 1, the majority of people in nearly all cultures understand that most of the kinds of corruption we will study—bribery, extortion, tax *arreglos*, police corruption, and so forth—are neither lawful nor customary. As elsewhere in social analysis, "cultural differences" may easily be abused as an explanation.

Too Much Capitalism

A nation of merchants, wrote the philosopher Immanuel Kant, is a nation of swindlers.[21] To some observers, including many intellectuals in developing countries, the root causes of corruption are capitalism and its

19. Herbert H. Werlin, "The Roots of Corruption–The Ghanaian Enquiry," in *Bureaucratic Corruption*, ed. Ekpo, 386.

20. John Waterbury, "Endemic and Planned Corruption in a Monarchical Regime," in *Bureaucratic Corruption*, ed. Ekpo, 359.

21. Kant said: "The Palestinians who live among us have the well-merited reputation of being sharpers, owing to the spirit of usury which holds sway amongst most of them. It is true that it seems odd to imagine a nation of swindlers but it is equally difficult to imagine a nation of merchants, by far the most important of which, bound together by ancient superstitions and recognized by the State which they inhabit, do not aspire to civic virtue but wish to compensate their shortcoming in this respect by the benefits they derive from deceiving people who grant them protection, and even by swindling one another. But a nation composed merely of merchants, that is to say of unproductive members of society, cannot be other than this" (Immanuel Kant, *Vermischte Schriften*, cited in Leon Poliakov, *The Aryan Myth: A History of Racist and Nationalist Ideas in Europe*, trans. Edmund Howard [New York: Basic Books, 1974], 172).

historical ally, colonialism. Socialist leaders decry the corruption that eats away at their nations—in recent years, Tanzania's Julius K. Nyerere has lamented "corruption growing like cancer."[22] They declare that a move away from capitalist values is needed to overcome the problem. Islamic leaders in Iran blamed the corruption of the Shah's regime in large measure on the evils of capitalism.[23] Commentators in the Soviet Union "generally attribute instances of corruption among Soviet officials today to 'vestiges of the past' that will wither away as the Socialist system becomes ever more firmly established."[24]

A good example of this style of explanation can be found in a fascinating study of Zaire. The author's research documented astonishing examples of corruption. For example, two thirds of the names on the civil service roster in Zaire were fictitious, accounting for 20 percent of the national budget in 1978. The bureaucracy is corrupt; because the bureaucracy was brought by the colonialists, the colonialists are largely responsible for the corruption:

> If readers have been persuaded that this bureaucracy was indeed a colonial creation—the result of the penetration into lineage-based society of the capitalist mode of production—then it stands to reason that systematic bureaucratic corruption is part of the same process. Bureaucratic corruption has taken on the function of reproducing conditions of the capitalist mode of production as it has progressed from the colonial political conjuncture to the present neo-colonial conjuncture.[25]

Too Little Capitalism

If methods other than the market are used to allocate resources, corruption will flourish. This line of explanation might be characterized as calling for more, rather than less, capitalism. If the market were allowed to replace the government wherever possible, corruption would be reduced.

22. Cited in Uma Lele, "Tanzania: Phoenix or Icarus?" *World Economic Growth*, ed. Arnold C. Harberger (San Francisco: ICS Press, 1984), 478n.

23. Shaul Bakhash, *The Reign of the Ayatollahs* (New York: Basic Books, 1984).

24. John Kramer, "Political Corruption in the USSR," *Western Political Quarterly* 30 (June 1977): 213.

25. David J. Gould, *Bureaucratic Corruption and Underdevelopment in the Third World: The Case of Zaire* (New York: Pergamon Press, 1980), 122. The reference to the largely fictitious civil service roster is on p. 71.

Box 8 Some Social Conditions Underlying Corruption

Political scientist Samuel P. Huntington in his classic book on political development put forth several propositions about the conditions favoring corruption in government.

□ Corruption tends to increase in a period of rapid growth and modernization, because of changing values, new sources of wealth and power, and the expansion of government.

□ There tends to be *less* corruption in countries with *more* social stratification, *more* class polarization, and *more* feudal tendencies. These conditions provide a more articulated system of norms and sanctions, which reduces both the opportunity for and the attractions of corrupt behavior.

□ In Latin America the "mulatto" countries have more corruption than the "Indian" or "mestizo" countries; black Africa also has a high degree of corruption. As the cause Huntington cites not race itself but rather the associated phenomenon in these countries of the "general absence of class divisions."

□ A country's ratio of political to economic opportunities affects the nature of corruption. If the former outweigh the latter, then people will enter politics in order to make money, and this will lead to a greater extent of corruption.

□ If foreign business is prevalent, corruption tends to be promoted.

□ The *less* developed are political parties, the more prevalent is corruption.

Samuel P. Huntington, "Modernization and Development," in *Bureaucratic Corruption in Sub-Saharan Africa: Toward a Search for Causes and Consequences*, ed. Monday U. Ekpo (Washington, D.C.: University Press of America, 1979), 313–24. This is an excerpt from Huntington's *Political Order in Changing Societies* (New Haven: Yale University Press, 1968).

An extreme version of this idea would turn a public service monopoly over to a private sector monopoly. The outcome might be no different. The same consumers might pay the same inefficiently high "price" for the service—only now it would be called the market price instead of a corrupt bribe.

This transformation could even be done with the collection of taxes. Indeed it has been done: in olden times, "tax farming" was commonplace.

Under this scheme the ruler sold to the highest private bidder the rights to collect revenue from specific sources. The winning bidder or "farmer" would create his own collecting agency, as well as the necessary enforcement apparatus. In colonial Singapore in the nineteenth century, such a system of local tax farmers was used by the British administration, in part because otherwise "the government would be brought into a frequent and odious collision with the natives, and compelled to employ a vile, expensive and corrupt crew of native excise officers."[26] But the "farmers" and their enforcers were themselves corrupt and coercive, and eventually the British did take over the tax collection apparatus. Privatizing, in this case, was no guarantee that abuses would diminish–though it apparently made a difference to the British authorities in the earlier years that the "corrupt crew of officers" were not in Her Majesty's own employ.

In many cases, therefore, letting a private firm, instead of the government, distribute goods and services does not necessarily reduce the harmful effects of corruption. If monopoly power and discretionary enforcement remain, consumers can expect to continue to pay too high a price. For instance, rent seeking will probably still occur. Thus, the key ideas regarding underlying conditions might not be capitalism versus state socialism, or the private sector versus the public sector, but rather *competition* and *accountability*. We'll return to this point later in the chapter.

These three theories about underlying causes–corruption-prone cultures, too much capitalism, and too little capitalism–have something in common. They are aimed at basic structures, values, and ideologies. To carry out their goals requires changing those structures or values or ideologies, and this is notoriously difficult. Recognizing this, one may resort to a shrug of the shoulders: "If you can't change the structure or values of a society, you can't do anything about corruption."

Although this view has some merit, we are glad that Justice Plana did not succumb to it. He had been appointed to the top of a corrupt organization, in the midst of a corrupt society, with national leadership that itself was corrupt. He could easily–and understandably–have concluded that there was nothing he could do. But because he did not reach such a conclusion, he was able to accomplish a lot to reduce corruption.

26. C. M. Turnbull, *The Straits Settlements 1826–1867* (London: Athlone Press, 1972), 204.

Box 9 **Unhelpful Advice?**

When it considers anticorruption policies at all, the literature on corruption in developing countries gives advice that sounds fatalistic. It is not that the advice is false, only that it may overlook policy tools that can be used in the meantime to reduce, though not to eradicate, various kinds of corruption. For example:

> The cures for corruption in developing countries are these:
>
> The passage of time, during which, given steady economic progress, loyalties will gradually move from family, clan and tribe to nation-state.
>
> The spread of education, which will enable people to understand what politics are about, instead of regarding them as a tribal or partisan form of excitement; which will help also in the development of a scientific approach to the problems of government and administration.
>
> The evolution of a public opinion, which must follow the spread of education, which rejects corruption either because it is morally wrong or because it is scientifically inefficient, or both.
>
> The growth of commerce and industry, which will strengthen an element in the middle class which is at present weak, and which, historically, has been opposed to corruption.
>
> The further growth of the professional class, and its resolve to raise its ethical standards by increasing association.
>
> The diffusion of power, wealth and status now enjoyed primarily by politicians through society as a whole.
>
> The recognition of the fact that democracy which is worth having is a mature concept, and that in developing countries *local* democracy must by definition be immature; and, consequently, calls for a continuance of central control and inspection, exercised by the civil service.
>
> The raising in prestige and the increase in the number of skilled accountants and auditors, and the recognition of their equal status in development programmes with administrators, engineers, industrialists and agriculturalists.
>
> The rigorous enforcement of the laws concerned with inspection.
>
> The personal witness of individuals who are opposed to bribery and corruption.
>
> There are no shorter cuts than these.

Ronald Wraith and Edgar Simpkins, *Corruption in Developing Countries* (London: George Allen & Unwin, 1963), 208.

His case raises the possibility that other policymakers, too, can undertake measures to reduce corruption in their agencies. Short of contemplating broader social changes, though, how can policymakers get a handle on policies to combat corruption?

PRINCIPALS, AGENTS, AND CLIENTS REVISITED

A useful framework for analyzing corruption is the principal-agent-client model briefly outlined at the beginning of the last chapter. A principal, such as Justice Plana, employs an agent, such as a tax collector. The agent—who for convenience sake is referred to with the feminine pronoun—interacts on the principal's behalf with a client, such as a taxpayer. The principal-agent-client model asks us to take an economic approach to corruption. An agent will be corrupt when in her judgment her likely benefits from doing so outweigh the likely costs. Similarly, a client will engage in bribery or other forms of illicit behavior when the benefits to him outweigh the costs to him.

Suppose the agent has two choices: to be corrupt or not to be corrupt. If she is not corrupt, she receives a payoff that is the sum of her regular pay plus the moral satisfaction of not being a corrupt person.

If she is corrupt, she gets a bribe. She also suffers what we might call the "moral cost" of being corrupt. This cost depends on her own ethical, cultural, and religious standards; it may depend on what her peers and colleagues are doing; and it may depend on how big a bribe she gets for how large a deviation from her responsibilities to the principal. For an unscrupulous person in a corrupt subculture, the moral cost of being corrupt may approach zero.

Something else may happen to the corrupt agent: she may be caught and penalized. She has to weigh this prospect when making her decision. The penalty could include the loss of her pay and her job, a criminal penalty, the disgrace to her name, and so forth.

Here, then, is the agent's choice:

> If I am not corrupt, I get my pay and the moral satisfaction of not being a corrupt person.
>
> If I am corrupt, I get the bribe but "pay" a moral cost. There is also some chance I will be caught and punished, in which case I will also pay a penalty, and lose my pay.

> So, I will be corrupt if: the bribe *minus* the moral cost *minus* [(the probability I am caught and punished) *times* (the penalty for being corrupt)] is *greater than* my pay plus the satisfaction I get from not being corrupt.[27]

When the agent is corrupt, she receives private benefits but generates costs—or "negative externalities"—for the principal. The principal therefore wants to induce the agent to undertake the optimal degree of productive activity *and* the optimal degree of corrupt activity. If the principal has perfect information about the agent's productive and corrupt activities, he can easily persuade the agent to act as he desires. The principal simply pays the agent the value of her marginal product, in the case of her productive activities; and in the case of her corrupt activities, the principal taxes such behavior just as he would tax any externality-generating activities.

The principal's problem grows difficult when, as is usually the case in the public sector, he has poor information about the agent's activities,

27. A more complicated version of this calculation is featured in James Q. Wilson and Richard J. Herrnstein, *Crime and Human Nature* (New York: Simon and Schuster, 1985), 41–62 and 531–35. The amount of crime undertaken (B_c) by an individual and the individual's "avoidance of it, noncrime (B_n)" can be modelled with two equations:

$$B_c = \frac{p_c R}{p_c R + R_e + D_i}$$

$$B_n = \frac{p_n m R}{p_n m R + R_e + (D + \Delta)i}$$

where: R = net reinforcement for the criminal behavior—the tangible and intangible gains less the tangible and intangible contemporaneous costs; R_e = the total reinforcements being obtained, exclusive of those conditional on B; m = the ratio of the reinforcement for the noncrime (i.e., the legal and other penalties forgone by resisting the crime) to that for the crime; p_c = the probability of successfully executing the crime; p_n = the probability of receiving the legal and other penalties of the crime, if it is committed; Δ = the average delay between the reinforcers for the crime per se (i.e., R) and the penalties issuing, directly or indirectly, from apprehension, conviction, imprisonment, and so forth. Besides the legal penalties are the losses of prestige, earnings ability, association with family and friends, and so on; D = the time interval between B_c and R (i.e., the delay of the criminal act's reinforcer); and i is a parameter for "impulsiveness," a kind of discount rate for future benefits and costs (i is assumed to be the same for B_c and B_n). From these considerations the authors derive a few conclusions that enrich the simpler model presented in the text. For example: "It may be easier to reduce crime by making penalties swifter or more certain, rather than more severe, if the persons committing crime are highly present-oriented" (p. 62).

Box 10 **A Simple Decision Tree for the Potentially Corrupt Agent**

Let k be the agent's pay and $R(0)$ the moral satisfaction she takes from not being corrupt. By not being corrupt, the agent receives a payoff of $k + R(0)$. Let x be the bribe (or payoff from being corrupt), p the probability the agent is caught and punished if she is corrupt, f the size of the penalty, $R(x)$ the moral cost to her of taking a bribe of x, and U the utility of the agent involved.

Then the agent's decision tree is as shown in Figure 2.

Figure 2 **An Agent's Decision Tree**

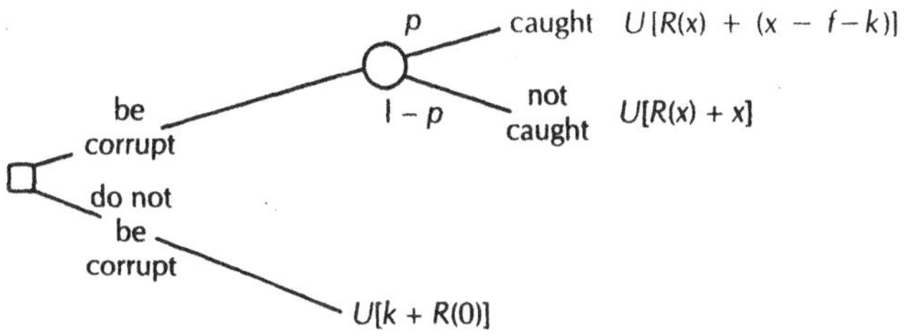

The expected utility to the agent of being corrupt is

$$EU = U/[R(x) + p(x - f - k) + (1 - p)x].$$

If this expression is greater than her payoff from not being corrupt, she will take the bribe.

either productive or corrupt. In real life the principal cannot tell how much of the outcomes he observes are due to the agent's activities on his behalf. And it is costly for the principal to find out more about what the agent is doing. The agent knows what she is doing, but the principal can't believe what she says. After all, the agent has incentives to mislead the principal into thinking she is working only on productive activities, never on corrupt ones. The principal understands this fundamental *asymmetry of information*. At the heart of the principal-agent problem are divergent incentives and asymmetric information; and these make the principal's problem difficult indeed. He has to set the agent's pay and penalties without perfect knowledge of the agent's marginal productivity and externality-generating behavior. He may decide to set up systems for gathering information about the agent's activities, but these systems will be costly in themselves.

(A similar analysis could be made of the principal's problem vis-à-vis the client. Here, too, the principal would like to structure the rewards and penalties for corrupt behavior to induce just the right level of good and bad activities by the client. Here, too, the principal faces imperfect and asymmetric information.)

The principal-agent model has been an active topic of research in economics for the past decade. For relatively simple situations, economists have analyzed how the principal should pay and punish the agent[28] and what information-gathering strategy the principal should follow.[29] The principal-agent framework has been used in various forms to study problems ranging from insurance to sharecropping; a book from the Harvard Business School explores its application to management.[30]

Closer to our topic, political scientist Edward Banfield used a principal-agent model in his important 1975 analysis of why corruption would tend to be more severe in government than in the private sector.[31] Since his paper and the pioneering work of political economist Susan Rose-Ackerman,[32] there have been numerous theoretical advances on

28. For example, Steven Shavell, "Risk Sharing and Incentives in the Principal and Agent Relationship," *Bell Journal of Economics* 10 (Spring 1979): 55–73.

29. For example, Frøystein Gjesdal, "Information and Incentives: The Agency Information Problem," *Review of Economic Studies* 49 (1982): 373–90.

30. Milton Harris and Artur Raviv, "Some Results on Incentive Contracts with Applications to Education and Employment, Health Insurance, and Law Enforcement," *American Economic Review* 68 (March 1978): 20–30; *Agency: The Structure of Business*, eds. John Pratt and Richard Zeckhauser (Boston: Harvard Business School Press, 1985). This work is intimately connected with the theory of nonzerosum games so effectively developed by Thomas C. Schelling (e.g., *The Strategy of Conflict*, 2d ed. [Cambridge, Mass.: Harvard University Press, 1980] and *Choice and Consequence* [Cambridge, Mass.: Harvard University Press, 1984]).

31. Edward C. Banfield, "Corruption as a Feature of Governmental Organization," *Journal of Law and Economics* 18 (December 1975): 587–605; reprinted in *Bureaucratic Corruption*, ed. Ekpo and in Edward Banfield, *Here the People Rule* (New York: Plenum, 1985).

32. Susan Rose-Ackerman, *Corruption: A Study in Political Economy* (New York: Academic Press, 1978); J. M. Montias and Susan Rose-Ackerman, "Corruption in a Soviet-type Economy: Theoretical Considerations," in *Economic Welfare and the Economics of Soviet Socialism: Essays in Honor of Abram Bergson*, ed. Steven Rosefielde (Cambridge, England: Cambridge University Press, 1981).

Box 11 **A Depiction of the Principal-Agent-Client Relationship**

1. *P* selects *A*
2. *P* sets *A*'s rewards and penalties
3. *P* obtains information from *A* and *C* about efforts and results
4. *P* structures the *A* – *C* relationship
5. *P* affects *A and C*'s "moral costs" of corruption.

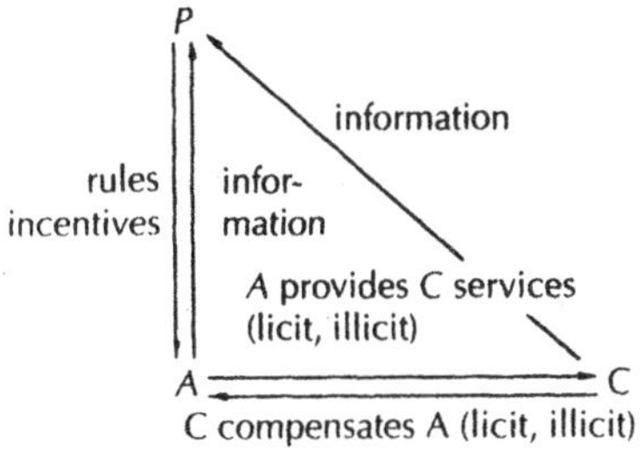

The principal (*P*) enlists an agent (*A*) to provide a service to *P* himself or to a client (*C*). *A* has discretion over that service. *A* may use that discretion in an illicit manner for a personal gain; doing so may create harm to the principal. Information about what *A* and *C* do is asymmetric, and it is expensive for *P* to overcome this asymmetry.

The principal may use several sorts of tools. He may

1. Select which agents work for him
2. Set the agent's rewards and penalties (also, perhaps, the client's)
3. Collect information about the agent and the client
4. Restructure the principal-agent-client relationship
5. Affect attitudes about corruption, changing the "moral costs" to the agent and the client of being corrupt

the principal-agent problem. But it is fair to say that several features of corruption as it is encountered in real life have yet to be incorporated in the economic models: the need to induce the agent to produce both optimal amounts of legitimate, productive behavior *and* optimal amounts of corrupt behavior; the multiplay nature of the principal-agent-client game; and, most important, the range of policy measures available to the principal. These latter include but go beyond the parameters of the usual principal-agent model (the setting of schedules of pay and penalties and the gathering of information). The following discussion tries to incorporate these additional features in a qualitative way.

A simple principal-agent-client model suggests several conclusions with regard to corruption. Illicit activities will be greater when agents have monopoly power over clients, agents enjoy discretion, and accountability is poor. Clients will be most willing to pay bribes when they reap monopoly rents from the service provided by the agents. The principal—this means you, the policymaker—has to analyze the extent of various kinds of corruption, assess their costs and possible benefits, and then undertake (costly) corrective measures up to the point where the marginal benefits in terms of reduced corruption match the marginal costs of the corrective measures.

Our model enables us to go one step further. It helps us to array and analyze the alternative policy measures available to the principal. The model suggests five clusters of such measures: selecting agents, changing rewards and penalties, gathering information, restructuring the principal-agent-client relationship, and changing attitudes about corruption. We'll examine these clusters in turn.

GENERIC POLICIES FOR REDUCING CORRUPTION

Selecting Agents

Typically we think of the task of selecting agents as finding those most technically capable for the job at hand—the most talented accountants, the best engineers, and so forth.[33] This is the main motivation behind "merit systems" in government service. But in the words of public administration scholar Gerald Caiden, "In the quest to replace the evils of the spoils system with the virtues of the merit system, it was assumed too readily that clever people would also be moral people."[34] When fighting corruption, the principal may be willing to give up something in technical capability to get more of what might be called "honesty" or "dependability."

33. On the general problem of selection, see Robert Klitgaard, *Choosing Elites* (New York: Basic Books, 1985) and Klitgaard, *Elitism and Meritocracy in Developing Countries: Selection Policies for Higher Education* (Baltimore: Johns Hopkins University Press, 1986).

34. Gerald E. Caiden, "Ethics in the Public Service: Codification Misses the Real Target," *Public Personnel Management* 10 (1981): 145–52.

Box 12 The Basic Ingredients of Corruption

Illicit behavior flourishes when agents have monopoly power over clients, when agents have great discretion, and when accountability of agents to the principal is weak. A stylized equation holds:

CORRUPTION = MONOPOLY + DISCRETION − ACCOUNTABILITY

Screening for honesty. One approach is to look for ways to predict which agents will be "honest." For example, increasingly the U.S. government "pre-screens" contractors and institutions that might receive financial awards for their honesty and integrity.[35] Employers can check individuals' work records for suspicious signs of previous misbehavior. Psychologists have even developed tests of honesty: for example, the Reid Report and Trustworthiness Attitude Scale. Some evidence suggests that such tests have successfully predicted "integrity on the job."[36] According to the *Wall Street Journal*, sales of honesty tests in the United States are "booming."[37]

35. This includes "checking relevant information including credit history, to check on qualifications, creditworthiness and outstanding indebtedness to the Federal Government. Pre-award screening has proven to be a successful tool for individual agencies to identify applicants for financial assistance who owe debts to the agency, have a criminal history, have internal management problems which could have a negative impact on grant or loan projects, or have unresolved audit problems. The screening can involve requesting a name check by law enforcement officials, checking the potential recipient's financial status, and/or reviewing audit records. The use of suspensions and debarments as a technique for protecting the Government from dishonest and incompetent businesses is also going to be automated and strengthened" (President's Council on Integrity and Efficiency, *Addressing Fraud, Waste, and Abuse: A Summary Report of Inspector General Activities*, Fiscal Year 1983, First Six Months [Washington, D.C.: U.S. Government Printing Office, 1983], 2).

36. D. J. Cherrington et al., "The Role of Management in Reducing Fraud," *Financial Executive* 49 (March 1981): 23–34.

37. In 1981 in the United States, such tests cost from $6 to $14 per administration, which took about an hour. "They cover a variety of topics, from off-track betting to homicide, posing questions that job interviewers might neglect, or be too embarrassed to ask. What's your favorite alcoholic drink? What drugs have you tried? Did you ever make a false insurance claim?. . . Although no single question can determine honesty, test makers say that an entire exam can." (Susan Tompor, "More Employees Attempt to Catch a Thief by Giving Job Applicants 'Honesty' Exams," *Wall Street Journal*, 3 August 1981, 17.)

Outside guarantees of dependability. A spoils system—or an arrangement in which appointments go to members of one's family, clan, or tribe—has many obvious faults. But it may also have a virtue. In such a system the principal may be able to invoke outside guarantees of the agent's dependability. First, the principal may be able to use the clan or tribe for credible information about the agent's honesty. Second, the clan or tribe may be employed to punish an agent who turns out to be dishonest. Thus, the principal who uses such "networks" to recruit agents may get a more dependable agent—and an agent with additional incentives to stay that way. In this fashion nepotism and similar practices may help overcome the principal-agent problem. This advantage may be a reason for the prevalence of what economists call "internal labor markets."[38]

But nepotism, favoritism, and related devices for selecting agents can easily backfire. The principal may well end up with people who are relatively *in*capable in technical terms and relatively *dis*honest. The ties of clan and tribe may turn out to strengthen the agent's hand vis-à-vis the principal, empowering a greater degree of illicit behavior.

The principal may nonetheless search for ways of obtaining outside guarantees of dependability. Sometimes agents can be brought in from another department noted for greater probity and discipline, or from an outside firm or international agency. One reason why international accounting firms are sought in the developing countries is their technical capability, but another important factor is their track record for honesty and dependability. The same might be said for "experts" brought in under foreign aid grants or loans.

The honesty of agents is most important in positions where discretion is unavoidable, monitoring is difficult, and the stakes are large. Examples include those responsible for internal security, inspectors, and top officials.

When they consider the selection of agents to control corruption, policymakers might ask several questions. How can I influence the selection of agents? What methods are available for screening agents according to their likely incorruptibility as well as their technical competence? What analogies to outside guarantees of dependability exist in my

38. Peter B. Doeringer and Michael J. Piore, *Internal Labor Markets and Manpower Analysis* (Lexington, Mass.: D. C. Heath, 1971).

situation? How much would such measures cost? What possible disadvantages could they entail?

Changing Rewards and Penalties

A second group of policy tools involves rewards and penalties for agents. The rationale behind this tactic is to make it more attractive for agents to be productive—and to fight corruption—and less attractive to engage in illicit behavior.

Rewards. Observers often note that, because of unreasonably low salaries, officials are compelled to be corrupt.[39] Indeed corrupt income may replace pay hikes. A kind of wage equilibrium is reached because illicit income is part of an effective market-clearing salary.

It does not follow, however, that raising pay scales will significantly reduce corruption. If nothing else changes, the now slightly richer official still will see that he or she can make money by being corrupt. A salary increase will not make much difference to incentives at the margin.[40]

Instead of raising overall pay levels, a more effective strategy is to change the specific rewards that accrue to specific actions. For example, the U.S. government is using the need to fight fraud, waste, and abuse to justify movements toward merit pay and incentive schemes.[41] In campaigns against corruption there is often a "mismatch between incentives and opportunity to control fraud," observed political scientist John A. Gardiner. Officials at the middle and bottom levels of a government hierarchy have many opportunities to reduce fraud but few incentives to do so. The reverse holds for top officials.[42]

39. For example, Clive Gray, "Civil Service Compensation in Indonesia," *Bulletin of Indonesian Economic Studies* 15 (March 1979): 85–113.

40. The change in the official's income affects the utility for these benefits and costs, but in most realistic cases, these "income effects" will not be enough to overcome the incentives at the margin to be corrupt. At the margin the expected benefits of being corrupt will still outweigh the expected costs.

41. President's Council, *Addressing Fraud,* 10.

42. For example, he cited a study of local welfare offices that concluded: "Wage increases for superior performance can be earned, but performance is evaluated on a variety of activities; there is no direct reward for superior 'investigative' work. Increasing cancellations by uncovering ineligibility factors may help in keeping the caseload under control, but it is not clear that this works to the caseworker's advantage, because caseloads are periodically redistributed." (John A. Gardiner, "Controlling Official Corruption and Fraud: Bureaucratic Incentives and Disincentives" [Paper presented at the International Political Science Association, Research Committee on Political Finance and Political Corruption, Oxford, England, March 1984], 23).

Changing incentives is crucial. Public officials should try to reward specific productive acts, and particularly effective agents. When the agents are private firms, as in the case of government contracts, the principal may make rewards *contingent* on results, rather than paying a flat fee or awarding a cost-plus contract. The economic literature on the principal-agent problem suggests making the agent's rewards partly, but not entirely, contingent on the results of her activities.[43] The effectiveness of contingent contracts in practice depend on the information available to the principal as well as on institutional features; in most cases in the public sector, employees are not rewarded through contingent contracts.

A related possibility is to postpone some of an agent's reward. For example, if an agent has a large, nonvested pension that she may lose through corrupt behavior, she may have slightly greater incentives to stay clean.[44] Or an agent may be asked to post a bond that is forfeited if she later behaves in an illicit fashion.

A principal often will have at his disposal nonmonetary rewards: training opportunities, travel, special assignments, transfers, awards, favorable publicity, and simple praise. All can be used to focus agents' attention on controlling corruption.

Penalties. Surprisingly often, the only punishment for a corrupt official is the loss of the job. Indeed even firing such a person can be problematical.[45] Prison sentences for corruption, when awarded, are often modest.

Plato had a different idea. "The servants of the nations are to render their service without any taking of presents. . . . The disobedient shall, if convicted, die without ceremony."[46] Recent work in economic theory—no doubt independently—also suggests that "infinitely large penalties" are an optimal solution for certain principal-agent problems.

43. Shavell, "Risk Sharing and Incentives;" Harris and Raviv, "Some Results on Incentive Contracts."

44. Gary Becker and George Stigler, "Law Enforcement, Malfeasance, and Compensation of Enforcers," *Journal of Legal Studies* 3 (January 1974): 1–19.

45. Although this problem is especially severe in the public sector, it is increasingly prevalent in the business world. See, for example, Joann S. Lublin, "Legal Challenges Force Firms to Revamp Ways They Dismiss Workers: Termination Is Often Upset If Secure Job Was Implied or Fairness Was Lacking: Rewriting the Old Handbooks," *Wall Street Journal*, 13 September 1983, 1, 18.

46. Plato, *The Laws*, ed. Edith Hamilton and Huntington Cairns (New York: Pantheon, 1961), book 12, sec. d.

Most societies, of course, are reluctant to mete out penalties of Platonic proportions.[47] The power to punish can be devastating if it is abused or corrupted; consequently, governments tend to guard against punishments for civil servants. While this caution may prevent abuses, it also leaves most public managers with little authority to penalize the corrupt. Consider Edward Banfield's generalization: "A government agency . . . is usually run by a loose and unstable coalition of individuals each of whom has independent legal-formal authority. . . . The executive function is itself divided."[48] As another expert noted, this is fertile ground for illicit behavior: "Corruption thrives on disorganization, the absence of stable relationships among groups and of recognized patterns of authority."[49]

If the authority to penalize errant agents does exist, policymakers should calibrate penalties according to deterrent effects. For example, Rose-Ackerman argued that penalties for corruption should be a positive function of *the size of the bribe* for the government official and of *the size of the profit made through the bribe* for the corrupt client. Thus, for deterrence's sake, penalties should not be the same for all illicit actions of the same type; penalties should vary according to the stakes involved.[50]

The principal need not confine his attention to penalties like firing, prison sentences, and fines. He may be able to punish agents in other ways. Justice Plana tarnished the family names of corrupt BIR employees,

47. A theme in John T. Noonan's history of bribes is how seldom societies have enforced penalties against corruption. Typical is his assessment of the achievements of Pope Gregory's sixth-century reforms: "After fourteen years of the pontificate of the most determined foe of the sale of holy orders . . . it is hard to find a single case where an accusation of the simonian heresy had been made, proved, and the offender punished by the Pope. 'God's consul,' as his epitaph proclaimed him, legislated but did not prosecute" (John T. Noonan, Jr., *Bribes* [New York: Macmillan, 1984] 124).

48. Banfield, "Corruption as a Feature," 83.

49. Huntington, "Modernization and Development," 322–23.

50. See, for example, Gary S. Becker, "Crime and Punishment: An Economic Approach," *Journal of Political Economy* 76 (March–April 1968): 169–217; George J. Stigler, "The Optimal Enforcement of Laws," *Journal of Political Economy* 78 (May–June 1970): 526–36; and A. Mitchell Polinsky and Steven Shavell, "The Optimal Trade-off Between the Probability and Magnitude of Fines," *American Economic Review* 69 (December 1979): 880–89. Empirical analyses are scarce. The literature is reviewed in Sally T. Hillsman, Joyce L. Sichel, and Barry Mahoney, *Fines in Sentencing: A Study of the Use of the Fine as a Criminal Sanction* (Washington, D.C.: Government Printing Office, November 1984). Of particular interest is the Swedish and German system of "day-fines," where the amount of the fine is determined as a function of both the seriousness of the offense and the economic means of the culprit (ibid., Appendix C).

Box 13 **Crack Down but Give Raises**

Historian Thomas Macaulay provided a colorful account of a successful fight against corruption in India. Here are some excerpts.

Such were the circumstances under which Lord Clive sailed for the third and last time to India. In May 1765 he reached Calcutta; and he found the whole machine of government even more fearfully disorganized than he had anticipated. . . . The English functionaries at Calcutta had already received from home strict orders not to accept presents from the native princes. But, eager for gain, and unaccustomed to respect the commands of their distant, ignorant, and negligent masters, they again set up the throne of Bengal for sale. . . . The news of the ignominious bargain greeted Clive on his arrival. [He wrote to a friend:] "Alas, how is the English name sunk! . . . I am come out with a mind superior to all corruption, and I am determined to destroy these great and growing evils, or perish in the attempt."

The Council met, and Clive stated to them his full determination to make a thorough reform, and to use for that purpose the ample authority, civil and military, which had been confided to him. Johnstone, one of the boldest and worst men in the assembly, made some show of opposition. Clive interrupted him, and haughtily demanded whether he meant to question the power of the new government. Johnstone was cowed, and disclaimed any such intention. All the faces round the board grew long and pale; and not another syllable of dissent was uttered. . . .

Clive redeemed his pledge. He remained in India about a year and a half; and in that short time effected one of the most extensive, difficult, and salutary reforms that ever was accomplished by any statesman. . . . He knew that, if he applied himself in earnest to the work of reformation, he should raise every bad passion in arms against him. He knew how unscrupulous, how implacable, would be the hatred of those ravenous adventurers who, having counted on accumulating in a few months fortunes sufficient to support peerages, should find all their hopes frustrated. . . . At first success seemed hopeless; but soon all obstacles began to bend before that iron courage and that vehement will. The receiving of presents from the natives was rigidly prohibited. The private trade of the servants [i.e., employees] of the Company was put down. The whole settlement seemed to be set, as one man, against these measures. But the inexorable governor declared that, if he could not find support at Fort William, he would procure it elsewhere, and sent for some civil servants from Madras to assist him in carrying on the administration. The most factious of his opponents he turned out of their offices. The rest submitted to what was inevitable; and in a very short time all resistance was quelled.

But Clive was far too wise a man not to see that the recent abuses were partly to be ascribed to a cause which could not fail to produce similar abuses as soon as the pressure of his strong hand was withdrawn. The Company had followed a mistaken policy with respect to the remuneration of its servants. The salaries were too low to afford even those indulgences which are necessary to the health and comfort of Europeans in a tropical climate. . . . It could not be supposed that men of even average abilities would consent to pass the best years of life in exile, under a burning sun, for no other consideration than those stinted wages. It had accordingly been understood, from a very early period, that the Company's agents were at liberty to enrich themselves by their private trade. This practice had been seriously injurious to the commercial interests of the corporation. . . .

The Company was now a ruling body. Its servants might still be called factors, junior merchants, senior merchants. But they were in truth proconsuls, proprætors, procurators of extensive regions. They had immense power. Their regular pay was universally admitted to be insufficient. They were, by the ancient usage of the service, and by the implied permission of their employers, warranted in enriching themselves by indirect means; and this had been the origin of the frightful oppression and corruption which had desolated Bengal. Clive saw clearly that it was absurd to give men power, and to require them to live in penury. He justly concluded that no reform could be effectual which should not be coupled with a plan for liberally remunerating the civil servants of the Company.

Thomas Babington Macaulay, "Lord Clive," in *Macaulay: Poetry and Prose* (Cambridge, Mass.: Harvard University Press, 1967), 355–57.

creating a huge effective penalty through publicity. The principal may punish an agent by affecting her credit rating, professional license, or later job prospects. One scholar distinguished ten categories:

> The least coercive strategies include two forms of moral suasion designed to induce voluntary change in provider or recipient behavior: (1) public pressure through disclosure and "jawboning" and (2) institutionalized peer pressure. Potentially more coercive are four methods of tying reimbursement to "approved behavior": (3) prior review, (4) prior authorization, (5) concurrent review, and (6) postdelivery denial or payment. The most coercive options are administrative and judicial: (7) restrictions placed directly on recipient utilization and/or provider delivery, (8) cancellation of program affiliation, (9) payment retrieval proceedings and civil penalties, and (10) criminal prosecution.[51]

51. Bruce Stuart, "Utilization Controls," in *National Health Insurance: Conflicting Goals and Policy Choices*, eds. J. Feder, J. Holohan, and T. Marmor (Washington, D.C.: The Urban Institute, 1980), 458–59; cited in John A. Gardiner and Theodore R. Lyman, *The Fraud Control Game: State Responses to Fraud and Abuse in AFDC and Medicaid Programs* (Bloomington: Indiana University Press, 1984).

Thinking about this second cluster of anticorruption policies–changing rewards and penalties–the principal might pose several questions. How can I more clearly define the organization's objectives, including the control of corruption? How can I then improve the way agents' efforts and achievements are rewarded and punished? How can I make rewards contingent on an agent's performance? In particular, what rewards might make agents more sensitive to problems of corruption? Are the available penalties stiff enough and appropriately calibrated to deter corruption? How can I alter them, both formally and through such devices as publicity? What are the costs of these various ways of improving rewards and punishments?

Gathering Information

If the principal has information on what the agent and the client are doing, he may be able to deter corruption by raising the chances that corruption will be detected and punished. Unfortunately, information is often not cheap. Several kinds of informational policies deserve consideration.

Systems for gathering and analyzing information. Auditing and management information systems often can be used to find *evidence* that corruption has occurred. Accounting texts speak of transactions as the key unit of analysis, and corrupt transactions may be tracked down if the information system has created "audit trails." As in the Philippines case, information systems can be set up so that "red flags" pop up when corruption is likely. Sometimes statistical analyses of a large number of transactions can help detect corruption; such techniques have been used to look at bidding patterns, the awarding of licenses and certificates, and change orders on contracts.[52]

A management information system can be rendered even more effective if it is supplemented with inspections. Randomness is an important characteristic. To search for corrupt transactions, the principal

52. Examples are given in President's Council, *Addressing Fraud*; Michael D. Maltz and Stephen M. Pollock, "Analyzing Suspected Collusion Among Bidders," in *White Collar Crime: Theory and Research*, eds. Gilbert Geis and Ezra Stotland (Beverly Hills, Calif.: Sage, 1980); and Robert E. Richardson, "A Proactive Model for Detecting Political Corruption: As Applied to the Purchase of Goods and Services in Middlesex County, Massachusetts" (Unpublished paper, Harvard Law School, May 1983).

may take a random sample rather than carry out a complete census; because he is thereby raising agents' perceptions that they have a greater chance of being caught, the principal may deter corruption. Unannounced inspections of particular activities or records may have a similar effect. Public administration professor Ralph Braibanti stated, "Careful, scientific work-flow analysis and rigid ruthless inspection of work flow, diaries and time logs by competent roving inspection teams are probably the most effective practical means of dealing with corruption."[53]

Information systems may also be used to assess an organization's *vulnerability* to corruption. The objective here is not to find evidence of past misbehavior but to locate places in the agency that seem particularly vulnerable to fraud and abuse. As the principal-agent-client model suggests, the principal should look for places where the agent has monopoly power and discretion, and where it is difficult to monitor her efforts or outcomes.

Information agents. Auditors, evaluators, and inspectors are key figures in the fight against corruption. In 1984 several colleagues and I carried out a survey of public and private management in the nine countries of the Southern African Development Coordinating Conference. We were repeatedly told that remarkable shortages of trained accountants were a major factor in encouraging corruption.[54] Concerning Nigeria, one expert has written, "One of the simplest yet most overlooked reasons why poorer countries have structural tendencies to inefficient and venal bureaucracies is the nature of their auditing procedures."[55] When auditing is strong, corruption can be dramatically reduced even in what seem to be hopelessly corrupt surroundings. "What encouraged corruption in Ghana, more than anything else, was the inadequacy of controls," Herbert H. Werlin observed. "Where

53. Ralph Braibanti, "Reflections on Bureaucratic Corruption," in *Bureaucratic Corruption*, ed. Ekpo, 25–26.

54. Our team of ten Africans and Americans was invited by the Southern African Development Coordinating Conference to study management needs in SADCC's member states of Angola, Botswana, Lesotho, Malawi, Mozambique, Swaziland, Tanzania, Zambia, and Zimbabwe.

55. Ronald Cohen, "Corruption in Nigeria: A Structural Approach," in *Bureaucratic Corruption*, ed. Ekpo, 301–2. Cohen went on to describe the shortage of government auditors.

Box 14 Vulnerability Assessments

Where is the potential for corruption in an organization? To find out, many policymakers are taking advantage of a tool known as vulnerability assessment.

Assessors first divide the organization into functional programs or activities. Then for each activity assessors look at three broad issues:

- □ The "general control environment"
- □ The "inherent risk" of corruption
- □ The adequacy of existing safeguards

The U.S. government suggests that these questions be addressed:

A. Is the general control environment permissive of corruption?
   1. To what degree is management committed to a strong system of internal control?
   2. Are appropriate reporting relationships in place among the organizational units?
   3. To what degree is the organization staffed by people of competence and integrity?
   4. Is authority properly delegated—and limited?
   5. Are policies and procedures clear to employees?
   6. Are budgeting and reporting procedures well specified and effectively implemented?
   7. Are financial and management controls—including any use of computers—well established and safeguarded?

B. To what extent does the activity carry the inherent risk of corruption?
   1. To what extent is the program vague or complex in its aims; heavily involved with third-party beneficiaries; dealing in cash; or in the business of approving applications, licenses, permits, or certifications? (The more of any of these, the greater the risk of corruption.)
   2. What is the size of the budget? (The bigger the budget, the greater the loss if corruption exists.)
   3. How large is the financial impact outside the agency? (The greater the "rents," the greater the incentive for corruption.)

4. Is the program new? Is it working under a tight time constraint or imminent expiration date? (If so, corruption is more likely.)
5. Is the level of centralization appropriate for the activity?
6. Has there been prior evidence of illicit activities here?

C. After a preliminary evaluation, to what extent do existing safeguards and controls seem adequate to control corruption?

Assessors use readily available information such as documents about policies and procedures, interviews, and observations of the program in action.

After a vulnerability assessment, the policymaker considers further study of the most vulnerable areas; one possibility is a detailed analysis of procedures and controls. A vulnerability assessment may take days or weeks, while the detailed further study may take months.

Only at the end of this process are remedial steps recommended.

Adapted from Office of Management and Budget, *Internal Control Guidelines* (Washington, D.C.: OMB, December 1982), chap. 4.

proper controls existed, as in the Volta Dam project, corruption was insignificant."[56]

The principal may add information agents, make them more professional, and strengthen their role in the organization. He should not overlook specialists who may function as "intelligence gatherers" about illicit activities.[57]

Within the organization, the rank-and-file can be encouraged to provide information about corruption. The principal may take measures to cultivate and protect "whistle-blowers." He may also create conduits of such information, such as ombudsmen, audit committees attached to the principal, or an anticorruption branch.

56. Werlin, "The Roots of Corruption," 391.

57. A useful workbook for investigators is Leigh Edward Somers, *Economic Crimes: Investigative Principles and Techniques* (New York: Clark Boardman, 1984), which includes chapters on intelligence and economic crime investigation, investigating criminal financial transactions, and investigating computer-related crimes.

Third parties as sources of information. Third-party data can help the principal overcome informational asymmetries within his organization. Public records and bank records are credible sources of data. Less reliable but often useful are the press and the media.

Clients and the public. Clients are sometimes good sources of information about corruption. When they are victimized by government agents—as in extortion—they have an incentive to say so. On the other hand, clients who benefit from corruption will obviously tend to keep quiet about it. The principal can encourage clients and the public to report corruption by issuing guarantees of anonymity, setting up hotlines, getting testimonials from local political figures, and encouraging citizens groups against corruption.

The principal may also fight corruption by giving more information *to* clients. Clients who are ignorant of their rights or of the rules that apply to them are particularly subject to corrupt officials. In this regard, simpler laws and regulations have an informational as well as administrative dimension.

The burden of proof. Rules govern how information is used to establish guilt. Shifting the burden of proof to the agent to show she is *not* guilty, can be a powerful deterrent to corruption. (Of course, such a step has obvious drawbacks.) Several countries have promulgated laws stipulating that an agent with wealth apparently beyond his salary may be required to prove that this wealth was gained through legal means.[58]

As regards these various informational strategies, policymakers might ask several questions. How well do existing information systems enable me to detect productive and illicit behavior on the part of agents? How

58. For example, the government of Thailand has promulgated a decree containing this stipulation: "If there are circumstances showing that any State official has become unusually wealthy, the Commission shall conduct an inquiry and shall have the power to instruct him to declare his assets and liabilities according to such particulars, procedure and within such time as the Commission may prescribe. If it appears from the findings of the Commission that such person is unusually wealthy and he cannot show that his wealth has been acquired legitimately, it shall be considered that he has abused his power and duties" (Office of the Commission of Counter Corruption, "B.E. 2518 [1975]," official translation published by the Government of Thailand, n.d. [1982?], 8–9).

In contrast, new legislation in Mexico permits only the "inspection and auditing" of public servants with "exterior signs of wealth that are ostensible and notoriously superior to the legal income a public servant could have." The burden of proof is not shifted. (Secretaría de la Contraloría General de la Federación, *Manual General de Organización 1983* [Mexico City, 1983], 17; my translation.)

might information be used to find both *evidence* of past corruption and the *vulnerability* of the organization to future corruption? How can information agents be strengthened? How can third-party information be used to detect corruption? Likewise how can we make use of the organization's clients and the general public? Can the burden of proof regarding an agent's illicit behavior be shifted? What are the possible costs of such measures? Consider direct monetary costs plus the costs in terms of morale and red tape from increased information flows and more inspectors.

Restructuring the Principal-Agent-Client Relationship

A fourth cluster of policies tries to reduce opportunities for corruption through organizational change. The aim here is to avoid situations where an agent has monopoly power plus discretion, with little possibility of accountability.

Competition. The enemy of monopoly is competition. Competition can sometimes be induced by turning the agency's activities over to a group of different private firms. Such a step is most likely to be successful when the good or service is a "private" one in the economic sense, produced under conditions of constant or increasing costs. Under other conditions a private monopoly may replace the public one, resulting in no benefit to the clients, or private competition may reintroduce the "market failure" that was the motive for the government's involvement in the first place. Thus, privatization is not a panacea for corruption, although it has its place.

The principal may induce competition among government agents. A client may be able to avoid extortion if there are many government agents to whom he or she can turn for the service. In simple models honest agents may eventually drive out dishonest ones. On the other hand, if the corruption involves clients requesting illicit services from agents, then competition may have the opposite effect: clients will learn who the dishonest officials are and flock to them.[59]

The discretion of agents. Organizational and procedural changes can be used to cut back agents' opportunities for corruption. Policies can be more clearly defined, rules can be designed to be more easily monitored,

59. See the valuable discussion in Rose-Ackerman, *Corruption*, chaps. 7 and 8.

Box 15 When Do More Rules Lead to Less Corruption?

The Santhanam Committee Report on corruption in India said: "It is necessary to take into account the root causes of which the most important is the wide discretionary power which has to be exercised by the executor in carrying on the complicated work of modern Administration." This report suggests that more rules would help reduce corruption. On the other hand, experts like Thailand's Thinapan Nakata have depicted "laws and regulations as a tool for corruption." Can these apparently contradictory views be reconciled?

Consider the conditions under which corruption flourishes: monopoly plus discretion, and an absence of accountability. A rule that creates a monopoly will, as Nakata said, be a tool for corruption: for example, when a regulation gives an official the power to allocate scarce wheat. A regulation may be so complex that clients don't understand it, thereby giving the agent effective discretion.

But a rule may be used to reduce discretion, thereby reducing corruption: for example, a tax officer may be given no discretion about allowable deductions, or an admissions committee may be told to select students on the grounds of test scores. A rule may also be used to make accountability easier, which should help reduce corruption.

Thus, rules may create or reduce "rents"; they may delimit or increase effective discretion; they may help or hamper accountability. Rules are not inherently good or bad for corruption.

Santhanam Committee citation from Gunnar Myrdal, "Corruption as a Hindrance to Modernization in South Asia," in *Political Corruption: Readings in Comparative Analysis*, ed. Arnold J. Heidenheimer (New York: Holt, Rinehart & Winston, 1970), 237. Thinapan Nakata, "Corruption in the Thai Bureaucracy: Who Gets What, How and Why in Its Public Expenditures," *Thai Journal of Development Administration* 18 (January 1978): 104.

and decisions can be subjected to hierarchical review, perhaps on a random basis. Control systems are mechanisms for circumscribing discretion.[60] Agents may be required to work in teams, with tight supervi-

60. "The logic of *ex ante* control holds that constraining managerial discretion is the first purpose of budget execution." (Fred Thompson and L.R. Jones, "Controllership in

sion, so that no one agent has the chance to make big corrupt decisions on her own. Dividing decisions into pieces and separating the pieces is often advisable. In the words of U.S. government guidelines:

> Key duties such as authorizing, approving, and recording transactions, issuing or receiving assets, making payments, and reviewing or auditing shall be assigned to separate individuals to minimize the risk of loss to the government. Internal control depends largely on the elimination of opportunities to conceal errors or irregularities. This in turn depends on the assignment of work in such a fashion that no one individual controls all phases of an activity or transaction.[61]

Rotation of agents. Corrupt relationships between agents and clients usually take time to develop. Rotating agents, changing both location and function assigned, inhibits long-term "buddy-buddy" or "sweetheart" arrangements.

The organization's mission or product. Redefining objectives or activities can often lead to reduced corruption. Take procurement, for example. If a government agency wants to procure a custom-made good or service, procurement officers will find it hard to ascertain the competitive price; this difficulty, in turn, makes kickbacks and ripoffs more likely. Suppose that the agency could instead procure a standard good or service whose price and suppliers were well known. The standard good would be less useful to the agency than the custom-made one, but it might be the better choice, if corruption were simultaneously eliminated from the procurement process. Similar points hold in other domains. Possibilities for corruption may be affected by the choice between capital- and labor-intensive technologies, direct or indirect payment schemes, cash or in-kind transfer mechanisms, and taxes versus subsidies.

Sometimes "vertical integration" can be used to combat corruption. Suppose an agency is being cheated by corrupt contractors. It may decide to make the good itself, rather than buy the service on the market. The consequent redefinition of the organization's role can, of course, have

---

the Public Sector," *Journal of Policy Analysis and Management* 5 [Spring 1986]: 553.) Examples of *ex ante* financial controls include object-of-expenditure appropriations, apportionments, position controls, and fund and account controls.

61. Office of Management and Budget, *Internal Control Guidelines*, I-10.

costs; but it may also lead to the overcoming of a corrupt principal-agent problem.[62]

Client groups. Anticorruption drives have notoriously short life spans. The idea of fighting corruption may be on political center stage at one moment, only to be virtually forgotten a year later. One reason for the short life is that the constituents for an uncorrupt government – the common people – are not usually organized for that purpose. A principal can help organize citizen lobbying groups, provide information, protect themselves against extortion, and maintain the political pressure.

This fourth category of policy measures – redefining the principal-agent-client relationship – raises a host of questions. The basic question is, Which of these many measures will be effective enough to be worth the increase in red tape, expense, morale, and bureaucratization?

Changing Attitudes About Corruption

The principal may try to raise what we earlier called "the moral costs of corruption." Of course, higher penalties may have this effect, but here I wish to consider policies that work directly on attitudes.

Education and example. The targets may be agents or clients or both. Training and publicity campaigns can be used to raise consciousness about the existence and costs of corrupt behavior. Mexican president Miguel de la Madrid called for "a moral renovation" of Mexican society. "The Mexican people are profoundly moral, and they demand that I prosecute all forms of corruption. That is what I will do, and I will govern with their example."[63]

To many observers, the moral standards of the bureaucrats have to be recast. One often hears this opinion from citizens in the developing

62. For a general analysis of vertical integration and the principal-agent problem, see Oliver E. Williamson, *Markets and Hierarchies: Analysis and Antitrust Implications* (New York: Free Press, 1975). On the practical pros and cons of vertical integration, see Michael E. Porter, *Competitive Strategy* (New York: Free Press, 1980), chap. 10.

63. Miguel de la Madrid, *Renovación Moral de la Sociedad* (Mexico City: Secretaría de Gobernación, 1983), 23; my translation. Unfortunately, U.S. intelligence reports alleged that by mid-1984 President de la Madrid himself had taken more than $100 million out of Mexico (James S. Henry, "The Great Third World Debt Caper," *The New Republic*, 14 April 1986). The Mexican government denied the charges.

countries (and in the West). Gerald Caiden's appeal for a new official morality is perhaps an extreme example:

> The country studies in this volume point to an agenda for improvement:
>
> 1. A change of heart is needed in the public bureaucracy. Public officials should cease their self-serving behavior and become true public servants, i.e., servants of the public. They should end their exploitation of public office and their parasitism. They should weed out the unfit and the incompetent. Like born-again Christians, virtue not avarice should be their guide. Such moral revolution should come from within.
> 2. The new morality should lead to the suppression of corruption and "bureaucratic rot."[64]

Unfortunately, there seem to be few readily available methods for changing ethical standards or transforming official morality.

The unimpeachable integrity of the principal is often cited as a key precondition for cleaning up a corrupt organization (or nation). Writing around 122 B.C., the authors of *Huai-nan Tzu* put it this way:

> The power to achieve success or failure lies with the ruler. If the measuring line is true, then the wood will be straight, not because one makes a special effort, but because that which it is "ruled" by makes it so. In the same way if the ruler is sincere and upright, then honest officials will serve in his government and scoundrels will go into hiding, but if the ruler is not upright then evil men will have their way and loyal men will retire to seclusion.[65]

The BIR case is consistent with a weak version of this argument—Plana's probity was legendary—but not with the idea that nothing can be done about corruption unless the political leadership is lily white. Plana made a big difference during his term in office, even under a president whose probity was admired by no one.

Codes of ethics. At the end of a tough, revisionist paper entitled "What Is the Problem About Corruption?" sociologist Colin Leys described the "line of escape" from corruption: "a nucleus of 'puritans' applying pressure for a code of ethics."[66] Organizational codes of conduct are in-

64. Gerald E. Caiden, "Comparative Bureaucracy," in *Administrative Systems Abroad*, ed. Krishna K. Tummala (Washington, D.C.: University Press of America, 1982), 20–21.

65. Cited in Syed Hussein Alatas, *The Sociology of Corruption: The Nature, Function, Causes and Prevention of Corruption* (Singapore: Time Books, 1980), 77.

66. Colin Leys, "What Is the Problem About Corruption?" in *Bureaucratic Corruption*, ed. Ekpo, 150.

Box 16 **Moral Uplift in Zaire**

Partly in an effort to stem rampant corruption, Zaire's leaders tried to introduce a new ethic based on a cult of President Mobutu. "His thoughts and actions become the new ideology, the new truth—Mobutuism. Only 'He' can maintain order and bring prosperity." In the words of one poster:

To support the regime of General Mobutu means first:
—work conscientiously. Then:
—pay your taxes.

The campaign of moral uplift included mass meetings several times a month in each prefecture. Citizens were prodded to sing and dance to political tunes, described by the Department of Culture and the Arts in 1974 as follows: "The patriotic and revolutionary songs . . . contain the teachings of the Guide of the Zairean Nation, the core of his thought, the enumeration of his major achievements. The name of the Guide is sung with joy to render homage to him, to express to him profound gratitude of the Zairean people, and to assure him the blessing of our ancestors by these prayers of invocation."

But the moral campaign made little headway. One scholar reported his impression that "many of those who attend do not do so willingly, and, like most of the population, they are very cynical about policy initiatives and implementation." Another expert on Zaire argued that the campaign of moral uplift was simply an attempt to conceal the regime's own dishonesty. "The population has not been fooled either," he noted. "Practically all of the ideological slogans advanced by the party have been contradicted by present-day reality."

And by all recent accounts Zaire is awash in corruption.

Thomas M. Callaghy, "State-Subject Communication in Zaïre: Domination and the Concept of Domain Consensus," *Journal of Modern African Studies* 18 (September 1980), 471, 477, 479; David J. Gould, *Bureaucratic Corruption and Underdevelopment in the Third World: The Case of Zaire* (New York: Pergamon Press, 1980).

creasingly widespread. "If the unethical acts of others and the lack of written policy provides a rationale for misconduct," noted one scholar, "the current popularity of ethical codes seems to suggest that a formal policy can be beneficial."[67] Indeed, in the West there is increasing interest in such methods of creating more "moral" organizations.[68]

Organizational cultures. Business consultant and security expert Bob Curtis drew a major conclusion from his long experience with employee crime in the United States: only by changing employees' sense of identification with the company could such corruption be controlled. Curtis was vague on how to achieve such identification, but he lauded "integrative management," where the participation of employees in managerial decisions led them to *want* to be honest.[69] Recent studies have shown that "organizational cultures" can have dramatic effects on performance;[70] it would not be surprising that they could also affect corruption.

Moreover, a principal should realize that *how* decisions are made—about anticorruption efforts as in other domains—can make a big difference. As an organization moves to combat internal corruption, morale is likely to suffer. Positive efforts by the principal to boost participation, elevate attitudes, and promote an honorable organizational image may alleviate this suffering. Even if it does little directly to change attitudes, such efforts may make change easier to ingest.

Policymakers may pose several questions about this fifth cluster of anticorruption tools, the changing of attitudes. Will such measures work? How well and at what costs? Even if they don't work, might they create a helpful climate for the implementation of other new policies?

A FRAMEWORK FOR POLICYMAKERS

In most real situations policymakers will not have all these anticorruption tools at their disposal. And yet, it may be useful when thinking of

67. James S. Bowman, "Management of Ethics," *Public Personnel Management* 10 (1981): 61.

68. See, for example, Simcha B. Werner, "The Self-Moralizing Organization" (Paper presented at the Southern Association of Political Science, Savannah, Georgia, November 1984), and its many references.

69. Bob Curtis, *How to Keep Your Employees Honest* (New York: Lebbar-Friedman Books, 1979).

70. See especially Terrence E. Deal and Allan A. Kennedy, *Corporate Cultures: The Rites and Rituals of Corporate Life* (Reading, Mass.: Addison-Wesley, 1982), chap. 9. Also helpful are Thomas J. Peters and Robert H. Waterman, Jr., *In Search of Excellence: Lessons from America's Leading Companies* (New York: Harper & Row, 1982) and Stanley M. Davis, *Managing Corporate Culture* (Cambridge, Mass.: Ballinger, 1984).

a particular problem in a particular context to consider all possible policies in a systematic way. As an aid to thinking about tools for fighting corruption, Exhibit 1 provides a framework for policymakers.

Exhibit 1 **Measures to Control Corruption: A Framework for Policy Analysis**

A. Select agents for "honesty" and "capability"
   1. Screen out the dishonest (past records, tests, predictors of honesty)
   2. Exploit outside "guarantees" of honesty (networks for finding dependable agents and ensuring they stay that way)

B. Change the rewards and penalties facing agents (and clients)
   1. Shift rewards
      a. Raise salaries to reduce the need for corrupt income
      b. Reward specific actions and agents that control corruption
      c. Use contingent contracts to reward agents as a function of their eventual success or failure (analogies: forfeitable nonvested pensions, performance bonds)
      d. Use nonmonetary rewards (transfers, training, travel, publicity, praise)
   2. Penalize corrupt behavior
      a. Raise the general level of formal penalties
      b. Increase the principal's authority to punish
      c. Calibrate penalties in terms of deterrence (as a function of the size of the bribe and the size of the illicit profit)
      d. Use nonformal penalties (transfers, publicity, loss of professional standing, blackballing)

C. Gather and analyze information in order to raise the chances that corruption will be detected
   1. Improve auditing systems and management information systems
      a. Provide evidence that corruption has occurred (red flags, statistical analyses, random samples, inspections)
      b. Assess the organization's vulnerability to corruption
   2. Strengthen "information agents"
      a. Beef up specialized staff (auditors, investigators, surveillance, internal security)
      b. Create a climate where agents will report improper activities (e.g., whistle-blowers)

        c. Create new units (ombudsmen, special audit committees, anticorruption agencies)
    3. Use information provided by third parties (media, banks)
    4. Use information provided by clients and the public
    5. Change the burden of proof, so that the potentially corrupt have to demonstrate their innocence

D. Restructure the principal-agent-client relationship to remove the corruption-inducing combination of monopoly power plus discretion plus little accountability
    1. Induce competition in the provision of service (private sector, among government agents)
    2. Reduce agents' discretion
        a. Define objectives, rules, and procedures more tightly
        b. Have agents work in teams and subject them to hierarchical review
        c. Divide large decisions into separable tasks
    3. Rotate agents functionally and geographically
    4. Change the organization's mission, product, or technology to render them less susceptible to corruption
    5. Organize client groups, to render them less susceptible to some forms of corruption and to create an anticorruption lobbying force

E. Change attitudes about corruption
    1. Use training, educational programs, and personal example
    2. Promulgate a code of ethics (civil service, particular organizations)
    3. Change the organizational culture

I hope this framework has practical relevance in two senses. First, it can be used as a heuristic device for public managers to consider a series of alternatives, suggesting options that might otherwise have been overlooked. Second, when studying anticorruption efforts elsewhere, we may find this framework helpful for understanding why and how these efforts succeeded or did not. This is about as much as we should hope from any general analysis of corruption—or indeed from any conceptual model applied to public policies. If our goal is to be of practical use to policymakers, we academicians would do better to derive rough-and-ready frameworks and checklists instead of calculating theoretically "optimal" policies under highly restrictive and unrealistic conditions. We might think of our job as stimulating creativity, making sure promising options are not overlooked, and highlighting trade-offs—a much humbler stance than many social scientists and policy advisers are used to but, I think, the correct one.[71]

Exhibit 2 uses the framework as a means of classifying the anticorruption tools that Justice Plana employed in the Philippines' Bureau of Internal Revenue.

Exhibit 2 **The Framework Applied: Anticorruption Tools Used by Justice Plana at the BIR**

A. Select agents
   1. Investigated past records to weed out the dishonest. Used professional criteria for recruitment and appointment. Created new rules against nepotism
   2. Exploited external "guarantees" of honesty by using military and civilian intelligence personnel as information agents

B. Change rewards and penalties
   1. Rewards: Installed a new performance evaluation system, which provided incentives for more efficient, less corrupt tax collection. Cleaned up the personnel transfer system. Used prizes and praise
   2. Penalties: Raised the pain of dismissal by publicizing the names and stories of offenders

C. Gather and analyze information
   1. Implemented a red flag system for identifying possibly corrupt agents. Installed another system to spotlight possible tax evaders
   2. Strengthened the role of information agents (Internal Security Division, Fiscal Control Division)
   3. Used third parties to obtain credible information (Commission on Audit monitored tax remittances; intelligence groups inspected financial records and acted as undercover agents)

71. On the use of frameworks and checklists for policymakers, see Robert Klitgaard, *Economic Advice: Patterns in Argumentation over Microeconomic Policies, or What Happens When Theory Meets Practice: with Three Case Studies and a Checklist for Policymakers*, Discussion Paper Series No. 64D (Cambridge, Mass.: Kennedy School of Government, March 1979); and Klitgaard, *Elitism and Meritocracy in Developing Countries.*

4. Did not use clients or public to gather information
5. Did not change the burden of proof re: corruption

D. Restructure the principal-agent-client relationship
   1. Used performance monitoring and targets for tax collection to stimulate competition among agents; no involvement of private sector
   2. Reduced agents' discretion in several ways, including centralized handling of large cases; more controls over remittances, stamps, etc.; greater use of banks to collect funds; some changes in tax laws; greater supervision
   3. Rotated field agents geographically
   4. Did not redefine the organization's mission, product, or technology in order to reduce corruption
   5. Did not organize taxpayers or business groups

E. Change attitudes about corruption
   1. Through "reorientation seminars" and personal example, tried to change attitudes
   2. Promulgated values of public service but did not issue a new code of ethics or conduct
   3. Worked on changing the BIR's corporate culture in many ways, including created or revived toastmaster's club, glee club, athletic club, etc.; started morning masses at the BIR; used participatory management in creating the new performance evaluation system

---

In the following chapters we shall refer back to the framework of Exhibit 1, as well as to the discussion of objectives in Chapter 2. We shall be asking several questions. Which of these many kinds of policy measures are used, and which seem to be most effective, under what conditions? How do policymakers actually implement such measures—what strategies do they follow? The framework presented in Exhibit 1 is not "the answer" but a way to organize our investigation of specific cases.

4 | Graft Busters: When and How to Set Up an Anticorruption Agency

During the past two decades increasing numbers of developing countries have set up new organizations with the specialized mission of rooting out corruption. Under what circumstances does this step make sense? What safeguards should exist to prevent the abuse of such powers? How should such an agency be set up, and what can it do to control competition in government?

This chapter examines the most famous and powerful anticorruption agency in the developing world, Hong Kong's Independent Commission Against Corruption (ICAC). We look at why and how the ICAC was set up, and how it achieved success in cleaning up corruption in the Hong Kong police force. At the same time we illustrate the usefulness of the concepts developed in previous chapters for analyzing policies to control corruption.

THE PROBLEMS

Today the Royal Hong Kong Police are widely acknowledged to be among the most effective and least corrupt forces in Asia. But it was not always so. Indeed in the 1960s and early 1970s, corruption was found throughout the police hierarchy.

There were many examples in those days of police corruption:

□ *Drug trafficking*. Since the nineteenth century, Hong Kong had been a notorious center of drug processing and reexporting. In the early 1970s, an estimated fifty tons of opium and ten tons of morphine was coming into Hong Kong each year from the "Golden Triangle" area on the borders of Burma, Laos, and Thailand. Hong Kong itself had an estimated 80,000 drug addicts. Morphine base was selling for HK$10,000 per pound and No. 3 heroin for HK$2000 per pound.

Drugs were big business, and the cooperation of the police was often purchased for a share of the large profits. The half dozen underworld syndicates who ran the narcotics empire made regular payments to various units within the police force to ensure that their operations would not be disrupted. For example, one small retail drug syndicate established a corrupt relationship with police officers stationed in the district. Approximately HK$10,000 a day was paid to the police officers in return for their silence or advance warnings of raids planned by higher echelons. Mock arrests and seizures were commonly made to help police officers who had to satisfy their superiors.

The police had their own syndicates. In the western district of Kowloon one such syndicate collected money from drug dens and gambling dens through middle-ranking police officers. Higher-ranking officers received a sizeable sum for keeping their eyes closed. The parties worked out an elaborate scheme of distribution of "black" money, including hired accountants, payments to six banks, and foreign remission of funds.

□ *Gambling and prostitution.* Ties with corrupt police officers enabled gambling establishments to receive warnings of raids. An arrangement would sometimes be made for paid "actors" to substitute for the casino's staff and regular customers. When arrested, the actors had their fines paid by the syndicate and were released after a night in jail. Larger casinos in Hong Kong island paid up to HK$10,000 a day for protection while handling a daily volume of HK$600,000 in bets and making a daily profit of HK$25,000. Off-track horse betting dens paid HK$1500 to HK$3000 per week to the police, depending on betting volumes.

Police corruption regarding prostitution involved relatively small bribes from brothelkeepers. Police were bribed to overlook regulatory controls dealing with the recruitment of prostitutes, the operation of brothels and unlicensed massage parlors, and the solicitation of clients.

□ *Traffic violations.* Drivers of taxicabs, trucks, and lorries frequently bribed police to "fix" traffic violations, thereby obtaining immunity from prosecution or a lesser charge. About HK$65,000 was collected each month in this fashion, and the sum was divided in an organized and hierarchical way: HK$50 for a constable, HK$150 for a sergeant, HK$500 for an inspector, HK$1000 for a chief inspector, HK$3000 for the divisional superintendent, and HK$4000 for the senior superintendent.

Once the police got in the business of accepting payments, some looked for opportunities to extort. As a consequence the public was becoming fearful of the police, and the police were becoming arrogant toward the public, looking for payments for fixing everything from parking tickets to prosecutions. This pursuit of bribes was distorting the police force's efforts and creating a climate of distrust in the government. The distrust was particularly unfortunate since the Hong Kong police force's responsibilities included not only constabulary functions but also internal security. And the corruption was hurting Hong Kong's reputation internationally: a study showed that 70 percent of news stories about Hong Kong in the British press had to do with corrupt practices.

Ernest Hunt, a convicted police superintendent who confessed to accumulating over HK$5 million during his eighteen-year police career, summarized the situation this way: "Corruption in the Hong Kong police force is a way of life. I mean it is as natural as going to bed and getting up in the morning and brushing your teeth. . . . One of my senior colleagues fled to Canada with a personal fortune . . . as soon as the Anti-Corruption Laws were passed. A senior Anti-Corruption officer within the police force offered to sabotage the case against me for HK$500,000." The new governor of Hong Kong, Sir Murray MacLehose, decided that this situation could not go on. In 1973, he appointed Senior Puisne Judge Sir Alastair Blair-Kerr (the equivalent of supreme court justice) to assess the effectiveness of existing laws and policies and to suggest changes.

THE SETTING

Hong Kong is a British Crown colony with a land area of 400 square miles. It consists of the Hong Kong Island and the Kowloon peninsula—both ceded "in perpetuity" to Britain by China in the mid-nineteenth century—and the New Territories, leased to Britain for ninety-nine years ending 1997. The total population in the early 1970s was about four million, of which 98 percent were Chinese.

By 1973, Hong Kong had achieved tremendous economic success.

Policies of free enterprise and free trade—coupled with an industrious work force, a sophisticated commercial infrastructure, a fine harbor, a conveniently located international airport, and excellent worldwide communications—had turned Hong Kong into a leading manufacturing complex and major commercial center in Asia. Although it had practically no natural resources of its own, Hong Kong had emerged as one of the newly industrialized countries, and its citizens enjoyed one of the highest living standards in Asia.

Hong Kong was administered by a governor, an executive council, and a legislative council. All members of both councils were either ex officio members or nominated by the governor. In the early 1970s, only the urban council—which took care of the city's services for environmental public health, recreation and amenities, and culture—included both elected and appointed members. In other words, the scope of popular participation in the governmental process was limited, in part because, according to former Governor Sir David Trench, "China has made it pretty clear that she would not be happy with a Hong Kong moving toward a representative system and internal self-government."

The absence of popular participation had resulted in a communication gap between the government and the people. To an extent the people resented the government's high-handedness. In 1966 when the government raised the price of a ferry ride by five Hong Kong cents, officials were astonished when riots broke out. The government decided to institute new measures to improve communications with the people. One step was the establishment of the city district office, whose main task was to bridge the gap between the centralized government bureaucracy and the residents of each district.

Two other developments were noteworthy. In the late 1960s, the Cultural Revolution in the People's Republic of China spilled over into Hong Kong and resulted in a series of internal disturbances. The police had their hands full keeping the peace and quelling riots; meanwhile, crime and other social evils flourished. Moreover, the number of illegal immigrants soared, creating conditions for dishonesty, evasion, and crime.

During the same period there emerged a so-called "New Class" of educated, young professionals, whose sense of belonging and civic duties was greater than among the older generation. Some of them organized pressure groups to speak out on public issues, challenging the government to account for its policies. One of their concerns was governmental corruption.

It was in this setting that the Royal Hong Kong Police came under increasing scrutiny. In 1970, it was one of the largest per capita urban forces in the world, with over 10,000 officers. Its budget had always been one of the highest among government departments. In fiscal year 1970–71, for example, its budget was HK$180 million. In comparison, the 1970–71 budget for the medical and health department was HK$170 million; for housing, HK$50 million; and for social welfare, HK$22.5 million.

The Royal Hong Kong Police was under the command of a commissioner and a deputy commissioner and had five functional wings—special branch, criminal investigation, personnel and support, civil and administration, and field operations. Each functional wing was controlled by a director, who held the rank of senior assistant commissioner or the civilian equivalent. Below the five functional wings was a pyramid structure within headquarters, with specialized controlling, supervising, and coordinating functions in each of four districts. And although there were, of course, many honest police officers, in the early 1970s throughout this massive structure, there was systematic, even routinized, corruption.

Illicit activities in Hong Kong were not confined to the police force nor to the public sector. In the private sector there was a long-standing tradition of "commissions," which were often hard to distinguish from bribes and kickbacks but which were usually considered a socially legitimate means of promoting business.

Many analysts, both Chinese and non-Chinese, pointed to local traditions and cultural traits that led to, and were even confused with, corruption. In olden days Chinese civil servants were expected to supplement their salaries with "surtaxes" and "contributions." In a letter to the governor of Hunan province in 1709, the Chinese Emperor K'ang-hsi wrote: "It is impossible for any magistrate to support his family and to pay for the services rendered by his secretaries and servants without charging a single cash in excess. A magistrate charging ten percent in excess of regular taxes may be considered a good official."[1]

1. Cited in John Rochester Oldham, "Police Corruption: A Comparative Study of Proactive Control Strategies in Hong Kong and New York" (Unpublished senior thesis, Woodrow Wilson School, Princeton University, May 1979), 44.

Mindful of this "cultural trait" that sees corruption as neither good nor bad, a Hong Kong Government commission declared in 1907 that "in China the system of blackmailing is unfortunately a matter of everyday occurrence amongst government officials and the civil population. Any chinaman consequently settling here [Hong Kong] not only accepts but is prepared to find similar conditions prevailing in this colony as that which he obtains in his own country."[2] In Chinese a single character represents both "wealth" and "official status."

Both the "particularistic" values of Confucianism and the custom of gift giving were also said to create an environment favorable to bribery. Although citizens recognized that using personal ties or gifts to obtain public services illicitly was officially wrong, apparently many thought it was socially right—especially, perhaps, in the context of a colonial government.

Many people believed that corruption was deeply ingrained in the Hong Kong Chinese culture. Some drew fatalistic conclusions, saying that efforts to reduce corruption would be futile. The pessimists could cite the dismal record of past anticorruption campaigns. The cycle of scandal, legal reform, and renewed corruption had been played out many times over the century.[3]

For example, after the 1897 scandal involving a police-protected gambling syndicate, officials were purged, and a new ordinance was passed, providing for stiffer penalties. But corruption returned. In 1948, a Prevention of Corruption ordinance allowed the authorities to investigate a suspect's "bank account, share account, or purchase account . . . to corroborate the charge of a specific corrupt transaction." In 1959, this power was enlarged. A tribunal could examine a government official's "standard of living" and "control of pecuniary resources," and if these were deemed beyond his or her "official involvements," the official could be dismissed. This regulation had no precedent or equivalent in the commonwealth and the British dependencies.

But despite ever tougher laws, corruption persisted and, in the late

2. I am indebted to Frank Wong for this quotation.

3. The history that follows is based on Hsin-Chin Kuan, "The Legal History of Anti-Corruption in Hong Kong" (Preliminary paper presented at IDRC conference on negative bureaucratic behavior, Pattaya, Thailand, February 1977). Such cycles are a familiar phenomenon in other countries as well: see, for example, Lawrence Sherman, *Scandal and Reform* (Berkeley and Los Angeles: University of California Press, 1979).

1960s, grew. There were two explanations. First, criminal laws required proof of a particular advantage conferred through a corrupt transaction. And second, the responsibility for detection, investigation, and prevention was within the police force itself. As a 1961 anticorruption report argued, the police force's Anti-Corruption Branch (ACB) had limits on its effectiveness:

> 1. The public's fear of, lack of sufficient respect for, and reluctance to complain to, an anti-corruption unit attached to a Police Force which is itself thought to be corrupt;
> 2. The danger that the staff of the ACB will, on transfer to other sections of the Force, put to use techniques (blackmail, extortion, etc.) learned while investigating corrupt practices; and
> 3. The danger that an officer of the ACB might be called upon to investigate a former colleague and, out of "brotherliness," bury the case.[4]

Despite such acknowledgments, the government found it difficult to move anticorruption responsibilities out of the police force. The 1961 report resulted in no change organizationally. There were some good reasons for this reluctance. As the 1976 Salmon Report in the United Kingdom and the 1983 Stewart Commission Report in Australia concluded, severe practical constraints may stand in the way of locating an anticorruption office outside the police. Where would competent investigators come from? Would two police forces be created, leading to redundancy and organizational conflicts? And so it was that in Hong Kong in 1971, yet another set of legal reforms was accompanied by the rejection of arguments for an ACB outside the police.

THE GODBER AFFAIR

In 1971 the government passed a remarkable Prevention of Bribery ordinance. It broadened the categories of offenses. For suspects whose personal wealth exceeded their incomes, or who enjoyed standards of living beyond what their incomes would warrant, the burden of proof shifted: they would have to demonstrate their innocence. "In any proceedings against a person for an offense under this Ordinance the burden of providing a defense of lawful authority or reasonable excuse shall lie

4. *Sixth Report*, Advisory Committee on Corruption, Hong Kong, 29 December 1961, 46.

upon the accused." This was, in short, a reversal of the usual presumption of innocence in English law. And now "unexplained enrichment" was a criminal offense – not just grounds for administrative dismissal. Penalties were increased to a maximum of HK$100,000 fine and ten years in prison, in addition to paying the amount of the bribe received.

The police force's Anti-Corruption Department was upgraded to an office (the ACO), expanded, given greater autonomy within the force, and placed under new, impeccably honest leadership. The government also reorganized the ACO, giving a three-part Investigations Group prominence. The group's three parts were long-term intelligence gathering, investigations of day-to-day allegations of corruption, and the investigation of public officials who seemed to have assets disproportionate to their incomes.

These changes had an immediate effect. Within a year of the ordinance's passage 295 police officers, including two superintendents and twenty-six inspectors, took early retirement or resigned from the Royal Police Force. (Some of this change, of course, reflected normal turnover and attrition.) Unfortunately, many hurriedly left Hong Kong with their ill-gotten gains. The sudden disappearance of Chief Superintendent Peter Godber created a huge scandal, bringing anticorruption efforts to the center of Hong Kong's political stage.

Godber was the second "big fish" who was to be prosecuted under the 1971 ordinance; Police Superintendent Ernest Hunt, whose words were quoted earlier, had already been successfully prosecuted. The ACO had spent two years investigating Godber's finances, which included at least HK$4.3 million in banks in six countries. This sum was about six times his total net salary during his twenty years of police service.

On 4 June 1973, the ACO served Chief Superintendent Godber notice, as required by the ordinance, that he had seven days to prepare a written explanation of his excessive property. But four days later, using his skills and knowledge as a police officer to slip through the security barriers at the Kai Tak Airport, Godber escaped on a flight to London. Existing procedures did not allow the Hong Kong authorities to have him sent back from England, and Godber seemed set to enjoy his corrupt fortune outside the reach of the law.

The Hong Kong public was outraged. Students rallied to demand his return for trial. Radical elements accused the government of complicity in letting the "big fish" go free. Governor MacLehose, who had assumed office only the year before, appointed Sir Alastair Blair-Kerr as a one-man commission of inquiry, not only into the circumstances of Godber's escape, but also into corruption in Hong Kong and its cures.

Blair-Kerr was quick to respond. Three months later, in September 1973, he issued a report that exonerated the ACO from complicity in Godber's disappearance. He also painted a vivid picture of systematic corruption in the Crown Colony:

> The worst forms are what is described by the Anti-Corruption Office as "syndicated" corruption, that is to say a whole group of officers involved in the collection and distribution of money. For example, it is said that groups of police officers are involved in the collection of payments from pak pai drivers, the keepers of gambling schools and other vice establishments. Frequently the "collection" is far more than corruption in the true sense. It is plain extortion accompanied by veiled threats of violence at the hands of triad gangsters. The "collections" seldom take the form of direct payments to any member of the corrupt group of officers. Almost invariably there is the middle-man. He is referred to euphemistically as "the caterer." He receives the money; and in some cases, it is said that vast sums are involved.
>
> Opinions vary as to the extent of "syndicated" corruption; but it is widely believed that it exists in a number of departments, notably the police. It is said that in a number of cases these "syndicates" involve certain senior officers as well as those of intermediate and junior rank. . . .
>
> Many police officers, so it is said, have simply lost heart in their endeavour to deal with a number of "social" offences and have joined the ranks of those who "squeeze" the operators rather than take them to court. . . . It is also said that corruption exists in connection with recommendations for promotion—so much to become a corporal, so much to become a sergeant and so on. Of course, if this is true, it necessarily involves senior officers because the promotion boards are composed of very senior officers.
>
> It is said that Police corruption is, for the most part, "syndicated" and that corruption on an individual basis is frowned upon by the organizers of these "syndicates"—indeed anyone operating on his own is liable to be "fixed." The organizers are good psychologists. New arrivals in the Force are tested to see how strong is their sense of duty. The testing may take various forms—sums of money placed in their desks, etc. If an officer fails to report the first overture of this sort he is really "hooked" for the rest of his service, and is afraid to report any corrupt activities which may thereafter come to his notice.
>
> On a number of occasions during this inquiry I have been told that there is a saying in Hong Kong:
>
> 1. "Get on the bus," i.e., if you wish to accept corruption, join us;
> 2. "Run alongside the bus," i.e., if you do not wish to accept corruption, it matters not, but do not interfere;

> 3. "Never stand in front of the bus," i.e., if you try to report corruption, the "bus" will knock you down and you will be injured or even killed or your business will be ruined. We will get you, somehow.
>
> The reaction of honest young police officers hearing this kind of talk may well be imagined. They either join the "bus" or mind their own business. They may, so it is said, accept payments but nevertheless continue to do their public duty as conscientious police officers. In other words, they are paid, but do nothing for it.[5]

Blair-Kerr recommended a further toughening of anticorruption laws. He outlined the pros and cons of the ACO's being located within the police force but made no recommendations in that regard.

The ball was then in Governor MacLehose's court. Public and international pressure was building for him to do something. As the new governor, he may have seen this as a chance to establish himself as a bold leader tackling one of the problems left behind by his distinguished predecessor. But what policies should he promulgate, and how should he get them implemented?

THE INDEPENDENT COMMISSION AGAINST CORRUPTION

On 17 October 1973, Governor MacLehose announced to Hong Kong's Legislative Council that a new Independent Commission Against Corruption (ICAC) would be created. Among his reasons: "Clearly the public would have more confidence in a unit that was entirely independent and separate from any department, including the police."[6] The Anti-Corruption Office within the police force would be abolished.

The popular reaction was positive. In the words of one journalist, Peter Godber's "abrupt retirement to an English village instead of aiding his police colleagues in his own investigation woke the administrative and political elite in the Colony from complacent slumber."[7]

From the beginning, Governor MacLehose stressed that the ICAC should have strong investigatory powers but also should work to prevent

5. Excerpt from *Second Report of the Commission of Enquiry Under Sir Alastair Blair-Kerr* (Hong Kong, 1973), paragraphs 92, 93, 96–100.

6. Hong Kong *Hansard*, 17 October 1983; quoted in Oldham, "Police Corruption," 83.

7. Leonard Goodstadt, "Rude Awakening," *Far Eastern Economic Review*, 22 October 1973, 28.

corruption. Its efforts should not be confined to finding and punishing the corrupt. Thus, from the start the ICAC contained what one of its annual reports would call "an entirely new concept in public administration," a Corruption Prevention Department within the commission.

The governor's immediate problem was to set up the ICAC, which was to assume its responsibilities in February 1974. He had some difficulty finding senior staff; some government officials did not want to get involved in something as sensitive as fighting corruption. To do the job thoroughly, ICAC officials would have to step on many toes. They would be in the position of putting other people's careers and reputations at stake. At the same time such great public expectations had been created that it might be impossible to fulfill them.

With great effort the governor prevailed upon Jack Cater to head the new commission. After a distinguished career in Hong Kong government Cater had just recently left government service to become the general manager of the Hong Kong Telephone Company. For many years he had been secretary of commerce and industry, where he presided over Hong Kong's dynamic economic growth in the 1960s. He was very well liked by the local Chinese population, a quality that the governor considered important in the first ICAC commissioner, since it would lend popular support and credibility to the new body. Cater was a high-profile figure, a person thought to harbor ambitions to be the chief secretary to the governor or even the governor.

Jack Cater's new organization was given sweeping powers. All the ICAC needed to arrest someone suspected of corruption was to say that the commissioner had reasons to believe that the suspect had committed an offense. For exceptional cases, ICAC officers had powers of search and seizure without need of a warrant. The ICAC could require any person to provide any information that the commissioner deemed necessary. And the ICAC could issue a restraining order to freeze assets and properties. This last step, plus the right to seize travel documents, would ensure that no more big fish escaped with their Hong Kong loot.

But increases in legal powers had not previously been enough to deter corruption. In the past the office in charge of fighting corruption turned out to be ineffective and corrupt; Cater had to ensure this never happened to the ICAC. A key issue in its creation was ICAC's independence. To ensure this independence, the governor and Cater arranged that the ICAC would report directly to the governor, not through any legislative or executive agencies. Its employees would be entirely outside the civil service.

At the same time Cater had to make sure the public would be confident in the ICAC's own integrity—not fearful of it as a new super-police. From the beginning he set up citizen advisory committees that included government critics.[8] The attorney general, not the ICAC, would decide which cases would be prosecuted; this separation would, in one commissioner's words, "avoid suggestions that zealousness is clouding objectivity."[9] And over his new creation the governor maintained close scrutiny, acting as a guardian of its integrity.

Staffing and Organizing the ICAC

The public's confidence would also depend on who worked for the ICAC. Cater decided he could not simply assume the staff of the police force's Anti-Corruption Office. Nor could he rely solely on Hong Kong civil servants seconded from other agencies. Cater needed both capability and honesty. But where could he find them?

8. The members of these advisory committees were appointed by the governor with a maximum of six years' service. The committees consisted of leading members of Hong Kong's government, commercial, trading, and social services sectors, as well as "grass-roots" people. Five such committees were formed:

a. The Advisory Committee on Corruption, the top advisory committee on overall policy.

b. The Operations Review Committee, which analyzes the ICAC's investigations, practices, and procedures. An important member of this committee is the commissioner of police.

c. The Corruption Prevention Advisory Committee, which oversees the ICAC's assignments and reports on the prevention of corruption. A senior assistant commissioner of police is a member, as is the director of administration of the Hong Kong Government.

d. The Citizens Advisory Committee on Community Relations, which gives policy advice on publicity campaigns and educational and moral approaches to fight corruption. This committee has a housewife and members of the church among its members, as well as experts on public relations.

e. The "ICAC Complaints Committee," which receives complaints from the public about ICAC officers or the commission's practices and procedures and advises the ICAC on suitable punishments, changes in practices, and so forth. This committee largely consists of members of Hong Kong's Executive and Legislative Councils.

9. Peter Williams, "Concept of an Independent Organisation to Tackle Corruption" (Paper presented at International Conference on Corruption and Economic Crime against Government, Washington, D.C., October 1983), 33.

One answer was the United Kingdom. With the agreement of the British Home Office, Cater recruited experienced police officers. He also appointed several senior officers of unquestioned integrity from the Royal Hong Kong Police. In addition, Cater decided to find the best young Hong Kong Chinese possible, and give them formal training and, through working alongside their more experienced British counterparts, on-the-job training as well. To attract the ablest staff, the ICAC offered salaries about 10 percent higher than Hong Kong government officers of comparable rank. All recruits were subjected to intense background checks.

Then Cater organized the ICAC to ensure its incorruptibility. Rewards and punishments were heavy. Cater introduced renewable contracts of two and a half years and made sure renewal was based on effective performance. The commissioner sought, and was given, absolute legal power of dismissal of ICAC officers, if necessary "without cause assigned." An internal staff monitoring unit had power of covert access to officers' bank accounts in the event of reasonable suspicion; officers could be placed under surveillance if appropriate. Sumptuous life-styles were certainly not to be the order of the day for ICAC officers.

How should the ICAC be organized to fulfill its mission of combating corruption? Cater conceptualized that mission in three parts: raising the risk of being caught, restructuring government bureaucracies to reduce opportunities of corruption, and changing people's attitudes about corruption. Accordingly, he organized the ICAC into three corresponding departments:

- The *Operations Department* resembled the old Anti-Corruption Office in its functions. Its task was to investigate, arrest, and help prosecute corrupt individuals.
- The *Corruption Prevention Department* was something brand new. It aimed to carry out assessments of organizations' breakpoints, or where corruption would be most likely to occur. The ICAC had the power to "secure" changes in working procedures in government agencies in order to reduce the risks of corruption.
- The *Community Relations Department* was also new. It had two aims: to gather support and information from the public and to change public attitudes toward corruption.

The Operations Department (OD). The OD's objective was, in official terms, "to establish a real deterrent quickly, a force capable of striking fear into the hearts of the corrupt." The department had two branches. The General Targets branch investigated and prosecuted corruption in all areas and at all levels; it also followed up public complaints submitted through new hotlines and complaint centers. The Personality Targets branch looked into the finances of officials who seemed to be living beyond their means—a painstaking, time-consuming, and delicate endeavor.

A Chinese-language newspaper described the OD's investigative powers as follows:

> Indeed, the ICAC has, under the supervision of a retired secret agent, started to employ techniques modelled on those of the Americans' FBI and the U.K.'s M 15. Day and night surveillance of the suspects, and investigations sometimes take months and even years. . . . Anybody who comes in contact with a suspect is listed on file. They even "interview" relatives and friends of suspects and companies which have dealings with them. They have the power to order banks to disclose details about the suspect's accounts and even inspect safe-deposit boxes. Of course, they can bug telephones as well.[10]

The OD employed many new, multiple sources of information, including the media, the public, checks on bank accounts, undercover agents, and so forth. To the extent that "third parties" such as the media and the banks could be used for information, the data would be more credible than if provided by the police officers themselves or, in some cases, by members of the public who might have been involved in corrupt schemes.

The Corruption Prevention Department (CPD). In the words of one of its officers, the CPD was

> responsible for taking a good, hard, incisive look at practices and procedures within the Government and those public utilities/bodies defined in law. We do this through careful examination and analysis of systems, methods and even work approach and policies. The object is to eliminate, and simplify wherever possible or desirable, unenforceable laws, cumbersome procedures, vague and ineffectual practices conducive to corruption.

10. *Sing Tao*, 13 March 1975; cited in Oldham, "Police Corruption," 167–68.

> We want to cut down red tape and bureaucratic excesses. In particular, our CPD specialists will study areas of delays and inefficiency, also those areas where it is widely known or believed that corruption exists.[11]

The CPD identified areas of excessive or unregulated discretion, poor control systems, and unenforceable rules and regulations.

The ICAC's 1975 annual report called the CPD "an entirely new concept in public administration." In the prevention of corruption "there has been no bank of previous experience to consult or rely upon for guidance and advice."[12] The CPD had two examination divisions: a "people" division dealt with services and personnel function, and a "property" division worked with buildings, contracts, and land. Subunits carried out the specific vulnerability assessments.

At first these subunits were specialized according to various types of corruption. But experience taught the ICAC that such specialization could be a mistake because the subunits would tend to overlook corrupt practices outside their particular expertise. The ICAC broadened the subunits to include a cross-section of skills and backgrounds. Indeed within two years the CPD recruited about sixty-five specialists including administrators, architects, lawyers, surveyors, engineers, accountants, systems analysts, computer specialists, and management experts.

The Community Relations Department (CRD). The CRD set up local offices to gather information about corruption from local citizens as well as to engage in grassroots educational activities about corruption's evils. Through mass education and publicity the CRD sought to promote greater civic awareness and faith in good government, as well as to develop higher moral, social, and ethical standards in the society.

Hong Kong is above all a Chinese community. Having always held a great admiration for the youth of Hong Kong, Cater decided that the staff of CRD would be totally Chinese and young. He believed that this difficult area of work required a particularly high degree of imagination, devotion, and idealism. Those best suited to this task would be the bright, young Chinese graduates of Hong Kong's universities. The recruitment advertisements for these new jobs drew a huge response, and an unprecedented experiment began. To get anticorruption messages to the

11. I am indebted to Frank Wong for this interview quotation.

12. *1975 Annual Report by the Commissioner of the Independent Commission Against Corruption*, cited in Oldham, "Police Corruption," 173.

public, the CRD produced TV dramas, film strips, a phone-in radio program, special pamphlets, and exhibition shows. CRD liaison officers visited schools, hospitals, youth and religious organizations, and factories to explain the work of the ICAC on a personal basis and to receive feedback. In addition, the CRD cooperated with the education department to inject anticorruption messages into curricula in primary and secondary schools.

Success at Controlling Corruption

Cater apparently had two immediate strategic aims. First, he wanted to get Peter Godber back from Great Britain and put him in jail. Second, *syndicated* corruption was seen to be the heart of the problem in the police force. The ICAC had to use its powers to go after the syndicates; in the early years, that meant giving priority to the investigative powers of the Operations Department. And the OD had an immediate impact. Between 1974 and 1975, the ICAC investigated 2466 corruption complaints out of 6368 received. The number of cases brought to trial increased from 108 in 1974 to 218 in 1975.

As the most prevalent site of corruption, the police force felt ICAC's biggest bite. Of particular importance was the successful extradition and prosecution of former Chief Superintendent Godber. Cater worked with the attorney general and the governor to persuade the United Kingdom secretary of state—the person in charge of the colonies—to extradite Godber on corruption charges. Their efforts succeeded. Godber was returned and convicted in early 1975 and sentenced to four years in prison.

In addition, from February 1974 to October 1977, the ICAC arrested 260 police officers on corruption charges. By February 1977, the effort "to strike fear into the hearts of the corrupt" was so successful that Cater said: "We are now in a position where the greatest achievement of the ICAC so far is that it has impressed the public that policemen no longer dare to solicit bribes undauntedly." Syndicated police corruption had been broken.

The ICAC also investigated other government departments. With the ICAC's help the government prosecuted officials from the Departments of Fire, Housing, Immigration, Labor, Marine, Medical and Health, New Territories Administration, Post Office, Prisons, Public Works, Transport, and Urban Services. Moreover, ICAC investigations involved the private sector, too. For example, in 1975, the government convicted a well-known building contractor for bribery of officials in the Public Works Department for special favors in government contract awards. And in March 1976, the Hong Kong business community was shocked when one of the oldest and largest firms was fined HK$90,000 for offering commissions to employees of other companies. In 1982, over a third of the ICAC's corruption reports involved the private sector, making this an area of growing concern to the commission.

The ICAC did not eliminate corruption in Hong Kong. Indeed, after having declined from 3189 in 1974 to 1234 in 1978, reports of corruption began moving upward. Commissioner Peter Williams began the ICAC annual report for 1980 with questions that "have been concerning the Directorate and will continue to do so. . . . How does one interpret the fact that in its seventh year of existence the Independent Commission Against Corruption has taken more people to Court than ever before? Is corruption getting worse? . . . Is there something more the Commission should be doing?"[13] In the early 1980s, the ICAC annual reports cited a few recent cases of the same kinds of corruption that had been prevalent in the early 1970s. But the scale of corruption was nowhere near what it was before. The police force had been cleaned up. By 1981 the ICAC annual report could state flatly that "the dark days of large-scale vicious corruption so well described in the annual report of 1976, are no longer with us."[14]

The ICAC accomplished a great deal in the new areas of corruption prevention and community relations. Especially after the first few years' emphasis on the Operations Department, these two areas received increasing attention. By the end of 1981, the Corruption Prevention Department had carried out almost 500 studies on various policies and practices in government agencies. It had followed up many of these studies with full-scale monitoring reports on how well the recommendations were being implemented. Its training seminars on the prevention of corruption had been attended by over 10,000 officials.

Equally, by the end of 1981, the Community Relations Department

13. *1980 Annual Report by the Commissioner of the Independent Commission Against Corruption*, 9.

14. *1981 Annual Report*, 9.

had set up ten local offices, received more than 10,000 reports of corrupt activities, and held more than 19,000 special events such as seminars, camps, exhibitions, and competitions. It had produced everything from teaching kits for schools (with titles like "Your Government and You" and "Work of the ICAC and the Evils of Corruption") to television dramas on actual investigations carried out by the Operations Department. Indeed, in a short time the ICAC became the most visible governmental organization in Hong Kong—which had positive ramifications for citizens' feelings about government in general. In the words of one foreign student of the commission in the late 1970s, "Discussing ICAC with almost anyone in Hong Kong, it becomes obvious that in the less than three years that the Community Relations officials have been operating in the field, they have had more productive and amicable contacts with the public than any other group of public servants save, perhaps, the coordinators of the Government-backed Mutual Aid Committees."[15]

The ICAC also enjoyed great success as an organization. Its budget had grown from about US$2 million in 1974 to about US$14 million in 1982. Jack Cater left the ICAC in 1978 to become chief secretary of the Hong Kong government, and shortly thereafter he received a knighthood. Both honors were widely regarded as recognition for his five years as commissioner of the ICAC. And in 1982, when Governor MacLehose retired, many cited his greatest role as "father of the ICAC." His big, bouncing baby had become a preeminent legal, political, and moral force in Hong Kong—and probably the largest and most famous anticorruption agency in the developing world.

ANALYZING THE ICAC'S SUCCESS

We may discern in this case several corrupt principal-agent-client relationships. One relationship involves the police as the agent and the client as the public. Another association has the Anti-Corruption Office as the agent in charge of rooting out illicit behavior and the rest of the police force as its corrupt client. Cater had to worry about both relationships.

15. Oldham, "Police Corruption," 179.

Police – Public

Police work everywhere inevitably contains a large dose of both discretion and monopoly power. As we have seen, these are potent conditions for the emergence of corruption. Consequently, police officers everywhere are carefully screened and subjected to quasi-military discipline. Even so, when the costs to police officers of being corrupt are outweighed by the benefits, we expect corruption to result.

And corruption had become systematized in Hong Kong. In the dramatic words of a later ICAC commissioner:

> Our experience in Hong Kong suggests that a significant stage for the descent of society into a state of rampant corruption is reached when it becomes syndicated or institutionalized, that is to say, when groups of officials band together systematically to extort money from the public and share it amongst themselves. If this includes officers at a senior level, the result is virtually the setting-up of an alternative, illicit form of Government. The officials impose their own illegal rules of conduct on the public, and the lawful rules of the Government for which they work are blatantly ignored. When corruption reaches this stage, the situation is certainly grave, and inevitably produces a crisis in which either drastic counter-measures are imposed or society lurches further downwards.[16]

What "drastic counter-measures" might these be? Apparently the key dimension was to raise the probability that a corrupt police officer would be caught and punished. Concerning the police, the ICAC could pursue few of the other policy measures discussed in Chapter 3. It could not select new police officers nor greatly alter the rewards and penalties affecting the police.[17] The ICAC did not have the authority to reorganize the police to reduce the corruption-inducing combination of discretion plus monopoly.[18] And it was believed that attitudes about corruption among adults, such as police officers, could not be changed: "With the

16. Williams, "Concept of an Independent Organisation," 3–4.

17. In 1973–74, the government did institute a pay increase and a new pension scheme for recruits into the police force. The result was a 250 percent increase in the number of applicants. These financial steps plus the cleaner image of the police force have resulted in a more educated pool of recruits in the past decade.

18. But the police force's "mission" was altered when off-track betting was legalized through the Royal Hong Kong Jockey Club. Its convenient betting stations located throughout the colony plus phone-in betting services rendered the bookies redundant. Legalizing this activity also meant there was no need for corrupt payments to the police.

adult population, we often use the deterrent approach, that is to say, we exploit the fear of punishment. However, in the longer term, children and young people must be brought up with the proper attitudes toward corruption."[19]

The ICAC could, however, raise the probability of corrupt officers being caught. The commission accomplished this goal by gathering and analyzing information about police corruption. The ICAC opened new channels for the public to make complaints about corruption, including twenty-four-hour hotlines and complaint centers. Complaints could be anonymous, which was a safeguard for the complainant.[20] Commission officers used undercover surveillance. They investigated bank accounts. The ICAC checked those activities that were natural places to look for syndicated corruption: drug dens, prostitution houses, gambling dens, transportation networks, and the internal passing of funds within the police.[21] The burden of proof had also shifted. Those with "unexplained wealth" had to prove they acquired it licitly. This shift reduced the informational burden on the prosecutors of the corrupt.

These various informational steps, taken by a vigorous and independent agency, raised the chances that the corrupt would be caught. And this in turn deterred corruption.

Anti-Corruption Office – Police Force

But another principal-agent problem needed solving. The old Anti-Corruption Office was thought to have itself become corrupted. Cater had to make sure this did not happen to his new commission.

Here, because he was setting up a new agency, Cater enjoyed a freer hand than will most public managers. He also had the strong support of

19. Williams, "Concept of an Independent Organisation," 29.

20. Anonymous complaints also presented problems. Unless detailed information was provided, they were harder to follow up. Moreover, the ICAC was careful of the possible use of false complaints to tarnish reputations. It was made a criminal offense knowingly to render a false complaint.

21. It is often difficult to document actual corrupt transactions. In New York's successful clean-up of police corruption, Patrick Murphy knew this and followed a different informational track. He told his seven top commanders that he would judge the prevalence of corruption by the extent of illicit activities that could not easily exist without such corruption, such as prostitution, numbers games, open drug dealing, and the like.

the governor and the public, and he had the budget of a "Rolls Royce agency." Cater's actions can be usefully analyzed with Chapter 3's checklist.

He selected new agents. Fortunately—and, of course, atypically—he could import many of his agents from another country to help solve his senior staffing problems. He chose the imported officers, local staff, and new recruits with great care. He was also fortunate to have an ample local pool of accountants, auditors, systems analysts, and others to draw upon.

He set up rewards and penalties to attract the best and make sure they stayed clean. A special 10 percent pay allowance was added to the usual Hong Kong government rates, and civil service rules were not in force. Most employees were on two-and-a-half-year contracts and were carefully evaluated before being renewed. He relied little on short-term secondment from other civil service agencies.[22] Cater had the power to dismiss any employee at any time.

He used a remarkable system of internal controls and outside advisory boards to provide and analyze information about possible corruption and abuse of powers within the ICAC. These steps contributed both to the fact and the appearance of a "cleaner than clean" agency at the public's service—and helped avoid the image of a second police force or even, with the ICAC's strong powers, a secret police.

Finally, the ICAC had a strong internal code of conduct and extremely high morale, both of which raised the moral costs of being corrupt.

We should also take note of the sequenced strategy that Cater and the ICAC followed. Such an examination may allow us to appreciate both the *ostensible* problems of corruption faced by Hong Kong in 1974 and Cater's own *strategic* problems of implementation.

Ostensibly, the central problem was systematic corruption, especially in the police force. Strategically, Cater may have had several other considerations in mind. He had to establish the credibility of the new commission. And he had to have some immediate successes, especially with a "big fish" like Godber. ICAC Commissioner Williams drew this conclusion:

> An important point we had to bear in mind (and still have to) is the status of people we prosecute. The public tends to measure effectiveness by

22. Those who were seconded to the ICAC were occasionally ostracized upon returning to their original agencies. A police superintendent named J. J. English committed suicide upon his return, apparently out of frustration.

status! Will they be all small, unimportant people, or will there be amongst them a proportionate number of high-status people? Nothing will kill public confidence quicker than the belief that the anti-corruption effort is directed only at those below a certain level in society.[23]

Cater also had to make sure the ICAC did not at the outset bite off more than it could chew. Finally he did not want to alienate the other government agencies.

Cater's implementation strategy meant an early emphasis on the Operations Department plus a big political effort to extradite Godber. Only in 1976 and thereafter was a major effort made in the Corruption Prevention Department and the Community Relations Department.[24] The CPD worked with a variety of government offices in assessing vulnerability to corruption. Although it had the power to make changes in the practices at these agencies, the CPD was careful to take a low and cooperative profile. The department called the agencies it helped "clients," and it was attentive to requests for assistance by officials of these agencies; overall it acted more as a sympathetic consultant than a ferocious watchdog. The department was aided in taking this stance by its respected technical competence, the unwavering support of the governor, Cater's personal charisma and popularity, and the department's own authority to "secure" changes in policies and procedures if necessary. All of this helped the ICAC retain friendly ties with the other government agencies of government—an important strategic consideration.[25]

23. Williams, "Concept of an Independent Organisation," 23.

24. Cater said in his 1975 *Annual Report* that at the outset priority "in terms of resources had to be given to the Operations Department" to establish "a real deterrent" and the ICAC's own credibility. Once this was achieved, the ICAC could "undertake the more positive areas of our work—corruption prevention and public education." (Cited in Oldham, "Police Corruption," 169–70.)

25. Commissioner Williams described the importance of such cooperative relationships this way: "Other senior officials in the Government, politicians and other VIPs may also express interest in the work of the organisation, and this is to be encouraged. But the organisation should not be seen to be referring to them for decisions on its work but rather to be briefing them in general terms on problems, and receiving their assistance. There may be a need for the organisation to seek specific support from heads of Government departments in the face of what may well be a reluctance from the junior officers in those departments to cooperate fully with the new organisation. There is often an inertia in these matters and any help the organisation can gain from sympathetic senior officials overcomes such inertia that much sooner." (Williams, "Concept of an Independent Organisation," 31–32.)

The ostensible missions of the Community Relations Department were to garner support and information from the public and to change public attitudes about corruption. But the creation of the department also had strategic dimensions. When fighting corruption, the leadership does not want to take a wholly negative stance. And when the government is importing British investigators to clean up corruption in a largely Chinese police force, the administration is running certain risks—especially in a colonial setting not known for popular participation. Thus, by creating the CRD as a kind of moral public face of the commission and staffing it exclusively with Chinese, Cater strategically may have prevented a popular and even xenophobic reaction against the powerful new commission. Indeed, apparently the CRD assumed an even larger role than expected on the Hong Kong political scene, becoming the place for citizens to voice grievances of all sorts, not just about corruption.

The Pros and Cons of an Anticorruption Agency

To many, ICAC's success in controlling corruption could not have been expected. After all, the corruption was both systematic and related to "cultural traits" like gift giving and the exploitation of public office for private gains. Furthermore, previous reforms had failed. Thus, the ICAC's success, though not complete, provides an example of the potency of a specialized, powerful anticorruption agency.

On the other hand, setting up the ICAC carried large costs. The agency had a sizeable budget. Moreover, the law gave the ICAC powers that created such legal precedents as "guilty until proven innocent" and the right of the government to violate the privacy of individual citizens. In many contexts these precedents and the powers could themselves be subject to abuse. Who will guard the guardians?

In late 1983, ICAC Commissioner Peter Williams addressed an international conference. Under what conditions would it make sense for a country to set up an independent anticorruption agency? His answer makes a fitting close to this chapter.

> *First:* The state of corruption in the particular society must have reached a critical or traumatic level to be sufficient to persuade the authorities that a radically new law enforcement agency is needed to combat it.
> *Second:* To ensure public confidence in the new organization it must be

independent of political and executive Administration and responsible directly to the highest authority in the land.

Third: The staff and organization must manifestly have and retain the highest possible integrity.

Fourth: Corruption being the very difficult crime to combat that it is, the powers conferred on the new agency must be embracing if not draconian.

Fifth: A credible independent system to deal with complaints against the new agency must be created.

Sixth: All these considerations involve considerable resources and the state must be willing to set aside the funds to provide them.[26]

26. Williams, "Concept of an Independent Organisation," 43.

5 | Combining Internal and External Policies

A strong external agency like the ICAC is not sufficient to rid a government of corruption. Internal measures are needed as well. The case of Singapore's Customs and Excise Department is an apt illustration.

In the 1950s, corruption was widespread in Singapore. The Customs and Excise Department was one well-known site. Clearing customs routinely involved tipping. Large-scale imports often required large-scale bribes. On many occasions illegal goods were brought into the country under the friendly noses of corrupt inspectors.

The situation today is much different. Singapore is widely recognized as a squeaky clean government with very little corruption. By Western standards, the enforcement seems almost ludicrously strict: a campaign was recently under way to preclude taxi drivers from accepting tips. Public policies have controlled most corruption in government, including in the Customs and Excise Department.

This chapter presents a shorter and more schematic case study than that of Hong Kong's ICAC, but many of the same factors account for Singapore's success in controlling corruption. The case provides a further application of Chapter 3's framework for analyzing anticorruption policies.

CORRUPTION IN CUSTOMS WORK

Customs bureaus around the world present numerous opportunities for bribery. A client may want his or her goods to clear customs more rapidly than usual and may offer "speed money." The payoff procures a licit service, but more quickly than normal. For example, in 1976 two Singaporean officers were convicted for receiving a bribe in exchange for their underchecking imports in order to facilitate clearance.

Other examples of corruption in customs bureaus involve payment for illicit services. For example, a client may pay a customs official to tax his or her imports at a lower rate. Customs inspectors have some discretion, and the reporting system is not perfect. A client may be able to pay a bribe for a more favorable duty, or an inspector may threaten to charge an improperly high rate unless a bribe is paid. For example, in 1973, a Singaporean customs officer was sacked for taking a bribe to charge no duty on a consignment of dutiable pantyhose at the airport.

Corruption can also involve illegal imports. In exchange for a bribe officers may permit illegal imports to enter the country. Pornographic films, videotapes, and magazines fetch a high premium in puritanical Singapore. Firearms and explosives also command high prices. Because selling narcotics and other drugs can be so profitable, couriers risk their lives in bringing them across the causeway. (Drug trafficking can be punished by death.) In 1973, an officer was fined for being in possession of MX pills, presumably part of the payoff for allowing a shipment of this drug into the country. If the drug had been a narcotic, the sentence imposed would have been much more severe.

Sometimes corrupt payments play a part in the smuggling of legal but dutiable goods into Singapore. In 1974, for example, an officer was jailed for accepting a small bribe for allowing a ship officer to take out bonded goods.

Another form of corruption occurs when investigations are influenced via bribes. In an unsuccessful prosecution in 1973, the authorities alleged that a middle-level investigator demanded and received a bribe from a trader who had failed to pay duties on a consignment of imported brassieres. During the cross-examination another officer was implicated for having received a bribe for not levying duties in the first place.

Not all the corruption involves imports. Illegal distillers of *samsu*, operators of opium dens, and coffee shops selling liquor without a license may be willing to pay a bribe to be protected from harassment by Customs and Excise Department officials. For example, in 1966, an officer was jailed for eighteen months for taking a bribe from an opium den operator. In 1972, an officer was punished for demanding payments from a shop owner who had sold alcoholic drinks without a license.

These various kinds of corruption take place at different locations—for example, normal terminals of incoming trade and travel, residential and business areas, and courtrooms. They involve different branches of the Customs and Excise Department, and depending on the kind of corruption, they may involve low-level or high-level officials.

THE SETTING

Singapore is a city-state covering 239 square miles (618 kilometers), with a population in 1983 of 2.5 million. It has been led since 1959 by Prime Minister Lee Kuan Yew, whose firm rule has among other things led to Singapore's reputation as a place where corruption does not flourish.

Singapore's Customs and Excise Department has undergone several major transformations in its role and organizational structure since its inception in 1910 as the Monopolies Department. In those days its main role was collecting revenues from opium and liquor. For other commodities Singapore was a free port.

After independence in 1959, Singapore implemented protective tariffs, while simultaneously creating free trade zones to facilitate entrepôt trade. The Customs and Excise Department had responsibility for collecting the tariffs. The merger with Malaysia in 1963 again changed the import duties and the department's responsibilities; and secession from Malaysia in 1965 implied, among other things, the imposition of duties on commodities from Malaysia itself.

Since 1972, the steady reduction of import taxes has lessened the department's workload. The government has been removing duties and restrictions on the import of manufactured goods, and numerous protected industries have graduated from "pioneer status."

Even in a relatively free port the Customs and Excise Department is busy. Singapore restricts trade for several reasons:

□ *Morality.* Pornographic material—heavily demanded in Singapore—is banned.

□ *Security.* Imports of firearms, explosives, and fireworks are restricted. Subversive literature is banned.

□ *The protection of pioneer industries.* The government tries to promote strategic industries, such as electronics and computer software, through import restrictions and tariffs.

TABLE 3 CONTRIBUTIONS OF CUSTOMS AND EXCISE DEPARTMENTS TO THE REVENUES OF GOVERNMENTS IN THE FAR EAST IN 1980

Country	Percentage
Thailand	75
Sri Lanka	66
Malaysia	53
Bangladesh	45
India	38
Papua New Guinea	32
Philippines	27
Taiwan	24
Australia	22
Hong Kong	18
South Korea	18
New Zealand	16
Singapore	14
Indonesia	10*
Japan	3

SOURCE: *Far Eastern Economic Review Yearbook, 1981*

*60.9 percent of Indonesia's government revenues came from the petroleum industry.

□ *Consumption taxes.* Petroleum, liquor, tobacco, and certain luxury items are dutiable. Other items, such as automobiles, are also taxed because of congestion externalities.

In 1980, the department contributed 14.5 percent of the Singapore government's total revenue of US$2.35 billion, or US$350 million. As Table 3 shows, by Asian standards this percentage is quite low. Three major items–petroleum, tobacco, and liquor–each contributed about a quarter of the department's take. The other 25 percent was obtained from taxes on sugar, local entertainment, film rentals, licenses, taxes on warehouse rents, and other items. Fewer than thirty categories of goods were dutiable.

In 1981, the staff of the Customs and Excise Department numbered about 1800. A little over 80 percent were uniformed officers classified in divisions 3 and 4 of the civil service, which are lower levels. Supervisory staff and investigative personnel classified in division 2 accounted for about 15 percent, and only about 2 percent of the staff were classified in division 1. This allocation of personnel contrasted sharply with the 10,000-person police force of Singapore, where about 12 percent of the staff were classified in division 1, and the lowest ranking officer was in division 3. In addition, the Customs and Excise Department has recruited many young, well-educated candidates into the relatively senior ranks. This preference has led to experienced but less educated personnel serving under junior officers, with some consequent problems of morale.

The department was divided into eight branches:

1. *Revenue.* The classification of duties, the allocation of permits, and the appraisal of particular items.
2. *Special.* The investigation and prosecution of smuggling and revenue frauds; the recommendation of appropriate protective measures.
3. *Administrative.* Personnel, training, transport, and development projects for the department.
4. *Preventive.* Programming measures to prevent the evasion of duties.
5. *Control.* The supervision of divisions in charge of warehousing, excise taxes, exemptions, and petroleum.
6. *Enforcement.* The custody, disposal, and sale of confiscated goods; the supervision of divisions of radio control and airports.
7. *Inspections.* The supervision of licenses, entertainment duties, film hire taxes, and research on commercial intelligence.
8. *Special Duties.* The control of harbors and intelligence about customs.

At lower levels there was geographical specialization, and functional lines tended to overlap.

CLEANING UP CORRUPTION

Several policies were responsible for a dramatic turnaround in corruption in the Customs and Excise Department.

One of the most important was external to the department: namely, the Corrupt Practices Investigation Bureau (CPIB), Singapore's analogue to Hong Kong's ICAC. In fact, the CPIB was founded in the early 1950s, well before the ICAC; Hong Kong officials had studied the CPIB in a special trip in 1968 to consider anticorruption policies. It is considerably smaller than the ICAC, involving fewer than a hundred officers compared to around 1200 in the ICAC. But the CPIB also has extraordinary powers. Several features of Singapore's tough Prevention of Corruption Act of 1960 deserve special note:

- Section 17 empowers the public prosecutor to authorize investigation by senior officers of any bank, share, purchase, expense account, or safe deposit box, and it requires persons to disclose or produce documents asked for.
- Section 19 empowers the same prosecutor to check such records of an employee's wife, children, or any person believed to be a trustee or agent and to take copies of those records. Such power can be delegated to other senior officers.
- Section 20 extends the powers to require persons to furnish sworn statements about property and money sent out of Singapore. It allows checks on income tax documents and records maintained by the public sector and banks.

As a society Singapore is characterized by abundant record keeping, all of which is open to the CPIB's investigation. For example, the ownership of housing, cars, and other equity is recorded and easily checked by investigators. If a public official makes an expensive purchase, this information is passed along to the appropriate agency. Inspectors sometimes frequent race tracks and keep an eye out for government employees who may be wagering. A relatively recent measure requires government officials to make a biannual declaration of their assets. Furthermore, Singapore is such a small place that rumors of corruption and manifestations of unexplained wealth soon come to the attention of the authorities.

The Corrupt Practices Investigation Bureau has such a reputation for thoroughness and efficiency that the mention of the CPIB's investigating an officer is said to cause fear and trembling. In highly publicized cases the CPIB has demonstrated many times that it has the political heft to punish both the "big fish" of corruption as well as those accepting even $1 bribes. It has successfully prosecuted a minister of state, prominent lawyers and surgeons, numerous accountants, expatriates as well as Singaporeans, and low-level workers in the postal service and garbage collection department. Although the CPIB is small, it is widely credited with having deterred corruption throughout the government – including the Customs and Excise Department.

But that department also instituted its own measures to check corruption. They can be usefully analyzed with the framework of Chapter 3.

Changing Rewards and Penalties

Uncovering corrupt activities is made worthwhile. For lower ranking officials, monetary rewards, commendations, and better prospects of promotion are given to those who refuse bribes and turn in the client. Senior officials normally do not receive monetary rewards and must content themselves with favorable publicity. For example, in 1980 a police officer was commended publicly in court for refusing a bribe of US$15,000. In 1965, however, another high official refused US$500,000 but could not be named because of the sensitive nature of the job. Presumably, he reaped a promotion later.

Penalties against corruption vary. Managers have a good deal of authority to mete out administrative sanctions. The civil service has a number of rules to deal with illicit behavior. The specific law governing the Customs and Excise Department is the Public Service–Customs Officers (disciplinary proceedings–delegation of functions) Regulations of 1962. The government may pressure an officer to resign, but it cannot sack him or her without a hearing. It can, however, impose administrative punishments that affect promotional prospects. For example, even if a defendant in a court case is acquitted, he or she may be subject to departmental action if a departmental rule was broken. Punishments include forfeiting one's pension, being sacked, or retiring on a much reduced pension. More informally, prospects for promotion may be limited, and the officer may be informed of this fact.

An officer may also face prosecution in court. The judiciary takes a serious view of corruption among public officials, and sentences meted out have generally been heavy, usually including both a fine and a jail term.

Not only the corrupt are punished: so are their supervisors. The department's system of accountability makes supervisors answerable for their subordinates' misdeeds. This chain of responsibility is said to lead to greater vigilance and closer supervision.

The government makes it costly in two ways to lose a job because of illicit behavior. First, the government shares this information with potential employers, both public and private. A kind of informal blackball system results. Second, the government's generous gratuity for long service and its pension policy are attractive enough to induce most employees to stay with the Customs and Excise Department for a relatively long time.

Gathering Information

The monitoring of possibly corrupt activities raises the chances that such activities will be detected and penalized. For example, before assuming their duties each day, officers must record the petty cash in their possession and their personal effects. This procedure facilitates spot checks. An officer is presumed to have accepted a bribe if more than the recorded amount is found in his or her possession. The actual transaction need not be observed. This policy is thought to be especially effective in curbing petty corruption at points of entry. In 1978, for example, an officer was caught with an undeclared amount: he had been demanding a small bribe from truck drivers to expedite clearance.

The department also maintains elaborate systems of reporting and accountability, carries out frequent surprise checks, and practices close observation. Surprise checks of employees are done both internally and externally to the department—and with costs in morale. In 1973, 200 customs officers of the Harbour Division protested through their union that CPIB officers were searching them, sometimes in full view of the public.

Finally, the department seeks information from the public and the business community. Members of Parliament hold weekly "meet the people" sessions. Citizens with grievances can seek redress outside the bureaucracy, which increases the probability of detecting some kinds of corruption. The business sector has been asked to report requests for bribes.

Restructuring the Principal-Agent-Client Relationship

This restructuring has involved four categories of policy changes. First, as Singapore has reduced the number of dutiable goods, it has also reduced the number of clients who are willing to pay the department's agents for illicit services. Allowing a good to enter duty-free is analogous to the customs agency's withdrawing from that particular market, thereby eliminating one source of public-sector corruption.

A second structural change involves agents' discretion. Low-level officials have less discretion than before, although the job of a customs officer inevitably involves some. For example, an officer stationed at the customs point usually has discretion only on whom and what to check. He or she is guided by a quota, which typically is 5 percent at the airport and lower during peak hours. Tax rates and categories allow no discretion, although officers have some leeway in valuing particular items.

Discretion is constrained by the prospect of reviews up the organizational ladder. For example, the officer examining the manifests or checking vehicles leaving the free trade zone has the privilege of deciding which cargo should be detained for inspection. But if illegal imports are found or tax evasion is suspected, the case is referred to superior officers and investigators. In the case of raids on premises and vessels suspected of containing smuggled goods, investigators have considerable limits of discretion in gathering evidence and deciding who should be investigated, but again there are hierarchical reviews and occasional spot checks. Finally, superior officers have the discretion to close a corruption case without prosecution or to classify it as a less serious offense. Otherwise, the prosecution of minor cases might overwhelm the resources of investigators, the attorney general's office, and the courts. But here, too, internal control measures and hierarchical review help to check possible abuses.

A third structural change involves the agents' relationships with clients. Low-level officials work in pairs under most circumstances. This leads to higher costs, but it reduces one-on-one contacts between the agent and the client. Officers are frequently rotated, except for lower rank officers with specialized technical skills—for example, boat steersmen. These policies make it harder for corrupt personal ties to develop between particular agents and clients.

Fourth, Singapore's Audit Department examines the financial administration of every part of the government and reports its findings to Parliament. Department investigators highlight and make recommendations concerning weaknesses in existing control systems and monitoring procedures. (These activities resemble in many ways the "vulnerability assessments," discussed in Chapter 3, and they are akin to the endeavors of the Corruption Prevention Department in Hong Kong.) The public accounts committee of Parliament then questions officials whose agencies have been mentioned in a bad light. This procedure keeps the various departments on their toes, and it inserts other players in the principal-agent relationship at the Customs and Excise Department.

Changing Attitudes About Corruption

The Customs and Excise Department has not emphasized the raising of moral costs. Still some examples of their actions do fit into this category. For example, in 1974, the controller of Customs sent a letter to the business community, urging vigilance that employees not pay bribes, no matter how small the amount. "Tips" given to facilitate the movement of cargo would be regarded as "mistaken objects of generating goodwill."

DISCUSSION

One may tend to think of corruption in a customs bureau as consisting of relatively harmless, small-scale bribes at the "boundary level" between low-level officials and a random assortment of the general public. Corruption occurs because of discretion on both sides: citizens may easily understate the value of their goods, and corrupt customs officials may use their discretion to undervalue goods or place them in a lower duty category. Much of this discretion is inevitable; and small-scale corruption here is perhaps not the most damaging variety of corruption that one encounters in developing countries.

But other forms of corruption in customs bureaus are more harmful. Large-scale commercial traders and middle-level customs officers may have repeated contacts, leading to speed money, extortion, and fraudulent tariff rates. Exports may be understated, classified in lower duty categories, or "overlooked." Lost government revenues can run as high as 50 percent. Smuggling of socially harmful items such as drugs and armaments may be involved. If a customs bureau also has responsibility for some domestic licenses and excise taxes—as does the Inspections Branch of Singapore's Customs and Excise Department—officers may be willing to harass and accept bribes in exchange for overlooking violations.

One reason for corruption is to avoid delays in clearing customs. The costs of delay can be large, especially for perishables or goods vital to projects with deadlines. If corruption exists to speed clearance, governments may wish to instigate two policies: speeding up the service through greater resources or managerial improvements, and paying customs officers high enough wages that extorting speed money is not "necessary." Without such steps, cracking down on illicit speed money may create few social benefits.[1]

Import duties usually exist for good reasons, but they also impose an often overlooked cost. If duties imply delays, they can create large private costs. And if they open up opportunities for fraud and the like, the putative revenues from a tariff may be much less, or differently distributed, than a planner may surmise from a model of an ideal economy. To put it another way, Singapore's move toward becoming a freer port was also a move in the fight against corruption and bureaucratic inefficiency. (The same points may be made about taxes. Simpler tax systems covering fewer items will tend to reduce corruption and evasion.)

As in the case of police corruption in Hong Kong, success here in fighting corruption depended upon an external anticorruption agency. But we have emphasized that the Customs and Excise Department undertook a number of its own policy measures to control corruption. These measures can usefully be examined with Chapter 3's framework. Penalties and rewards were shifted to discourage corruption. Many anticorruption measures fall under the category of gathering and analyzing information on agents. The structure of principal-agent-client relationships was altered. Since "it may be virtually impossible to avoid giving monopoly power to low-level administrators such as policemen or inspectors of housing, grain, meat, etc."[2] or customs officials, the department limited discretion through new rules, hierarchical reviews, and spot checks.

The successes of Hong Kong and Singapore in controlling corruption contain common features. Both governments authorized remarkable

1. In 1977, Indonesian officials tried to eradicate this sort of corruption in the customs bureau, without taking the positive steps I mentioned. The result was "widespread delays," which "led the finance minister to appeal publicly for a speed-up" (Susan Rose-Ackerman, *Corruption: A Study in Political Economy* [New York: Academic Press, 1978], 90n).

2. Ibid., 88.

information-gathering activities. The financial records of officials and their families could be probed at will. If officials had "unexplainable assets," they had to prove they had acquired those assets through legal means. Thus, the government not only took measures to detect corrupt activities—for example, surveillance, undercover work, citizens' complaints, and spot checks—but they also gathered information to detect the *results* of corruption—namely, "unexplained assets." And with the burden of proof shifted to the suspected official, the latter sort of information could raise the chances of the corrupt being caught and punished. Thus corruption was deterred.

The CPIB's role was similar to the ICAC's. It was independent, "cleaner than clean," technically competent, politically potent, and armed with a full legal and investigatory arsenal. Lacking ICAC's large divisions dedicated to corruption prevention and community relations, the CPIB was much smaller. Also, the Singaporeans themselves cleaned up their corruption without any importation of British officials for the top ranks of the anticorruption effort. Foreigners are not a necessary ingredient.

A final point of comparison should also be emphasized: such strenuous efforts against corruption carried heavy costs in money, morale, and the potential abuse. Both governments' anticorruption agencies were granted scary powers. That neither agency has seemed to abuse them is encouraging, and a compliment to the staff, the leadership, and the people of the two countries.[3] But many nations will be reluctant to give a government body so much independence and so much power. The fear, of course, is that of a relapse into a deeper and more dangerous bout of corruption. But the success stories in Hong Kong and Singapore show that endemic corruption can indeed be controlled, if never eradicated.

3. Recent proposals in Hong Kong to fight organized crime—including expanding the investigative powers of the police and depriving certain suspects of specified legal privileges—have excited the opposition of civil rights activists. One worry is that such measures could easily be misused after the transfer of power to the People's Republic of China. "At a time we should be protecting civil liberties, we're talking about limiting them," complained a prominent lawyer (Patrick L. Smith, "Hong Kong Crime Clampdown Raises Fears for Human Rights," *International Herald Tribune*, 18–19 July 1986, 2).

6 | Corruption When Cultures Clash

Sometimes corruption cuts across national boundaries. Foreign firms bribe local officials or are extorted by local officials or both. One government uses illicit tricks to obtain the compliance of another. Indeed political scientist Hans Morganthau once characterized foreign aid as little more than a transnational bribe.

When the principal is from one culture and the agent from another, new problems arise. The principal may lack the power to select or penalize errant agents from another land. Information may be even more difficult to collect and interpret. Attitudes about corruption and its "moral costs" may not coincide. And if one party is playing dirty, the other party could have little choice but to do the same. When agreed-upon rules and penalties are scarce and unenforceable–and when informational asymmetries are particularly pronounced–anticorruption efforts can come down to bargaining and negotiating.

The case in this chapter describes the U.S. Army's efforts during the 1960s and 1970s to overcome collusion and corruption in its procurement activities in Korea. It analyzes the general problem of corruption in a procurement process, pointing to policies that might be used to combat collusive bidding and kickbacks. But it also shows that policy measures that work in the West may fail when cultures clash over corruption.

PROBLEMS OF PROCUREMENT IN KOREA

In the 1960s and 1970s, the U.S. Army in Korea could not procure local goods and services without encountering collusion and corruption. Korean suppliers consistently thwarted the Army's policy of competitive bidding by colluding to charge Uncle Sam 30 percent and more above competitive prices. The suppliers would also give gifts (including cash) to Korean cost estimators and accountants working for the Army, in exchange for higher "independent" cost estimates passed along to the Army brass. If gifts did not work, the suppliers threatened physical violence.

The Korean contractors were highly organized. Instead of reaching their bids independently, they held meetings called "dongoes" in which they decided the price that would be bid, who would be the low bidder, and how the profits of their collusive efforts would be shared. They even used standardized forms to record their decisions. Members enforced decisions through intimidation. Evidence even exists that until 1973 the Korean Central Intelligence Agency (KCIA) discouraged would-be competitors from entering the bidding, ostensibly in order to maximize Korean foreign exchange earnings from U.S. procurement. When the KCIA's involvement ended after an American protest, the colluders organized the Mutual Benefit Association, which had the same chairman and used the same offices as the Korean Hopkido Association. (Hopkido is a Korean martial art.)

The enforcement of collusive arrangements sometimes turned tragic. In 1972, Army officials encouraged a respected Korean supplier named Eddy Chang to bid on a contract to transport household goods. The Army was upset that in Korea it was paying about twice as much for these services as in Japan, and Eddy Chang was well known in the American community for high quality and fair prices. Eddy Chang was interested. He offered prices that were much less than half of what the Army was paying. The Army awarded him the contract.

But two days after the first order was issued on 9 February 1973, Eddy Chang passed along the word that he could not perform the contract, and he disappeared for an extended period. Sometime later newspapers reported that upright Eddy Chang had been arrested for illegally selling Korean antiques. His furniture store was closed down for several years. When it reopened and he could not regain his former success, Eddy Chang committed suicide.

The Eddy Chang case was the most dramatic known example of intimidation to enforce collusion. Other Koreans were threatened away, or were hospitalized after beatings. Despite various efforts to foster competitive bidding and follow proper procedures, the U.S. Army in 1976 faced the reality that its procurements were surrounded by collusion and corruption. How might the managers of the Army's procurement program usefully analyze these problems? Do policies designed for Western conditions retain validity for countries like Korea? What steps might be taken to control collusion, kickbacks, and intimidation?

GENERIC PROCEDURES TO FIGHT COLLUSION AND KICKBACKS

For years the Army practiced its version of well-known international procedures for competitive bidding. The version most likely to be encountered by developing countries are those published in 1983 by three of the largest development banks. The Asian Development Bank, the Inter-American Development Bank, and the World Bank jointly issued "sample bidding documents" for the procurement of goods.[1] Countries were urged to use these forms and procedures when buying things with money loaned by these banks. One purpose was to reduce the possibilities for kickbacks, collusion, and other corrupt schemes.

Kickbacks refer to payments by the suppliers to agents of the purchaser of the goods. The agents pocket cash in exchange for using their discretion to make sure a particular supplier obtains the contract or receives a higher price. The purchaser or principal loses, of course, because he or she has to pay a higher price than if competition induced the supplier to provide the goods at the lowest profitable price. The agent and the supplier split the extra profits from the higher price.

Collusion refers to agreement among possible suppliers before submitting their bids. Suppliers form a sort of cartel, which agrees on a bid price above the competitive minimum. One supplier is chosen to have the winning but artificially high bid; other firms submit still higher bids; and the additional profits are in one way or another divided among the participants.

Kickbacks and collusion are widespread problems in the procurement of goods and services. To try to keep these practices under control the three development banks published their standard forms and procedures. These standards require that potential suppliers submit sealed bids. Agents of the purchaser open the bids in public, and the winner is

1. Asian Development Bank, Inter-American Development Bank, and the World Bank, *Sample Bidding Documents: Procurement of Goods* (Washington, D.C.: The World Bank, September 1983).

chosen on "objective grounds," such as the lowest price. Agents of the purchaser are not allowed to negotiate with suppliers once the bids are in. They can ask for clarifications, but "no change in the price or substance of the bid shall be sought, offered or permitted."[2] And once the contract is awarded, the purchaser cannot accept anything less than the contract requires without being adequately reimbursed.

Thus sealed competitive bids are designed to elicit competition among the suppliers and, along with other rules, to delimit the discretion of the purchaser's agents, thereby reducing the opportunities for kickbacks.

Of course, no system can eliminate these problems. Collusion can take place before the sealed bids are entered. The agent's discretion can be reduced, but it cannot and for efficiency's sake should not be abolished. For example, other things matter to the purchaser besides "objective" features like price, and the agents may have to judge which bid does best on more subjective grounds such as "performance," "quality," and "adaptability."[3] After contracts are set, the purchaser may need to make changes. For efficiency's sake the principal may wish to give agents some discretion in deciding which changes are necessary and when they are to be implemented.[4] With these discretionary powers, opportunities arise

2. Ibid., 15.

3. "The Purchaser's Evaluation of a bid will take into account, in addition to the bid price, the following factors . . . :

a. cost of inland transportation . . . ;

b. delivery schedule offered in the bid;

c. deviations in payment schedule from that specified in the Conditions of Contract;

d. the cost of components, spare parts, and service;

e. the availability in the Purchaser's country of spare parts and after-sales services for the equipment offered in the bid;

f. the projected operating and maintenance costs during the life of the equipment;

g. the performance of the equipment offered; and

h. the quality and adaptability of the equipment offered" (Ibid., 16–17).

4. "The purchaser may at anytime . . . make changes within the general scope of the contract in any one or more of the following:

a. drawings, designs or specifications, where foods to be furnished under the contract are to be specifically manufactured for the purchaser;

b. the method of shipment or packing;

c. the place of delivery; or

d. the services to be provided by the supplier.

If any such change caused an increase or decrease in the cost of, or the time required for, the supplier's performance . . . an equitable adjustment shall be made in the contract price" (Ibid., 29).

for corrupt arrangements like kickbacks.

The U.S. Army in Korea had required competitive bidding and had placed numerous limits on the discretion of its procurement agents. But the military learned that it is one thing to have procedures and another thing to implement them successfully.

SOURCES OF COLLUSION IN KOREA

Collusion is always a possibility, but in some settings it is more likely than others. Features of a country's economic system may facilitate collusion. Such was the case in Korea. In the early 1960s, the Korean government started an ambitious and eventually successful program to boost export earnings. It formed large trade organizations, each specializing in a particular industry, under the supervision of the Minister of Commerce and Industry. The result was a kind of trade cartel. When competing against foreign countries, Korean industry would present a united front. Korean firms would not bid against each other, and export quotas would be divided among Korean firms by the trade organization, avoiding competition that might reduce the country's foreign exchange earnings.

The result was an economy that worked through what might be called "collusive" arrangements among potentially competitive firms. For the purpose of international trade, these arrangements made sure that Korea as a country enhanced its income from foreign sales. But the same scheme could undermine competitiveness in the domestic economy. Programs dependent upon competitive bidding, like the U.S. Army's, were easily subverted by a similar process of "cooperation" among potential suppliers.

In the view of many familiar with Korea, collusion and kickbacks were also facilitated by certain "cultural traits." The "emphasis on harmony" in Korean culture "is diametrically opposed to true competition," wrote George Martin, a former U.S. Army official in Korea, on whose monograph this case study draws heavily. "Competition requires a number of independent contenders each seeking to be the winner but with most finishing as losers. Koreans have a strong need to preserve face, and a loss in competition can undermine one's standing."[5] Cooper-

5. George Martin, *And Never the Twain Shall Meet. Cross-cultural Conflict in the Administrative Process: US Military Procurement in Korea*, a PASITAM Design Study (Bloomington, Indiana: International Development Institute, Indiana University, n.d. [1982?]), 8–9.

ative arrangements like the trade associations were more in tune with this attitude.

Moreover, the Koreans had a custom of gift giving, which Martin believed was "related to the traditional problem of corruption in the Korean government."[6] One expert put it this way:

> Koreans are among the most gracious and generous people one will meet. They are thoughtful and considerate, and try by every means to establish personal relationships before they conduct any business. . . . The giving and receiving of gifts are considered a normal operating commission for services rendered.
>
> In this context, every gift expects something in return. One rarely gives an expensive gift without a purpose. The purpose may be to establish an obligation, to gain a certain advantage, or merely to create an atmosphere in which the recipient will be more pliable to the requests of the donor. To accept a gift and then refuse the requested favor is considered insincere.[7]

Bribery and corruption were not applauded in Korean culture. On the contrary, the ideal was the "poor nobleman," a person of power whose poverty testified to his rectitude. But the line between gift giving and bribery was less clear in Korean society than in many others, such as the United States. Policymakers in the U.S. Army were faced with what looked like a deep-rooted problem—one that their usual procedures for competitive bidding could not seem to overcome. In the words of George Martin: "The U.S. sought competition, openness, equal opportunity for offerors, legal-bureaucratic relationships, corruption avoidance, and fair and reasonable prices, all under the rule of law. Korean businessmen preferred cooperation, covert dealings, a hierarchy among offerors, personal relationships, gift-giving, and the promotion of export earnings, all governed by personalities and traditional mores rather than by law."[8]

How Collusion Took Place

Sometimes the collusion among Korean bidders was unmistakable. Three prospective contractors on a steel project offered almost identical prices—and they divided the items so that when their separate proposals

6. Ibid., 11.

7. Paul Crane, *Korean Patterns* (Seoul: Hollyn Corp., 1967), 75–76; cited in Martin, *Never the Twain*, 10.

8. Martin, *Never the Twain*, 12.

were added up, the three proposals combined to offer two feet more than the total of 9 million feet of steel. Another obvious case of collusion involved three bidders for the purchase of socks. One bidder was much higher than the other two, who each offered to provide exactly half of the socks, with identical prices for each of the three kinds of socks in the contract.

Investigators of collusion around the world look for such patterns in bidding. Collusive bidding comes in at least four varieties: price fixing on a particular bid; dividing a bid among various suppliers; dividing geographical regions among suppliers to create local monopolies; and dividing government agencies among suppliers, again creating effective monopolies or oligopolies. Increasingly, investigators use computers to sift through past bidding records, looking for patterns that may indicate these various kinds of collusion. If they discover such patterns, investigators can follow up using more traditional methods of intelligence gathering.

Exhibit 3 provides helpful indicators for ascertaining whether collusion or kickbacks are taking place. Such indicators have been successfully applied in the United States. One author found that only three weeks of one person's work, using public records, were sufficient to uncover several collusive bidding schemes in Massachusetts.[9] The U.S. government has recently had good success detecting collusion by using large-scale computer analysis of bidding patterns.[10]

But most Korean cases of collusion were not easy to prove. Korean businesspeople put on a charade of competition.

Here is how the process usually unfolded. The Army would solicit bids from five to seven eligible contractors. Three to five of the contractors would respond with pre-bid "proposals." The Army would negotiate

9. Robert E. Richardson, "A Proactive Model for Detecting Political Corruption: As Applied to the Purchase of Goods and Services in Middlesex County, Massachusetts" (Unpublished paper, Harvard Law School, May 1983), 26.

10. "Automated auditing is a third category which is being developed as a prevention technique. . . . One of the most successful applications of this advanced computer technology has been undertaken by the Departments of Transportation and Justice in their joint investigation of highway contract bid rigging. Using computers to identify bid rigging patterns, this effort has resulted in a total of 188 indictments, 134 convictions, and $17 million in fines" (President's Council on Integrity and Efficiency, *Addressing Fraud, Waste, and Abuse: A Summary Report of Inspector General Activities, Fiscal Year 1983, First Six Months* [Washington, D.C.: Government Printing Office, 1983], 3).

Exhibit 3 **Indicators of Possible Kickbacks and Collusion in Bidding**

A. Indicators of Possible Collusion
   1. Identical bid prices for contract
   2. Evidence same person prepared all bids (e.g., same handwriting or typeface)
   3. Patterns in bids over many contracts
      a. Same vendor gets a particular kind of contract
      b. Regional or agency pattern to bids
      c. Pattern of rotation among winning vendors
   4. Information that prices charged are greater than competitive prices
      a. Prices for same or similar contracts elsewhere
      b. Market information
      c. Informers among contractors
      d. Internal or third-party estimates of costs

B. Indicators of Opportunities for Kickbacks
   1. Large contract
   2. Few bidders on contract
   3. Discretion in awarding a contract
      a. Agency may award contract to other than low bidder
      b. Agent has discretion to avoid competitive bidding in a contract
      c. Agent can negotiate with bidders
   4. Discretion after contract awarded
      a. Agent can issue "change orders"
      b. Agent can award additional work to contractor without bids

C. Indicators of Possible Occurrences of Kickbacks
   1. Large contract
   2. Few bidders
   3. Specifications of contract
      a. None or vague when bidding opened
      b. Bidder helped set specifications
      c. Particular brand of equipment mandated
      d. "Emergency" contract
   4. Awarding of contract
      a. Not to low bidder
      b. Contract awarded without bidding

   c. Modification of bid after submission
   d. Contract put to bid for second time
5. After contract awarded
   a. Cancellation of award
   b. Unexplained delay in executing contract
   c. Many change orders
   d. Further work on contract without bids
   e. Lots of overtime on project
6. Character of agent and contractor
   a. Presence of small-scale corruption in area
   b. Presence of "suspicious individuals" in system
   c. Vendor has made questionable payments in past

---

with the bidders, trying to get a lower price. (This latter step was a departure from the usual procedure that no negotiation would take place once bids were in. We'll discuss this departure further in a moment.) The high bidder would lower his or her price but not enough to threaten the lowest bidder. All but the lowest two bidders would drop out of the negotiations. These two would engage in what looked like serious negotiations with the Army. But the bidder who started with the lowest bid would virtually always end up with the lowest bid.

The contractors retained consistent rankings through these "competitive negotiations," because occasionally a contract would be awarded without negotiations. The Koreans did not want to risk the contract going to someone not already chosen by themselves.

How did the Koreans choose? When a contract was put out by the U.S. Army, prospective contractors would be organized by the contractor's association. Before any bids were submitted, the Mutual Benefit Association would hold a *dongo*, usually in a coffee shop, a tea room, or a restaurant. At the *dongo* all the potential bidders decided upon a collusive price. The choice of the winning bidder-to-be could be determined in several ways. On small contracts sometimes the *dongo* held a lottery among those present. More often–and in a more characteristically Korean vein–the decision was by consensus. The biggest contracts often went to the most influential companies; they had the greatest clout in the process of consensus building. (This power frustrated some of the smaller contractors, who later became informers for the U.S. Army.)

Connoisseurs of irony will appreciate a third method that the contractors used for choosing the winner: competitive bidding. After agreeing on a collusive price, contractors would bid against each other to determine who would give the largest cash contribution to the Mutual Benefit Association, the other contractors present, or a charity. For example, in 1975, a *dongo* met in a Seoul restaurant to arrange a collusive bid on a contract to provide ammunition storage bunkers. Each contractor submitted a sealed bid saying how much the company would give to the group if it were allowed to win the contract, which was valued at about $400,000. The winner was the Ah Jong Construction Company, which contributed $79,395 to the others in the *dongo*.

If all these methods proved unsatisfactory, the head of the Mutual Benefit Association would take the responsibility for picking the winner. The price in every case was a collusive rather than a competitive one; the later show of multiple bids and negotiations with the Army was to meet the letter of the Western process of competitive bidding.

The U.S. Army did not know the details of the Korean collusive bidding system until the early 1970s. Rumors had occasionally surfaced, but because the Koreans' collusive arrangement was so well enforced, firms did not report on their colleagues. The arrangement was lucrative to the firms. It fit into an economic system that supported trade associations and "gifts," so that side payments were unremarkable. The country enjoyed foreign exchange benefits by the suppliers' milking the U.S. government through inflated prices. Reluctant firms were sometimes informed through official channels that it was their patriotic duty not to bid the price too low. Profits, bribes, force, and patriotism conspired against the U.S. Army's competitive bidding procedures.

ATTEMPTS TO MAKE COMPETITION WORK

In the early 1970s, the Army took three general steps to try to make competition work: they attempted to increase the number of Korean bidders, break up the contractors' cartel, and enter direct negotiations with a single contractor rather than pursue competitive procurement.

Increasing the Bidding

One policy initiative encouraged other Korean firms to enter the bidding for U.S. Army contracts. If enough smaller firms were involved, the Mutual Benefit Association might find it difficult to enforce collusion. Like all cartels, a collusive arrangement is always under the threat that its monopoly profits will be an attractive lure for one or more firms to enter or to break ranks, make a lower bid, and pocket big profits.

The Army had to overcome two problems. One was legalistic. In 1962, when the Korean government launched its export drive and created the trade associations, it initiated a procedure for registering firms that wanted to supply the military. It also created a military contractors' association "to establish order in the trade and/or for their common interest." All firms that wished to bid on U.S. military contracts had to register with the Korean Ministry of Commerce and Industry.

The possibilities for collusion here—and for bribery among ministry officials who had the discretion to allow firms to register—are obvious. And yet, it is common in contracting situations to have certain "eligibility requirements" for firms to be able to bid. The purpose is not to reduce competition but to make sure that those who bid have a good chance of delivering what they promise. A procurement system would be disastrous if unscrupulous, inexperienced, or foolish firms bid low but promised more than they could deliver. The result might be noncompliance, delays, low quality, or other problems. The U.S. government, as well as the three development banks, require evidence that the bidder is qualified to perform the contract if the bid is accepted.[11] The Korean government could argue it was doing the same. Still the Army became increasingly convinced that this registration process was restricting competition and thereby facilitating collusion.

The second problem was the powerful enforcement mechanism developed by the Korean suppliers. New bidders might be attracted by the potential profits from cartel-busting, but they themselves might be busted in a more literal sense by the Korean CIA or the Hopkido (Mutual Benefit) Association.

In 1972, the Army launched an aggressive attempt to increase the number of competitors. For the first time they publicly posted procurement solicitations, no longer issuing them solely to the registered mem-

11. Among the three clauses pertaining to bidders' qualifications, the three banks' sample bidding documents let the purchaser require whatever evidence they like "that the bidder has the financial, technical and production capability necessary to perform the contract" (*Sample Bidding Documents*, 11).

bers of the suppliers' association. The Army simply circumvented the Korean regulation, and they hoped that such a step would make collusion impossible to enforce.

In the Korean business community, havoc ensued. Old-line suppliers and new entrants competed in some rather remarkable ways. For instance, a small firm called Won Hyo Motors Corporation bid against a large company called Korea POL on a contract for the painting of railroad cars. At first Won Hyo told Korea POL it would not compete if Korea POL would make a side payment. When Korea POL refused, both companies competed frantically to win the award. Negotiations with the Army led to lower and still lower prices. The Army began to fear that the price was so low that neither company could make money. Worrying that the contract would later go unfulfilled for this reason, the Army hesitated to award a contract. George Martin mused: "There seems to have been something in the Korean psyche that would not allow them to give up on a procurement once there was genuine competition. Perhaps open competition was such a blatant affront that one could not surrender easily without losing face. In any event those involved in actual competition viciously cut prices."[12]

But, according to Martin's account, this effort did not bring lasting improvements. The colluding contractors violently suppressed "greedy, unpatriotic" would-be competitors. The Eddy Chang case was one example that came to light; many others were not uncovered until later. Thus, prices did not generally decline because of "increased competition." And when prices did fall because small "suitcase contractors" forced bids downward, the Army was often faced with defaults, delays, or poor quality in the work performed.

Breaking Up the Cartel

Typically, a government agency victimized by collusive bidding can call on its Ministry of Justice to go after the colluders. The American Army in Korea found itself in a different position. Not only did it have a difficult time proving that collusion existed, it could not tell a Korean justice agency what to do. Nonetheless, the Army decided to try to document

12. Martin, *Never the Twain*, 51.

the existence of collusion and then ask the Korean government to crack down on the practice.

Here entered a remarkable figure, John Guss of the Army's Criminal Investigation Division (CID). Guss was a detective, complete with trench coat and drooping cigarette. He succeeded in the early 1970s where others had failed. Through personal observation and a network of informants he infiltrated the contractors' collusive bidding system and documented its methods of operations.

John Guss started small. Among his first informants was the chauffeur of one of the contractors. Little by little he hooked up with dissidents within firms, and he induced some contractors to give testimony against the others. Sometimes he gathered data firsthand. "Guss's personal courage emboldened his informants. At times he would lurk outside the building where a collusive meeting of contractors was to take place and photograph the participants as they arrived. Or, in a demonstrable lack of tact, he would walk in on such meetings uninvited and unwanted."[13]

The Army procurement agency reinforced Guss's efforts. It debarred some of the firms that had won collusive bids; it also solicited more often those firms that cooperated with Guss, or it gave them sole-source contracts. (We'll describe these sole-source contracts later in this chapter.) As Guss increasingly dispensed rewards and punishments, more informants came forward. By thoroughly documenting the role of the Mutual Benefit Association, the Army at last had more than circumstantial evidence of collusion.

In 1975, the Army representative to the U.S.-Korean Status of Forces Agreement Committee sent a strong letter to his Korean counterpart, with a copy delivered by the American Ambassador to the Korean Foreign Minister. The letter cited "conclusive and ever-mounting evidence of continuing attempts by Korean military supply associations and organizations, with the acquiescence and assistance of agencies of the Government of Korea," to thwart competitive bidding. The letter said that a Korean government official had unofficially confirmed that U.S. contracts typically contained an extra profit of 30 percent. The letter concluded by warning that the U.S. General Accounting Office might investigate the collusive contracting system.

13. Ibid., 21.

The Korean government responded on two levels. Through military channels came an official answer denying all improprieties and disclaiming any governmental connection with the Mutual Benefit Association. But another response came on 26 June 1975, when a special team of police assigned to Korean President Park Chung Hee raided the Mutual Benefit Association and the homes of its officers. The police seized documents and detained two top officers. A month later the Korean government directed that the Mutual Benefit Association be disbanded. A new leader of the Korean contractors was named, and the contractors were left without their enforcement arm.

The government saved face through the official denial, while with the raids it hoped to squelch the problem and avoid a diplomatic incident. The use of President Park's own "Blue House" police in the raids demonstrated how strong the forces of collusion had become.

With the Mutual Benefit Association gone, reported incidents of violence against contractors virtually disappeared. But while the U.S. Army "could reasonably demand that the Korean government not be involved in or sanction collusive bidding, it was far less reasonable to demand that the government force private contractors to practice [the Army's] competitive methods."[14] The *dongos* kept on meeting; the new leadership of the contractors organized them. The CID reported that most bids were still collusive.

Negotiating with the Bidders

The Defense Department allowed its procurement officers overseas to negotiate with prospective contractors. This procedure differed from the usual practice of allowing no discussion once bids had been received. After getting a first offer, the Army in Korea could hold discussions with all contractors who stood a reasonable chance of being awarded the contract. The Army would explain ambiguous or difficult areas of the contract. More importantly, it would bargain with the contractors over price. Then the Army would ask for a best and final offer from the bidders.

This procedure gave the Army a chance to reduce the harmful effects

14. Ibid., 36.

of collusion by bargaining down the price. The Army could balk, delay, or even threaten to withdraw the contract. But to make its negotiating position credible, the Army needed some independent idea of how much the contract should cost. So it employed its own cost estimators.

Procurement agents often use independent cost estimators as a device to guard against both collusion and kickbacks in procurement. In this case the Army employed Korean cost estimators and accountants to make two sorts of independent estimates. They made one estimate before bids were received, basing it on an engineering approach, including piece-by-piece estimates of the contract's costs. A different set of estimators carried out the second estimate after bids were in. They examined the bidders' prices for each part of the contract, looking where possible at Korean market prices as points of reference. Koreans filled most of these estimating and accounting positions, since local language capability was necessary for researching trade publications, markets, and so forth.

When these independent estimates were routinized in the early 1970s, the Army pressed contractors to meet them. And the tactic worked: prices dropped. But the contractors soon had their own response. They bribed, cajoled, and threatened the Korean accountants and others working for the Army so that they leaked cost estimates, made higher estimates, and altered bids submitted by noncolluders. The contractors thus managed to corrupt the "independent" estimates.

The case of Mr. Kim illustrates the role of threats. Kim worked as a contract specialist for the Army. When threatened by the contractors' group, he altered the bid of a dissident competitor. Fortunately, the ever-vigilant John Guss had got wind of this possibility, and he dusted the dissident firm's bid page in the Army records with phosphorescent powder. The next day Guss discovered that a new bid page had been inserted—with a price twice that of the dissident firm's true bid. Phosphorescent powder was found on Kim's hands.

Caught ultraviolet-handed, Kim confessed and was fired. Later he sought reinstatement. But even when trying to be rehired, Kim was reluctant to talk about why he had committed the offense. He wrote that he would help "as much as possible within the limitation which would not directly endanger living status in Korea." He had been threatened several times, he said, and defying the contractor's group would result in "irrevocable disaster."

The Army's Korean accountants and contract specialists were vulnerable to corruption because their salaries were not high. Moreover, gift giving was customary in Korea, and their private-sector counterparts frequently received "presents." They found themselves stretched between loyalty to their employer and a perceived disloyalty to their country. In one documented case the Korean CIA called an auditor several times and "informed him that as a Korean he had a patriotic duty to prevent unnecessary low prices."[15] And the threat of violence lurked, indeed scarcely lurked, all around them.

Choices in 1976

So the Army entered 1976 with a problem. Despite its efforts, systematic collusion and kickbacks were still adding large costs to Korean procurements. Given its past experience and unusual status as a foreign body in a developing nation, what might it try next?

A visiting team from the United States suggested one radical alternative: obtain all goods directly from the Korean government. The plan here was to let the Koreans do the subcontracting to the colluders. This tactic would place the responsibility for avoiding collusion with the Korean government, which in theory could do much more to combat collusion than could the U.S. Army. The team had been impressed by what President Park had done to disband the Mutual Benefit Association. If President Park wanted something done, the team reasoned, it would be done. The Army would ask President Park to make sure that fair and reasonable prices were provided.

The Army's procurement staff in Korea put forward a second, equally radical alternative: abandon competition. In this case the strategy was to solicit only one contractor on each procurement. This option would beef up the American staffing of procurement, with particular emphasis on better estimates of prices and effective surveillance by CID. The staff argued that competitive bidding had become time consuming and had restricted the Army's ability to negotiate with the colluders.

> Instead of wasting time on multiple sources, only one of whom was a serious contender, [the Army] could focus on getting a better price out of the

15. Ibid., 28.

> one source selected for negotiations. Because only one source would be solicited (and that source would be selected by [the Army]), there should be little reason for the Korea Military Contractors Association to exist, since it functioned primarily during the pre-award stage of procurement. The proposed system would possibly eliminate some payoffs, since other contractors would not be solicited and there would be no need for them to be compensated. It focused the procuring agencies' attention on the right goal–getting proper supplies and services at fair and reasonable prices–rather than on the impossible–obtaining competition.[16]

These were the two choices on the table in 1976. Few on the scene were prepared to endorse the status quo.

DISCUSSION

A key to this problem is bargaining. Ordinarily, procurement agents and contractors *avoid* bargaining, because it creates opportunities for corruption. The sample bidding documents designed by the three development banks preclude bargaining. They assume that the contractors will submit sealed bids, the procurement agents will make a rather mechanical choice among the bids, and no negotiation will be allowed.

But what happens if the bidding is not competitive but collusive? Then the sample bidding documents virtually force the procurer to take the "low" bid, eliminating any possibility of the procurer using its own bargaining strength to secure a lower price.

Faced with this problem, the purchaser has several broad options. One choice is to *induce competition and break up collusion*. In theory, competition leads to the most efficient supplier getting the contract and the purchaser getting the best price. In a world with uncertainty, however, this happy outcome may not always occur. The lowest bid may not be the best bid. It is likely to be the lowest partly because the bidder has underestimated the true costs of providing the good or service. Notice, too, that the supplier bears all the risks of the uncertain cost being higher than anticipated; one might instead want to share that risk between the supplier and the purchaser. Enter once again the principal-agent problem, with conflicting incentives, uncertainty, and asymmetric information.

16. Ibid., 38–39.

The Army had tried to induce competition in Korea. They were thwarted because the colluders had remarkable powers of enforcing collusion, while the Army, as a foreign entity, had virtually none of the powers a government usually has to punish colluders.

A second option is a *cost-based contract*. The reasoning here is as follows. If costs are *ex ante* uncertain, let us look at them *ex post*. The contractor is paid based on the actual costs incurred. Here the purchaser bears all the risk. Moreover, the supplier may have an incentive to raise the costs—a problem called "moral hazard."

A third option is *vertical integration*. The purchaser solves the principal-agent problem by absorbing the agent, or becoming his or her own contractor. Problems can arise here, too. The purchaser may sacrifice efficiencies of specialization. And even when the contractor becomes part of the purchaser's organization, there still may be incentives to mislead on costs; as we have seen, the principal-agent problem often occurs within an organization. Of course, when the principal is from one government and the agent from another, the alternative of vertical integration is seldom open.

Other options also exist. Using Chapter 3's framework for policy analysis, Exhibit 4 lists possible measures for combating collusive bidding.

Exhibit 4 **Possible Policies to Deal with Collusive Bidding**

A. Select Bidders
   1. Screen for honesty (surveillance showing noncollusion; background checks on contractors; performance on past contracts)
   2. Exploit outside guarantees of honest bids and faithful performance
   3. Allow only one firm to bid and negotiate ruthlessly

B. Change the Rewards and Penalties Facing Bidders
   1. Shift rewards to favor honest bids (later payment depending on costs and quality; incentive contracts)
   2. Change penalties to make collusion less attractive (disbar colluding firms; employ criminal sanctions; use publicity to damage company name)

C. Use Informational Strategies to Raise the Likelihood that Collusion is Detected and Punished

1. Use systems for detecting collusion (see Exhibit 3)
2. Strengthen agents for gathering information (undercover work, surveillance, market prices, cost estimation)
3. Involve third parties to obtain credible information (industry newsletters and consultants, independent cost estimates, auditors)
4. Use bidders as sources of information (disaffected employees, losing bidders, nonbidders)

D. Restructure the Procurer-Bidder Relationship
1. Foment competition among bidders (invite new firms, wider publicity, lower barrier to entry, risk-sharing contracts, requirements to share contract information)
2. Reduce the discretion of own agents (rules about change orders, follow-ons, "emergencies," sealed bids, decision rules for deciding among bidders, hierarchical review of decisions)
3. Rotate own agents
4. Redefine the organization's "product" (more standardized goods with market prices; choosing inputs, outputs, and modes of payment with an eye to corruptibility; vertical integration—make it rather than buy it)

E. Change Attitudes about Collusion
1. Disassociate collusion from acceptable practices (such as export cartels) and goals (such as maximizing foreign exchange earnings)
2. Educate contractors about how competitive bidding works elsewhere
3. Promote the bidders' identification with the social or public purpose of the contract

---

As the Army discovered, many of these options run into unanticipated problems when cultures clash over corruption. The Army did not have many of the powers of the usual "principal"; in particular, they could not punish colluding "agents." This dilemma led to the consideration in 1976 of the two radical options.

The Army staff in Korea proposed a radical extension of an option with which they had experimented. This alternative would *estimate costs in advance and bargain with the bidders*. If bidders collude or if a single bidder is chosen by the Army, it makes no difference in one sense; the

Army still faces a monopolistic supplier. But by doing away with the competitive apparatus, the Army frees its own hands to play hardball with that supplier. The problem changes to a monopolistic supplier bargaining with a monopsoistic purchaser. The purchaser is likely to do better than if he or she were forced to take whatever bid the monopolist made. The outcome is likely but not guaranteed: notice how much depends on the Army's own agents. The cost estimators and negotiating officers will have a significant impact on the price that is negotiated (unlike the ideal case of competitive bidding, where their discretion and monopsony powers are virtually eliminated). These agents will face powerful incentives to make corrupt deals with the supplier.

The visiting team from the United States proposed an equally radical recommendation. Their plan also took the clash of cultures very seriously, but it would have the hardball played exclusively among Koreans. The visiting experts recognized that the Korean side also contained principal-agent problems. First, they had the remarkable effort by the military contractors' association to enforce collusive discipline among its members using agents like the Mutual Benefit Association (and its martial arts capabilities). Second, they had the relationship between the Korean Government—with a capital *G*, personalized by President Park—and the contractors' association. The team hoped it could solve the Army's principal-agent problem by using President Park to control the colluders. The team was right that the U.S. Army had few powers to punish the colluders, whereas Park had many.

But the visiting team's recommendation had several problems:

- The team "overestimated the Korean President's power in relation to the Korean bureaucracy. Park could not simply proclaim fair prices." Indeed the Korean government was itself being ripped off by colluding contractors. In FY 1976, the Korean Board of Audit alone discovered 687 cases of "irregular activities" by officials in awarding construction contracts.[17]
- The Korean government did not have strong incentives to get low prices for the U.S. Army. The higher the prices, the more foreign exchange for Korea.
- All procurement squabbles would have the potential to become

17. Ibid., 37.

diplomatic incidents. "Diplomatic channels," noted George Martin, "are extremely inefficient for resolving contractual disputes."[18]

□ The U.S. government would lose all control of procurement. This consequence had a significant bureaucratic dimension: the Army procurement people in Korea, and their local-hire staff, would be practically out of business. Contrast this possibility to the effects of their own proposal—to abandon competition and use only single-source contracts. Under the latter scheme the Army staff in Korea would grow in personnel, budget, and power.

Between the two proposals on the table the visiting team's came in second. In 1977, the U.S. Army in Korea initiated a system based on sole-source procurement and heavy bargaining. For each procurement Army staff prepared a report that included a list and description of potential Korean contractors and a recommendation of the most suitable. The report was submitted to a Source Selection Board, made up of three top U.S. procurement officers, an attorney from the Staff Judge Advocates office, and the deputy to the assistant chief of staff. This board selected the contractor. Just over half the time it did this by random selection; the rest of the procurements were done on the basis of the contractors' qualifications. "Vital to the success of the innovation was the process for choosing a source," Martin wrote. "The Army team wisely adopted a method that emphasized the prevention of favoritism over speed."[19]

Then the Army would negotiate with the selected contractor. The Army beefed up its capabilities to estimate the likely costs of the contract. Price was one issue. The Army also used its new leverage to obtain better service during the contract period from suppliers who wanted repeat contracts and could no longer count on a collusively low bid to get it. If a contractor would not bargain, the Army did not have to reinitiate a cumbersome bidding process; they would simply select another contractor.

In the short run the results of this new policy were positive. The Army shifted resources from the investigation of collusion, which had ceased in

18. Ibid., 37.

19. Ibid., 39. Random selection was not used "when there was one outstanding contractor for a particular task or on recurring contracts where there was no reason for changing from the incumbent."

the new system, to the assessment of costs and the negotiation process. Violence among Korean contractors stopped. Data on prices are available only for the first years. On construction contracts – where there is often a "custom-made" element, so market prices are hard to ascertain – the Army saved 10 to 15 percent. On large-value projects procured through the district engineer, the savings were around 30 percent. George Martin observed:

> Such better prices should result from an intelligently administered single source system, because this should have eliminated some payoffs. In addition, government negotiators can now spend more time analyzing the procurement, and the contractor's cost data rather than expending time on imagined "competitors." Also, since a selected offeror's failure to negotiate a fair and reasonable price can result in [the Army's] cancelling his solicitation and going to another offeror, contractors have a greater incentive to bargain in good faith.[20]

Data are not available on the longer run. Some problems may be anticipated. How will new firms enter into the group of eligible suppliers? Can the cost estimates be kept free from corruption? Most crucially, can the sole-source process itself be kept free of corruption? Perhaps the U.S. military has enough controls and sufficient internal discipline to overcome the new system's obvious susceptibility to kickbacks. In other contexts the Army's "success story" in Korea might be an invitation to even greater, if differently shared, collusion.

Notice what the clash of cultures – the fact that two sovereign states were involved – can do to the choice of anticorruption policies. The principal's usual repertoire of tools may be radically reduced: he or she has less control over rewards, punishments, and information. New sorts of costs, such as the prospects of diplomatic incidents, may arise. Policies may boil down to selecting agents and restructuring the principal-agent relationship. The Army adopted this strategy in Korea, and it resulted in hard-nosed bilateral bargaining – effective if the principal plays well but having plenty of potential for escalation and, indeed, for a new level of corrupt behavior.

20. Ibid., 45.

7 | Implementation Strategies

Recent studies have investigated the extent to which patients follow the advice and prescriptions given to them by physicians. The answers have been remarkable. Even victims of heart attacks seldom did what their doctors advised. Fewer than 20 percent kept to their prescriptions. Given this phenomenon, what should doctors do?

One response is as follows: "I'm a doctor. My job is to diagnose the illness and tell the patient what to do if he or she wants to get rid of the illness. If the patient doesn't want to, well, that goes beyond medicine."

But a more sophisticated, and difficult, response would be the following: "If my objective as a physician is to improve my patient's health, I have to take seriously his or her unwillingness to do what I say. To be effective, I must go beyond the usual confines of medicine."

Similar problems arise in many areas of economic policy. For example, in a recent book Arnold Harberger collected a fascinating set of studies of economic policy and performance in a number of countries. Harberger and his colleagues offered guidance on the objectives of economic policy and the tools that can be employed to attain those objectives. In a concluding chapter Harberger regretfully observed that policymakers often do not follow the good advice that economists give them: "Economic policy professionals are also well accustomed to frustration. Proposals aimed at improving policy must run a veritable gauntlet of hazards and obstacles on their way to implementation. Most proposals do not survive, and of those that do, many emerge so mutilated or distorted that they no longer serve their intended purposes."[1]

1. Arnold C. Harberger, "Economic Policy and Economic Growth," in *World Economic Growth*, ed. Arnold C. Harberger (San Francisco: ICS Press, 1984), 428.

Unfortunately, Harberger and his colleagues had little to say about how to induce economic policymakers to seek those objectives or use those tools—how to get the patient to take the medicine.

There seem to be three stages in the evolution of thinking and writing about a given policy issue. In the first stage we realize we have a problem. In the case of corruption much of the academic literature is stuck here: witness the battle between the moralists and revisionists over the harmfulness of corruption.

In the second stage we consider which policies would best address the problem. The discussion in Chapter 3 was intended to move us to the second stage regarding corruption. This issue of determining effective policies has certainly occupied our attention for most of the book.

According to the usual evolutionary pattern, we next arrive at stage three, where we notice that the policies are not being implemented very well. Here we begin asking questions about how to get policymakers to listen to good advice, or how to get reluctant bureaucrats to implement the policies, and so forth. The matter goes beyond objectives and policies to *implementation strategies*. Seldom has this step been reached with regard to corruption. Perhaps we can make a start on implementation strategies for controlling corruption, and indeed we already have done so in the cases we have reviewed. In this chapter we'll begin by examining the true story of a shrewd policymaker who used a variety of policy measures to fight corruption but failed because he lacked an implementation strategy.

CORRUPTION IN THE NATIONAL FOOD ORGANIZATION

As Rafiq Shabir left work one evening during his first week on the job, he was overheard grumbling, "I am going to wring the neck of every corrupt official I come across. I am going to salvage the image of this organization if it's the last thing I do."

Shabir, only twenty-nine, had just been appointed to the powerful post of director of the National Food Organization (NFO) in Ruritania province. (In this chapter all names and some data have been altered to preserve confidentiality. But the case is real.) The NFO had a reputation as one of the most corrupt organizations in Ruritania. Shabir quickly appreciated how lucrative an NFO position could be. Most employees owned cars. A majority possessed bungalows. Some officials were almost legends in their own time:

□ Deputy Manager (DM) Buqsha worked in the small town of Elve, near one of Ruritania's ports. In his mid-forties, Buqsha had been a DM for twelve years and had refused two opportunities to be promoted and move from Elve. He was known to enjoy wine and women and was frequently found in the high-rolling Beach Hotel in the port city. On one occasion he was seen walking out of the nightclub after having lost his wallet. "Oh, it doesn't matter," he said, "there were only 5000 polas in it." (The pola is the local unit of currency.) Buqsha's annual salary from the government was P6000.

□ District Food Controller (DFC) Nyunt worked in the coastal district of Kilchon. He was asked to remove about 1000 gunny bags of defective wheat from the NFO warehouse and destroy them. Instead he removed 1000 bags of perfectly edible wheat and sold it in the interior of the province for a fabulous sum. The people of Kilchon continued to receive bad wheat. Finally, a citizens' delegation traveled 400 kilometers to the Minister of Food's office in Milang, the capital of Ruritania province, and protested. The minister visited Kilchon and saw the defective wheat in the ration shops; he ordered that something be done about it. Nyunt's fate was a transfer to Milang, where he was often seen enjoying his shiny new car.

□ Maguma had recently joined the NFO in Dipawa district. "Anyone who does not make money in this organization is a fool," he was quoted as saying. "When I joined I did not know where I would get my next meal. But now I own a motorcycle and have shifted to a three-bedroom house." Maguma was in charge of one of the wheat procurement centers. He was said to have agreed with local farmers to procure only 50 percent of their wheat, allowing them to sell the rest on the black market. In exchange he received kickbacks. When questioned by the DFC about the low procurement figures, Maguma could come up with no reasonable explanation. The DFC reported the matter to the District Manager, who was quoted as saying: "Maguma is a young man. He has a lot to learn. Ask him to be careful in what he does." Nothing else was done, and Maguma continued his scheme.

Shabir's predecessor as director was himself famous for corruption. He had appointed to key positions cadre members loyal to him. He had sometimes used his powers of summary proceedings to threaten or banish employees who were not loyal–incidentally showing higher officials that actions were being taken against "the corrupt." Employees of the NFO considered this situation a normal phenomenon and accepted it. At least it was normal at the time that the director was sacked and Shabir was brought to the post.

Shabir had been appointed director by the top civil servant in Ruritania, Chief Commissioner Rahimtoola. The chief commissioner himself had only recently come to his post through a routine transfer from the same position in another province. Rahimtoola's first concern in office had been to ensure that the NFO, which procured, stored, and distributed wheat and sugar through Ruritania, was working well.

To his horror, he discovered from NFO Commissioner Portilo that the organization was infested with corruption. The incumbent director was corrupt, Commissioner Portilo told the chief commissioner, but Portilo had been unable to take action because of the director's political connections and a lack of support from the previous chief commissioner. Indignant, Rahimtoola helped Portilo to remove the incumbent director, who ultimately was found guilty of corrupt behavior and dismissed from government service.

Chief Commissioner Rahimtoola consulted with Portilo about naming a new director. Portilo warned him that corruption within the NFO was widespread and that Deputy Director Mahfooz was tired and inefficient. Portilo suggested the appointment of an outsider. He mentioned Rafiq Shabir, whom he had met socially and knew to be one of the bright young stars of the country's civil service. The chief commissioner met Shabir and agreed. Despite his youth and inexperience, Shabir was appointed to the director's job.

Shabir had been raised in an adjoining province in a well-established family of many doctors, lawyers, and engineers. After attending private schools, he broke with family tradition and obtained a master's degree in business administration. He worked for a while in a pharmaceutical company but became attracted to government work. The public sector interested him because he believed that far-reaching decisions affecting his nation were made there. He foresaw that the government was eclipsing the private sector in importance. Passing the difficult civil service examination, Shabir was selected to join the elite cadre of general public managers.

Upon entering the civil service, he was trained in law and public administration. He spent three years in the Ministry of Planning and Programming, reporting to the commissioner. Then he was promoted to a post in a public enterprise in Ruritania, where he reported to the chairman of the corporation. In both jobs his colleagues were members of the same elite service. In the last job he was under the general jurisdiction of Ruritania's chief commissioner.

After Chief Commissioner Rahimtoola took over and removed the director of the NFO for corruption, he called in Shabir for a meeting. He expressed his desire to appoint Shabir to the Directorship. He told Shabir of the importance of the job and his desire to "straighten things out" in the NFO. Rahimtoola and Commissioner Portilo were reported to be men of integrity. They promised Shabir their support in his mandate: to rid the NFO of corruption, while ensuring the timely delivery of staples.

Although Shabir had only five years' experience—and that in staff positions—he had a reputation for toughness and honesty. A large, rugged man with a quick mind and an ability to work with people, Shabir was tabbed for a post that customarily called for at least ten years' experience within the NFO's own independent administrative cadre. His appointment raised eyebrows within and outside the organization. The NFO's rank and file did not know what to expect from the neophyte director, who, like Rahimtoola and Portilo, was not from their province, ethnic group, nor the NFO's own administrative cadre.

RURITANIA PROVINCE

Ruritania was an arid, mountainous province, covering an area larger than Ecuador, Ghana, or Romania. It had about 2.6 million inhabitants, a larger population in 1979 than 63 of the 142 "developing countries" (excluding Oceania).[2] It was known for political unrest, tribal turmoil, and grinding poverty. The government was constantly waging war, sometimes literally, against quasi-feudal rulers, autonomy-seeking linguistic and tribal groups, and the harshest forms of rural deprivation.

Farmers in Ruritania produced only about 10 percent of the province's wheat requirements and virtually no sugar. To ensure the

2. Organization for Economic Cooperation and Development, *Development Cooperation 1979 Review* (Paris: OECD, November 1979), table H.3.

TABLE 4 APPROXIMATE PRICES FOR WHEAT AND SUGAR

	Price in Polas/Kg	
Types of Prices	Wheat	Sugar
Official purchase	1.1	5.5
Official sales	0.75	4.0
Black market sales	2.5	15.0
Sales in neighboring countries		
Serradia	1.1	6.0
Pokal	1.25	6.5
Levistana	1.5	3.8

equitable and efficient distribution of such basic foodstuffs, the government had for some time instituted two major policies.

First, it controlled the purchase and sales prices of wheat and sugar, as indicated in Table 4. Despite these controls, a black market accounted for about 10 to 15 percent of the volume of wheat and sugar distributed in Ruritania, and food was smuggled to adjacent lands.

Second, the National Food Organization controlled the procurement (including imports), most of the storage, and the distribution of wheat and sugar. The NFO's main jobs in Ruritania were to arrange through private contractors the timely delivery of wheat and sugar, often to remote locations, and to manage about seventy-five storage facilities. The NFO also supervised the ration card system. Consumers obtained ration cards from local NFO officials. A card entitled a Ruritania resident to purchase a fixed amount of wheat and sugar at the subsidized price. The actual distribution of wheat and sugar to consumers was carried out via some 2500 private ration dealers, whose licenses were granted by the NFO. Finally, the NFO supervised the procurement of locally grown wheat at the controlled price.

When Rafiq Shabir took over, it was widely believed that uncontrolled prices would lead to an unfair and inefficient outcome. The government was committed to its interventions in the marketplace for food, both in setting prices and in running the distribution system. These

Figure 4 **The Functions of the National Food Organization**

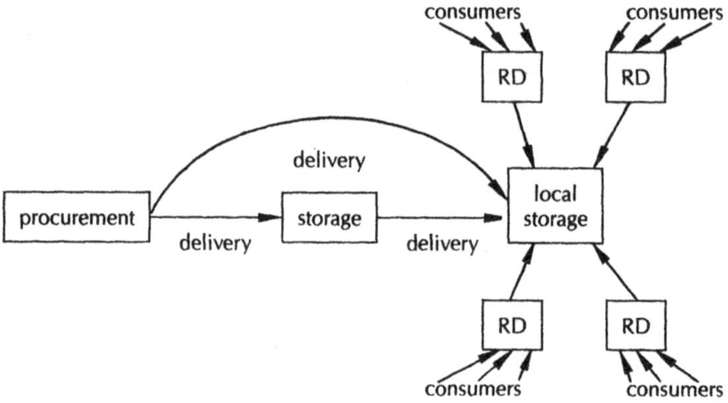

Procurement	Storage	Delivery
From NFO outlets in other provinces From local farmers	Manage seventy-five warehouses and open-air storage facilities	Contract for major and minor deliveries, to and throughout the provinces License and inspect ration dealers (RD) Issue and control ration cards for consumers

interventions were carried out in Ruritania as well as in the nation's other provinces.

THE NATIONAL FOOD ORGANIZATION

Figure 4 displays NFO's activities in procurement, storage, and distribution. In Ruritania its annual budget of P100 million included about P65 million for wheat procurement, P10 million for sugar procurement, P5 million for wages and salaries, and P20 million for distribution and administrative costs.

Procurement

Procurement took place in two ways. About 90 percent of Ruritania's wheat and virtually all its sugar were obtained from NFO outlets in other provinces. An NFO official would travel to the outlet and watch over the weighing and loading for transport. The first delivery point was usually the provincial capital of Milang, where another NFO officer (an inspector) would check the weight and quality.[3] The other 10 percent of the wheat was purchased from local farmers, who were legally required to sell their crop to the NFO official procurement centers. Most of Ruritania's wheat was grown in Dipawa district, which had thirteen procurement centers. Procurement was big business in the other provinces, where it was the NFO's most crucial task; but in Ruritania, storage and delivery were relatively more important.

Storage

The NFO operated about sixty huge warehouses and fifteen storage platforms throughout the province. While traveling through Ruritania's hinterlands, one would find a village of mud huts with a giant concrete NFO building looming in the background. The fifteen open-air platforms, inside compounds surrounded by walls, were located in areas with especially sparse and seasonal rainfall. Their stocks were covered with enormous tarpaulins for protection against freak weather or other mishaps. The NFO employed guards in all these compounds. Many of the ration dealers had their own, much more modest storage facilities.

Delivery

Transportation in Ruritania was arduous. Although its coastal region had several small ports, bad weather and rudimentary vessels handicapped sea travel. Railways and a few paved roads existed, but since the province's population was so widely dispersed, many deliveries had to be made over dirt roads, across deserts, and on camel trails. A severe rainstorm could render some areas unreachable for many days.

The NFO divided delivery routes into three categories, based mostly

3. Quality had several dimensions. Imported or "red" wheat was considered less desirable than locally grown wheat; most of the red wheat in Ruritania was delivered from the country's major port in another province to small coastal ports in Ruritania. Wheat might also be broken up or mixed with lesser grains or spoiled by moisture or pests.

TABLE 5 CATEGORIES OF ROUTES AND CONTRACTORS

Routes	
A	Major deliveries to large storage centers; 15–20 routes.
B	Smaller volume deliveries; 40 routes.
C	The smallest routes; often into remote areas; more than 2000 routes.
Contractors	
A	At least 15 trucks owned by firm; P2 million in collateral and cash deposit with NFO; about 40 eligible contractors on record.
B	At least 10 trucks; P1 million in collateral and cash deposit; about 50 eligible contractors on record.
C	At least 5 trucks; P500,000 in collateral and cash deposit; about 100–150 eligible contractors on record.

on the amount of grain and sugar per shipment. It contracted for individual shipments along these routes with private transport companies, which were also divided into three categories based on size (see Table 5).

Contractors were permitted to bid only on routes with the same letter; for example, only B contractors were eligible to make deliveries on B routes. This limitation was traditional, and it apparently stemmed from two arguments. First, efficiency: if the bidding were opened to all, small contractors who could not really do the job would bid, or some contractors would overextend themselves, resulting in nondelivery of essential food. Second, equity: small routes were retained for small, usually local contractors, who under this system would not be competed into oblivion by large transporters.

The NFO requested tenders on hundreds of deliveries per year. Each major delivery on each route was open for bid. Government regulations required that the lowest bid be accepted, unless a written justification were signed by the director. All contracting was handled by the NFO's Budget and Accounts Section, just down the hall from Shabir's office.

The NFO district offices supervised two other aspects of the delivery system: the regulation of the ration dealers and the issuance of ration cards. The regulation involved checking the quality of stocks, accuracy of weights, and records of ration dealers. The dealers moved the wheat from the NFO's storage centers, first to local flour mills and then to their shops. NFO officials issued ration cards and were supposed to check their records with the local Revenue Department, whose responsibility it was to keep data on residents, landholdings, areas under various crops, and so forth.

Chain of Command

The NFO in Ruritania employed 280 people, about half in professional positions of GS-8 and above. It was a "quasi-independent agency." As such, its administrative cadre was separate from the usual civil services, and its employees were governed by its own rules and regulations for appointments, efficiency, and discipline. The rules provided for summary proceedings against an employee if the prima facie evidence were overwhelming. Guilty employees would simply be dismissed from the NFO.

The NFO's organization chart is given in Figure 5. The *director* had many powers. He was the appointing authority through GS-11; higher-level appointments were the province of the commissioner. Appointments could not be made, however, without a vacancy in an authorized position, and the rules showed a "preference for duly qualified" members of the NFO cadre. The director could suspend and initiate proceedings against officials for reasons of prima facie evidence of corruption, misuse of authority, or even complaints about inefficiency. He or she could transfer employees, but employees could not be sent outside the NFO unless they were dismissed. The director could blacklist contractors for vaguely defined offenses such as tardiness or nonfulfillment of contracts. Blacklisting carried no penalties, but it did render contractors ineligible for future tenders for a period ranging from months to many years, depending on the director's discretion. Through the Budget and Accounts Section, the director had authority over the awarding of contracts, and, to some extent, their timing and design. The director enforced rules and regulations regarding storage, quality control of stocks, ration cards, recordkeeping, and the rest of the NFO's operations.

Figure 5 Organization Chart of the National Food Organization in Ruritania Province

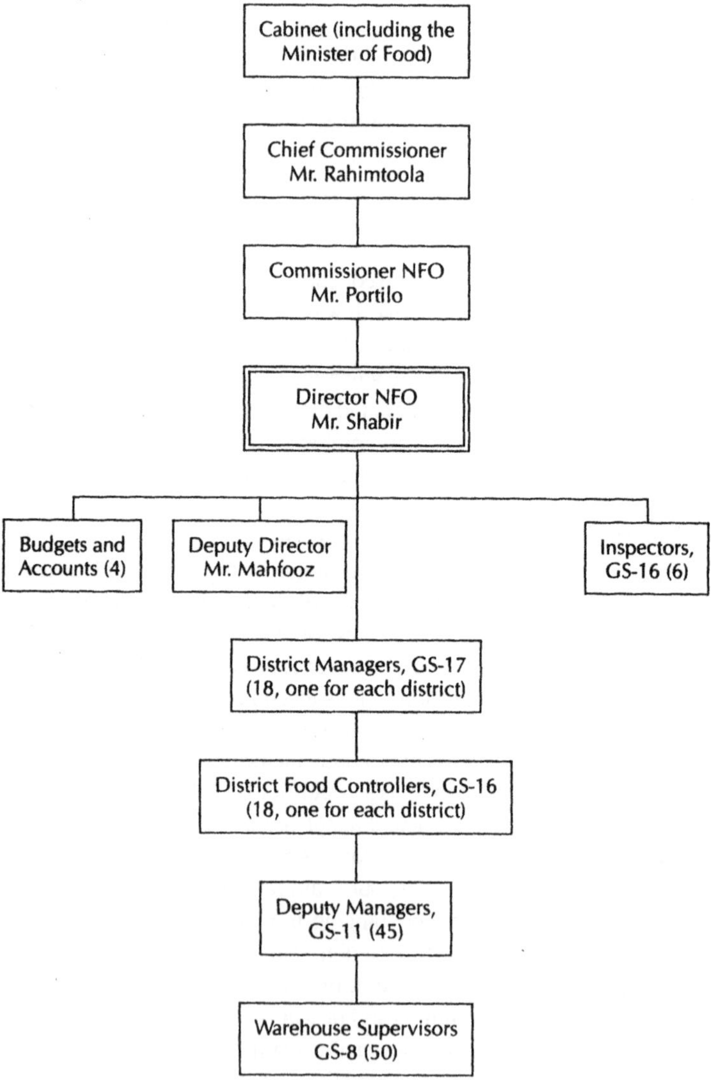

The inept *deputy director*, Mr. Mahfooz, had been put to pasture by the previous director. He spent most of each day sipping tea and talking with other officers and contractors. The six *inspectors* checked both deliveries to major storage areas and the storage facilities themselves. The *Budget and Accounts Section* had only four employees to manage the contracting procedures and to maintain accounts on all central-office activities.

The *district manager* in each of Ruritania's eighteen districts supervised a *district food controller* (DFC). Together they ensured that food was supplied, issued ration cards, and oversaw the storage facilities. Much of the day-to-day administration of the storage areas fell to the *deputy managers* (DMs) and *warehouse supervisors*; they had no responsibilities for deliveries. The DFC and DMs in Dipawa district supervised the procurement of wheat from local farmers.

The cadre of the NFO was almost entirely drawn from longtime residents of Ruritania. Even down to the GS-8 level, the officials were sometimes closely linked with tribal leaders and top politicians. Everyone seemed to know everyone else.

TYPES OF CORRUPTION

Shabir spent his first weeks on the job learning as much as he could about the NFO's activities. He discovered that perhaps half the wheat on the black market was from local farmers and the other half from NFO deliveries and stocks. Almost all the black market's sugar originated at NFO. Wheat and sugar were also smuggled to neighboring nations. He convened meetings of groups of district managers at headquarters in Milang. He took several long trips to major and minor storage areas around the province. He examined records in ration shops, district offices, and the Budget and Account Section. In surprise visits he encountered warehouses with literally no records. Large stocks of wheat were unaccounted for in several district offices. On the other hand, Shabir's impression was that a substantial minority of NFO district officials were competent and eager to help. He found that many contractors had not delivered correct quantities of wheat, and several were chronic offenders. Frequently in the evenings he would talk with Commissioner Portilo, who told him what he had learned during his year and a half in office. Portilo emphasized problems with contracts and ration cards, but Shabir found evidence of corruption in virtually every aspect of the NFO's operations.

Procurement

Shabir heard that kickback schemes like Maguma's were widespread in Dipawa. Less often procurements from NFO outlets in other provinces were falsely recorded, allowing wheat and sugar to be pilfered and then sold on the black market. In transit to Milang, gunny sacks were sometimes slit, turning an eighty-five-pound bag into a seventy-five-pounder. When the shipment arrived, the perpetrators would bribe an inspector, put the spilled wheat or sugar into other sacks, and sell it. Shabir learned of a flourishing market for new and used gunny sacks.

Storage

Several kinds of corruption existed in the warehouses and open-air storage platforms:

□ DMs and warehouse supervisors had the power to lodge reports about wheat or sugar that had been spoiled due to rain, lack of pesticides, and other reasons. Upon authorization the spoiled stocks were destroyed and a certificate issued for replacement. Especially in the open-air platforms such reports had become frequent. Shabir visited some of these sites after a record-breaking downpour and discovered that the tarpaulin had provided effective protection. Not a single bag of wheat or sugar had been damaged.

□ As in Nyunt's case, poor-quality wheat was sometimes substituted for good-quality wheat.

□ Straightforward theft and collusive deals with ration dealers did take place but were thought to be rare.

Delivery Contracts

Several sorts of corruption could be distinguished:

□ Although many contractors were eligible to bid on each delivery, only a few actually did so. Contractors knew each other well, and there were reports of collusive bidding. Shabir discovered from the records of the Budget and Accounts Section that in the past three years delivery costs for the same routes had risen 450 percent. He could not easily estimate how much this increase reflected higher petroleum prices and general inflation, but he guessed that collusion raised the bids by 25 percent over a "competitive" price.

□ Contractors sometimes delivered inferior qualities of wheat, provided less than agreed upon, were late in deliveries, or simply did not deliver at all. Shabir learned that such episodes occurred in 15 to 20 percent of all deliveries. But rarely were actions taken against contractors—and then only against the smallest transporters.

□ The Budget and Accounts Section had occasionally published announcements of contracts only three days before the deadline. Favored contractors would be given earlier notice in exchange for bribes. Occasionally, contracts were designed so that only one transporter could fulfill its terms. Preference was shown in the awarding of contracts to those residing in a particular village or area, but usually this practice did not involve corruption.

The Budget and Accounts Section seemed weak and ineffective. Its members had clamored for additional personnel, claiming that with hundreds of tenders and other duties the section was understaffed. The previous director had ignored these pleas.

Ration Cards

These cards had evident economic value. Because they entitled the bearer to a quota of provisions from a specified ration dealer at a subsidized price, people were willing to pay to acquire them. Occasionally, cards were obtained on fraudulent grounds by citizens who said their cards were lost or destroyed. In legitimate cases the previous card was to be cancelled by the NFO, the ration dealer informed, and entries made in the relevant registers. But often duplicates and new cards were issued without following these procedural requirements. As .officials learned how easy it was, this dishonest practice had escalated.

Shabir asked the district managers to collect their figures on ration cards and submit them to his office. To his surprise, Shabir discovered that in a province of 2.6 million people, the NFO had issued 4.2 million ration cards. The federal government had been allowing the NFO in

Ruritania to procure wheat and sugar for 4.2 million people, perhaps because it did not want to contemplate the effects of providing for only 2.6 million people when 4.2 million ration cards were outstanding.

SHABIR'S PREDICAMENT

With this information Shabir was poised to act. He had the support of the commissioner and chief commissioner to clean up corruption in the NFO. If he wished, he could draw upon the Anti-Corruption Agency, an independent government body. The agency's office in Ruritania was headed by a senior police official and staffed by about twenty investigators, mostly on deputation from the police. He could also use the Revenue Departments in each district for information about landholdings, family size, and crops. He heard that some of these departments, too, were rife with corruption, so that their data might be unreliable.

Shabir's position was tenuous. The importance of wheat and sugar to the diets of rural people and the sensitive logistics of delivery meant that he had to take care not to disrupt the system in a way that would leave people even temporarily without food. The province was politically volatile, and food was a major ingredient in stabilization efforts. Shabir was an outsider in several respects. He was younger than most of his subordinates, came from a different province and ethnic group, belonged to a different administrative service, and had no experience in food policy and management. His deputy had been passed over for the directorship and was somewhat resentful of Shabir, but Mahfooz wielded almost no authority in the NFO. Many NFO officials were closely tied to powerful political or tribal figures.

When Shabir took over, he was immediately surrounded by subordinates offering their advice and assistance. Many NFO officials regarded him as a greenhorn who could be easily bent. Instinctively, Rafiq Shabir wanted to dissuade them of this erroneous belief.

Instant Impact

Shabir's first step had been to gather information about the NFO's activities and the types and extent of corruption. He was shocked by the absence of basic record keeping in many warehouses and district offices. His review of the previous year's delivery contracts convinced him that several large contractors, who were certainly guilty of late deliveries and other defects in performance, were also colluding in bids. He was astonished to learn that the NFO had issued 4.2 million ration cards for a province of 2.6 million people.

"My initial reaction when I took over as director," Rafiq Shabir wrote to me, "was that I had landed myself into a quagmire, that the whole ruddy department was in a mess and that half-hearted measures would not make any impact at all. This department was reputed to be amongst the most corrupt, and this image was strongly imprinted upon my mind. In addition, I was specially sent with the mandate to 'clean it up,' and I was keen to dispel any doubts about not 'meaning business.'"

Shabir came out swinging. He made two unannounced inspection trips around the province and suspended sixteen employees at the district food controller and deputy manager levels in nine different districts. "In proceeding against the sixteen," Shabir wrote, "I took action on the spot. The gross negligence and the absence of records was totally inexcusable. I personally handed over show-cause notices to nine of the sixteen. The rest I dealt with when I got back to headquarters."

Later Shabir called in the Anti-Corruption Agency to investigate eight cases of serious corruption, including two district managers. Five DMs, including Buqsha and Nyunt, were either retired or dismissed. Three others, including Maguma, were returned to their positions. Maguma was exonerated because of "inconclusive evidence."

Commissioner Portilo was worried about the sudden firings. "He was perturbed by the possibility of a breakdown in the distribution system," Shabir said. But during his meetings with district managers on his trips, Shabir had found some good, honest officials. To avoid disruptions as well as to promote honesty, Shabir immediately reassigned some of these capable officials to the newly vacant positions. In some cases he placed people in posts for which their ranks and experience seemed not to qualify them. With Portilo's support Shabir simply promoted them as necessary.

Other Actions

Shabir quickly beefed up the Budget and Accounts Section, adding three additional people in new slots authorized by the commissioner. His new staff helped him review the records of chronically low-performing contractors. Among these delinquents Shabir blacklisted five whom he also suspected of corruption and collusive bidding. One of the blacklisted contractors was the largest contractor in Ruritania, a firm that had enjoyed a virtual monopoly on deliveries to the coastal area and also had tight links with tribal and political leaders.

Shabir began other actions as well:

□ He initiated a review of the contract procedures. He ensured that tenders were widely publicized well in advance of the deadline for submission. He began thinking about how to promote more competition in bidding. One idea, which was shot down by the minister despite Portilo's support, would have allowed contractors of all three categories to bid on all tenders. (The minister believed that some contractors would overextend themselves or would bid irrationally, leading to a risk of nondelivery—and chaos.) Another idea was to remove or reduce truck ownership requirements.

□ Accompanied by the district manager in Dipawa, Shabir visited the local Revenue Department in order to learn exactly what records were available. Shabir devised a simple scheme to estimate wheat production. The Revenue Department had records of each farm's acreage under wheat. By multiplying these figures by the average wheat yield per hectare, the NFO could obtain a usable estimate of the expected intake for each of its thirteen procurement units in Dipawa district. The district manager was told to study this possibility and report back to Shabir.

□ A similar idea occurred to Shabir regarding the ration cards. The NFO could cancel existing ration cards and issue new ones in strict accordance with the detailed records maintained by the local Revenue Departments.

□ The surprising findings of his own unannounced visits to warehouses and district offices led Shabir to question the current inspection system. He wanted to have inspectors and people from his office make lightning visits without previous notice. He thought this tactic might promote efficient management and deter corruption.

Newton's Third Law of Motion

Shabir was contemplating these steps—and what to do with his deputy director, Mahfooz—when he received a call from Chief Commissioner Rahimtoola. Shabir and the chief commissioner met. Rahimtoola explained that Shabir was to be transferred, after only four months as director, to a "very coveted and cushy post" near the border of Serradia.

The meeting lasted only a short time. The chief commissioner did not explain the transfer in great detail. He praised Shabir's work as director. The new post, he said, was a promotion. As deputy administrator of an important district with significant smuggling problems, Shabir would have vital and challenging responsibilities.

But the message was clear. The repercussions of Shabir's two-fisted actions had rocked not only the NFO but others in positions of power and influence. Although the chief commissioner said he was proud of Shabir's actions and still supported the fight against corruption, Shabir was transferred because of what he had done.

Reflecting on the experience, Shabir wrote me, "I knew that I could not annihilate corruption totally, but I was committed to mitigating it as far as possible. I did not know and could not tell as to how long it would take me to 'clean up.' In fact, even 'cleaning up' was some ethereal concept whose level I had to determine myself.

"Now when I think back, I realize that I did not have a predetermined plan to tackle the issue of corruption. I acted on the spur of the moment, always remembering that the system mustn't break down."

DISCUSSION

This case does not end successfully. True, Rafiq Shabir did a creditable job uncovering the sources of the many kinds of corruption he encountered in the NFO, and some of his proposed solutions look promising. In Chapter 3's terms, he did a good job of analyzing the ostensible problems of corruption and suggesting policy measures. But he failed because he seemed to overlook his strategic problems of implementation. He moved on too many fronts at once, without garnering political and bureaucratic backing. Rafiq Shabir was sent to a border post; corruption in the NFO remained behind.

Let us consider once again Rafiq Shabir's difficult assignment as he takes over the NFO. The NFO provides food to a large, poor, conflict-ridden province. If food supplies are interrupted, the consequences—both economic and political—could be grave. Making sure that food is delivered is the NFO's top priority. This objective is also crucial to the politicians: the central government is trying to keep Ruritania under control, and the provincial government's stability is doubtless greatly affected by the NFO's success in delivering food. Notice, for example, that the central government gives the NFO funds to supply 4.2 million ration cards. Surely, it is recognized that only 2.6 million people live in Ruritania. The central government is presumably willing to provide the extra funds in order to help keep the rebel-infested province calm.

But delivering the food is not Rafiq Shabir's only aim. He has been brought in with the specific mandate to clean up a corrupt organization. The previous director has been sacked, an act that has sent a shock wave through the NFO and indeed the whole provincial government. Shabir's immediate superior, Portilo, and the man who brought in Shabir, Chief Commissioner Rahimtoola, have promised Shabir support in his efforts to control corruption, while ensuring the timely delivery of staples.

These two aims may conflict. For example, if Shabir moves against those who contract for deliveries, he may provoke a short-run interruption in deliveries. If he tries to revoke the existing ration cards, he may stir up public resentment and resistance. It is not so much that corruption and other illegal activities are efficient in delivering food. Rather, fighting corrupt or illicit arrangements may involve costs and reactions that threaten to upset the distribution of wheat and sugar.

Not to mention the distribution of power. Shabir's organization is almost entirely staffed by Ruritanians, many of whom are linked with tribal leaders in that province. Also, in a poor, rural province like Ruritania, the category A and B delivery contractors are no doubt powerful economic figures, who perhaps are also well-connected politically and tribally. Certain forms of the existing corruption benefit these people. Attacking corruption, therefore, may attack these people, resulting in political consequences that Shabir should try hard to foresee.

Shabir is not particularly well equipped at the outset to deal with these political ramifications. As a newcomer, he is not intimately aware of the many probable linkages mentioned in the previous paragraph. He needs to educate himself. Portilo is one source of knowledge. So, perhaps, is the subset of conscientious officials he has met in his first weeks on the job. Moreover, Shabir has some political disadvantages. He is unusually young for such a responsible post. He is not a Ruritanian, nor is he a member of the NFO's own administrative cadre.

By playing the role of the new leader, he may be able to turn some of these handicaps into a sort of advantage. Shabir can turn his lack of expertise into an excuse for briefings, policy reviews, and other educational activities. And, as a newcomer, he may be given a grace period or honeymoon, where he can institute some large changes and be given a chance to see how they work. He may also be able to make some mistakes and be forgiven. Then again, as Shabir's fate revealed, he may not.

Types of Illicit Activities

Shabir discovered several distinct categories of corruption. How might he have analyzed their severity, causes, and possible cures?

Procurement. Let us focus on wheat, the NFO's major commodity in Ruritania. Dipawa district produces about 10 percent of the wheat distributed by Ruritania's NFO; the other 90 percent is shipped in from other provinces. The NFO's distribution makes up about 90 percent of Ruritania's entire wheat market, with the other 10 percent taking place on the black market.

About half of Dipawa's wheat production is estimated to go to the black market: this quantity is that last 10 percent of all wheat sales in Ruritania. What amount of wheat and money are we talking about?

To obtain some approximations, we will begin with the NFO's budget. Of P100 million, about P65 million goes to wheat procurement. If we assume that this 65 million covers the difference between the NFO's official purchase price of P1.1/kg and the sales price of P0.75/kg, then about 186 million kilos of wheat are procured by the NFO each year. (This is P65 million divided by P0.35/kg, the net cost per kg to the NFO.) Ten percent of 186 million is roughly 18 million. Farmers in Dipawa are producing about twice this amount–half going to the NFO and half to the black market.

Selling to the black market is much more lucrative (P2.5/kg). On the simplifying assumption that farmers would receive this price for selling on the black market, the loss to farmers from selling to the NFO instead is P1.4/kg. In the current arrangement Dipawa's farmers make about 18 million kg at P1.1/kg + 18 million kg at P2.5/kg = P65 million. If they were forced to sell the entire 36 million kg at P1.1/kg, they would get about P40 million. The current illicit scheme allows farmers to obtain 63 percent more revenues—some of which they give to NFO officials to be allowed not to sell all their wheat at the official price.

To the NFO officials the kickbacks could be big money. The case gives no estimate of the size of the payments from farmers to NFO officials like Maguma. But imagine that 10 percent of the farmer's benefits from selling wheat on the black market goes to kickbacks. This is 10 percent of P65 million − P40 million = P25 million, or P2.5 million. Compare this to the NFO budget, which allocates P5 million to all wages and salaries for 280 employees, half of whom are professionals.

Who is hurt and who is helped by the kickback scheme? Clearly the Dipawan farmers and their NFO collaborators are better off. What about the poor consumer for whom the ration system was presumably designed? The first reaction is to say that this consumer is worse off. But it depends. Suppose the federal government has already allowed for this scheme in setting the budget for the Ruritanian NFO. That is, if the amount of imported wheat now compensates for the lower procurement from Dipawa, and if higher Dipawan procurement figures were simply compensated by lower imports, than the poor Ruritanian consumer would be no better off by removing the kickback scheme. Indeed the Ruritanians who now buy Dipawan wheat on the black market would be worse off! (Imports for the black market might take place, but presumably the price would be higher than for Dipawan wheat.) The central government and those who fund its budgetary contributions to the NFO are financially worse off because of corruption in procurements. To a carefully calculating Rafiq Shabir, the central government's budget may seem a remote beneficiary, whose benefits do not outweigh the benefits now accruing to Ruritanians from the kickback scheme. At least, this trade-off should be considered.

What are the causes of this particular kind of corruption? Clearly at the heart of it is the price differential between the black market and the subsidized purchase and sale prices. Without the price differential there would be no incentive for the farmers to pay off the NFO officials for the privilege of selling their wheat on the open market. This problem, however, is outside Rafiq Shabir's control. No director of a provincial office will be allowed to reverse that major national policy. Shabir might ask his superiors to engage in a study of this problem, but it is not something on which he can be expected to take unilateral action.

Other causes and conditions lie behind the kickback scheme. One cause is the higher level government officials' lack of information about the amount of wheat that Dipawan farmers grow. For example, record keeping systems that allowed estimates of potential crops of these farmers would provide a check on the actual amounts sold and reported by the NFO officials on the scene. Better monitoring and information would help crack down on this kind of corruption. The Revenue Department may be of use in this regard.

Storage. Several kinds of corruption occur in this stage of the NFO's operations. For instance, wheat is stolen and then sold on the open market. This theft directly affects the consumers, since it forces some outlets to have less wheat than was originally anticipated. Thus, some consumers simply do not find the wheat available when they come to buy. The extent of theft is hard to estimate from the case. We can notice, in terms of causation, that the propensity to steal will be enhanced by a much higher open market price. But even if the open market and ration prices were the same, there would still be a straightforward gain from ripping off the system.

Sometimes theft takes place under the cover of legitimate bureaucratic operations. For example, government officials will claim that wheat was spoiled and then will sell the supposedly ruined goods for personal profit. To combat this sort of corruption, the NFO needs better administrative systems. Investigators might check a sample of the claims of damage or despoilation. Managers might keep records that compare various warehouses in terms of their propensity to have such accidents and losses. High performers could be rewarded, and low performers could be investigated. When Rafiq Shabir visited many of the local offices and warehouses and found virtually no record keeping, he saw this absence as a sign that basic administrative systems had broken down in at least some locales. Rip-offs would be less likely with such systems intact.

Another form of corruption at the storage level involves what might be called mislabeling. Bad wheat has been occasionally passed off as good, as in the case of Kilchon and Nyunt. This kind of corruption has a high visibility to the public—it had already prompted a citizens' delegation to travel 400 kilometers to the Minister of Food's office in Milang to complain. We have little idea from the case of the extent of this problem, but it is clear that in a political sense, and in terms of serving NFO's primary mission of delivering food to the people, this mislabeling could be a serious problem. The current administrative systems are apparently ineffective in fighting this kind of corruption. The NFO could consider several steps. Consumers could be organized to present their opinions on the quality of the food they receive. (This is one kind of corruption where the clients themselves will be happy to complain about the malfunctioning of the system.) Penalties could be increased; in this and other kinds of corruption in Ruritania, the penalties appear to be too low. District Food Controller Nyunt was simply transferred to Milang. Such punishment may have little deterrent value when large sums of money are at stake.

In short, problems of corruption occurring at the storage level appear to be quite serious from the point of view of the NFO's relations with the public. These instances have already been brought to the minister's attention; he understands that this sort of corruption is hurting him. Administrative changes under Rafiq Shabir's control could help in fighting these rip-offs. The director could consider inspections, better information systems, involvement of the clients and consumers, and stiffer penalties.

Delivery. The NFO spends P20 million each year in "distribution and administrative costs." Presumably most of these expenditures are payments to the private contractors who carry out the deliveries. Collusive bidding is estimated to add 25 percent to these payments. If three-quarters of the P20 million goes to the contractors and this P15 million is 25 percent too high, then the net cost of the collusion to the NFO is P3 million. (If only half the P20 million goes to contractors, the net cost is P2 million.)

Contractors were sometimes late in their deliveries, but such delays may or may not have been due to illicit activities. Delivering inferior quality wheat probably did generally involve corruption. A total of 15 to 20 percent of the deliveries were affected, which is serious; but such problems are prevalent in almost all delivery systems in developing countries, especially in rural areas.

Apparently some collusion did take place between the Budget and Accounts Office and potential bidders. Part of this collusion occurs because the office can credibly claim to be overworked – thus "excusing" late announcements of contracts, for example. It is hard to estimate the costs of these "occasional" acts.

Who is hurt and who is helped? Again, part of the answer depends on how the NFO's budget is determined by the central government. Would the P3 million of potential savings redound to the NFO and thence to Ruritanian consumers? Or would the savings simply result in a lower allotment from the central government? Clearly the contractors who collude are better off, as are the cooperating Budget and Accounts officials.

Competition is one possible cure for collusion, but competition has potential costs as well. In the short run especially, the current colluders may have built up so much capacity as to drive out other potential entrants. The NFO's A and B categories of contractors imply certain barriers to entry. The NFO will find it hard, particularly in the near term, to induce new, qualified, noncolluding firms to bid for delivery contracts in Ruritania. (In this regard note the chief commissioner's negative reaction to Shabir's suggestion that the bidding be open to contractors of all categories.)

Theft during delivery was a problem. "Sometimes" the gunny sacks containing wheat would be slit open, and an eighty-five-pound bag would turn out to weigh only about seventy-five pounds. Hypothetically, if this happened in about 10 percent of the deliveries, then about 10 percent of this 10 percent, or 1 percent, of the wheat would be lost. This amount might add up to about 2 million kg of wheat per year. The inspectors were apparently not doing their jobs, but obviously a problem of security en route also existed. Who is liable for such shortfalls? Could inspectors be more effectively monitored, and at what cost? Could the contractors be made directly responsible for losses en route, creating incentives for them to be more vigilant? Or is this much leakage through theft inevitable in large-scale delivery systems? These are some of the questions that Shabir might pose.

Collusion seems the biggest problem in deivery, but Shabir must be careful in fighting it. He must assess the net losses to Ruritania, which depend on the central government in the way described above, and to the central government's budget. And he must balance them against the possible political and economic costs of acting against the colluding contractors.

He might begin with small steps. For example, he might initiate studies of delivery costs, so that he could lay down guidelines or specifications and could negotiate delivery prices with contractors. He might announce a new policy that late or short deliveries would result in penalties to those responsible. More adventurously, he might study the forward integration of NFO's activities into the delivery stage: the NFO might have its own trucks, boats, and camels. Even a partial entry into the delivery process might enable the NFO to gather valuable information and, by directly competing with them, induce efficient behavior by private contractors. (Of course, this step also entails obvious costs.)

Ration Cards. Ruritania's 2.6 million inhabitants possess 4.2 million ration cards. Evidently, the central government funds 4.2 million rations of wheat. If only 2.6 million rations were allocated, the NFO's wheat budget of P65 million would drop to $(2.6/4.2) \times$ P65 million $\cong$ P40 million, a saving of about P25 million.

But who would gain and who would lose? It depends on who has the extra ration cards. Imagine that they were distributed fairly uniformly across the Ruritania population, perhaps having been given to the people for a bribe. Then the reissuing of "only" 2.6 million new cards would make the typical Ruritanian worse off. (Per capita consumption is currently about 71.5 kg per year; if only 2.6 million ration cards were supplied, this would drop to about 44 kg/year.) If, however, the extra cards were mostly in the hands of elites (or NFO officials), then the reissuing would leave most Ruritanians unaffected. Notice, too, that once again much depends on the central government's behavior. If savings could be made through the removal of extra ration cards, where would the benefits go? To larger rations for the eligible? Or to the budget in the central government, far away? Shabir's calculation of the severity of this kind of corruption presumably depends in part on the answers.

Several causes can be cited for corruption in ration cards. At the most fundamental level the existence of nonprice rationing itself creates incentives for corruption: the ration ticket has an economic value approximately equal to the difference between the subsidized price and the "free market" (= black market?) price. There is economic room for the officials who control the issuance of ration cards to extort money even from the deserving or to accept bribes from the undeserving. Such bribery is common with rationing systems. And to Shabir, the existence of ration cards is probably a given, a policy beyond his power to change fundamentally.

Poor information is also a problem. If complete information were readily and costlessly available on each transaction of wheat through the system, then multiple cardholders could be spotted and punished.

Apparently, even rudimentary record keeping is problematic in Ruritania, which allows this corruption to thrive.

Shabir might investigate several steps. *If* he decides the benefits of doing so outweigh the costs—which from a narrowly Ruritanian perspective may not be the case—he might reissue all ration cards. (This step actually took place a few years later in the nation of which Ruritania is a part.) He might investigate who actually holds the extra ration cards. If they are in the hands of NFO officials, the severity of this form of corruption could be grave, and the solutions might focus on internal procedures and penalties. Shabir might implement policies to try to ensure that even more cards were not issued in the future. (For example, he might collect information on how many cards were held in each locality, the average rates of card loss and internal migration, and so on. Then he might promulgate upper limits on the amount of growth in wheat and sugar shipments that would be allowed in each locale, with increases above those limits subject to special investigation.)

Table 6 summarizes the discussion of the kinds of illegal activity. Other dimensions could be added. For example, for which kinds of corruption might Ruritanian citizens be important sources of information? Which kinds of corruption would be reduced if wheat and sugar were not subsidized but were simply sold at an open market price?

IMPLEMENTATION STRATEGIES FOR FIGHTING CORRUPTION

In many ways Rafiq Shabir's choice of anticorruption policies made sense according to the framework in Chapter 3. He effectively diagnosed many of the causes of corruption in the NFO, and he moved on a variety of fronts to attack those causes. But the lesson of this chapter is that plausible policies are not enough; the corruption fighter needs an implementation strategy as well.

"Now when I think back," Shabir wrote me after being removed as the head of the NFO, "I realize that I did not have a predetermined plan to tackle the issue of corruption. I acted on the spur of the moment."

Shabir lacked a strategy for implementing his anticorruption measures. He seemed to overlook politics. In Ruritania, as elsewhere, corruption makes some people better off even as it hurts others. The corruption

TABLE 6 SUMMARY OF SOME KINDS OF CORRUPTION IN THE NATIONAL FOOD ORGANIZATION

Activity	Magnitude	Helps	Hurts	Causes	Cures
Procurement in Dipawa district (kickbacks)	~P25 million	Dipawa farmers; NFO in Dipawa; black market buyers	Federal budget; Ruritanian consumers(?)	Price differential; bad info. on crops, incomes; low probability of discovery; low penalties	Raise probability through better info.; stiffer penalties
Storage (theft and mislabeling)	"Small"?	Corrupt NFO officials	Consumers; political figures	Poor records; poor inspection system; low penalties	Obtain info. from clients; better record keeping and inspection; stiffer penalties
Delivery (collusion)	~P3 million	Contractors	Central govt. budget(?); consumers(?)	Lack of compet. bidding; poor info. on costs; low penalties	Induce competition; get better info. on costs; bargain with contractors; forward integration; stiffer penalties
Ration cards (fraud)	~P25 million in wheat alone	Consumers(?); corrupt NFO officials	Central govt. budget; consumers(?)	Price differential; poor records; low probability of discovery; penalties(?)	Reissue cards; improve record keeping and control systems

fighter must not fail to figure out who the winners are for different kinds of illicit activities, how they might resist anticorruption efforts, and how their resistance might be preempted or countered. Rafiq Shabir seemed to overlook these aspects of controlling corruption. He did not garner political support from the minister or the chief secretary, nor did he clear politically loaded decisions with them. He did nothing to mobilize the people's support for his policies, such as the potentially popular effort to fight theft and mislabeling.

Moreover, he attacked his organization. Despite being a new director and an outsider organizationally and ethnically, his first steps were consistent with what he was overheard saying during his first week on the job: "I am going to wring the neck of every corrupt official I come across." His approach was negative; while this tactic is not always a mistake, it was perhaps predictable that before long his organization would turn against him. He did not take steps that seemed to most NFO officers in their interest; he did not draw upon the good people in the organization to help him design or implement anticorruption measures; he did not demonstrate to most of his subordinates that the new measures would help them do their jobs better. Rafiq Shabir moved on all fronts at once in a kind of blitz on corruption. He did not sequence his actions in order to achieve some early, clear-cut successes and at the same time begin to rebuild the NFO's capabilities. Perhaps in a more favorable environment, he might nonetheless have succeeded. As it happened, the political and organizational resistance to Shabir's blitz led to his downfall.

Could Rafiq Shabir have succeeded with a better implementation strategy? Suppose he had moved first against the abuses in storage. Suppose he had singled out just a few notoriously corrupt officials for punishment, perhaps doing so with a new committee made up of efficient and honest NFO officials, a few political figures, and some citizens. Suppose Shabir had obtained the minister's advice often, especially in dealing with the contractors. Suppose he had gathered information and support from citizen's groups, even the tribes, especially on the issue of bad wheat being substituted for good. Would these steps have led to a more favorable outcome? Nobody knows for sure. But Rafiq Shabir and I think so.

Let us turn to the more general question of developing a strategy for implementing an anticorruption campaign. We have talked about the kind of policies that can help control corruption. What can we now say about strategies for getting such policies implemented?

1. *Distinguish between "ostensible" and "strategic" issues in fighting corruption.* The ostensible issue for a physician is what treatment (or what policies) will help the ailing patient the most. The strategic issue includes such matters as how to get the patient to follow (or to implement) the treatment. A similar distinction holds for fighting corruption (and for almost all policymaking). As we have seen in Chapter 3, the ostensible issue in fighting corruption involves in principle these steps:

□ Analyze the various kinds of costs (and the possible benefits) of various forms of illicit behavior.

□ Array possible anticorruption techniques (such as those in the checklist developed in Chapter 3 and applied in several of the subsequent chapters).

□ Consider the benefits in terms of reduced corruption, and the direct and indirect costs, of implementing these anticorruption techniques to various extents.

□ Choose anticorruption policies and implement them to the point where, metaphorically, the marginal benefits of reduced corruption are equal to the marginal costs of reducing it.

The strategic question goes further. It asks how such policies can be implemented in practice. How can allies be mobilized? How can potential resistors be neutralized or even coopted? How should policy measures be sequenced? Other relevant questions pertain to one's own career and to bureaucratic politics. For example, how will the choice of policies in this domain help or hinder the policymaker's role (or his organization's role or his superior's role) in other important domains?

As I mentioned earlier, these generic questions go well beyond the choice of anticorruption policies. As such, they cannot be given a thorough treatment here, especially since a number of valuable books and articles on implementation can readily be consulted.[4]

4. See, for example, Graham T. Allison and Morton H. Halperin, "Bureaucratic Politics: A Paradigm and Some Policy Implications," in *Theory and Policy in International Relations*, ed. Raymond Tanter and Richard Ullman (Princeton: Princeton University Press, 1972); special issue of *Public Policy* on implementation, Spring 1978; Daniel A. Masmanian and Paul A. Sabatier, *Implementation and Public Policy* (Glenview, Ill.: Scott Foresman, 1983).

2. *Cultivate political support.* Who gets hurt and who gets helped from various kinds of corruption – and from various measures to fight corruption? How can the various beneficiaries of anticorruption activities be made to see those benefits in advance, to support such activities, and to make their political influence felt by others? How can those who will lose be kept from seeing the fact in advance, or have their political influence neutralized?

The answers to these questions provide foundation stones for mobilizing political support. It is a truism in public policy analysis that policy reforms depend on political support. (Sometimes this is simply a tautology, because political support is not independently defined.) If top-level politicians stand behind anticorruption efforts – as they did in Singapore and Hong Kong, for example – it is a big plus. Sometimes from the point of view of a public manager, the level of such support is a given. But our cases also show that such support, like a delicate plant, can and should be cultivated. Jack Cater kept the governor of Hong Kong well briefed on the ICAC's activities, and no doubt many key decisions were vetted with the governor before being implemented. Justice Plana met often with the minister of finance, and occasionally with the president, to inform them and obtain their support. The U.S. Army procurement people in Korea had to garner the approval of the Department of the Army in Washington before inaugurating their new approach to fighting collusion.

You get support by showing another how he or she is being, or will be, helped by what you do. "Helped" here means according to his or her lights, not your own. Recall how the ICAC packaged its corruption-prevention activities vis-à-vis various other public agencies in Hong Kong in a low-key, collaborative way. Their actions did not say, "We are here to tell you what you are doing wrong and what you have to do." Instead their policies gave the message, "If you would like our help to solve your problem, we will be pleased to work with you, giving you the credit." Presumably Justice Plana obtained the backing of Ferdinand Marcos in part because the president could see higher tax revenues as a benefit to himself.

Politicians have to be educated; they must be shown how anticorruption efforts can help and hurt them. I mentioned in Chapter 2 that corruption sometimes has political utility; it follows that sometimes anticorruption efforts have political disutility. But there is a positive side as well. Around the developing world perhaps no other issue can be guaranteed to galvanize the support of the common man and woman to such an extent. And so, if politicians can be made to see that their popular support will rise with the control of visible, publicly onerous corruption, they will be more likely to put their muscle behind the battle against illicit activities.

3. *Get the public behind anticorruption efforts.* The public is thus a key, not only because the people's cooperation is important for uncovering and prosecuting illicit acts, but because public pressure may be vital in the politics of fighting corruption. How can the public be involved? Let's look at three effective tactics.

First, if you are lucky enough to ride a wave of popular indignation against corruption, as often occurs in periodic anticorruption "campaigns," try to institutionalize that indignation.[5] Create a public oversight board. Help the public to institutionalize its interests and create linkages with the legislative branch – for example, by requiring biannual hearings before an appropriate parliamentary committee.

Second, publicize and publicize some more. Let the people know your intentions, make clear the rules and the penalties, and trumpet your successes. Use the press, the schools, the politicians to convey your message.

Finally, convince the public that you are serious. As the Hong Kong and Philippines cases demonstrate, catching a few top officials and prosecuting them is an excellent device for showing that the new anticorruption efforts are serious. This is the principle of the "big fish."

4. *Break the culture of corruption in your organization.* Even in the most egregious cases corruption is seldom carried out openly; by its nature it relies on secrecy, collusion, and a measure of confidence that illicit transactions will not be reported. Metaphorically, one can speak of a culture of corruption, which requires not that everyone is corrupt but that almost everyone will be unwilling to report on the corrupt. The Blair-Kerr report in Hong Kong compared corruption to a bus: not everyone in the police force was required to get on the bus, but they had better not stand in front of it.

An organization or society that has suffered widespread corruption

5. Amitai Etzioni, "The Fight Against Fraud and Abuse," *Journal of Policy Analysis and Management* 2 (Fall 1982): 26–38.

usually has become cynical. People have heard a lot of talk before about how evil corruption is, about the need to follow rules, and about the supposed consequences to those who transgress. But it has been just that—talk. Thus, the would-be reformer who simply *announces* tougher penalties or a greater likelihood that the corrupt will be caught and punished does not automatically deter illicit behavior.

Breaking the culture of corruption, therefore, has two parts. First, the administrator must upset the climate of confidence and trust that is necessary for corrupt transactions. Second, he or she must combat cynicism, which means that words, being all too cheap, must be backed by action.

What can be done to upset the climate? The administrator may plant informants in key slots, perhaps coupled with wide-ranging and periodic rotation of officers. Surveillance, including inspections, is important. The organization can give rewards to those who report corruption (perhaps in confidence). Just as bacteria breed in warmth and darkness, so corruption multiplies in a "friendly" setting with little light. This tactic does not imply terror. It does mean that the "us and them" attitude of the corrupt group in the Bureau of Internal Revenue must be changed, and Justice Plana's initiatives of undercover agents, rotation, surveillance and review, inspections, rewards, and publicity were effective steps.

And what about overcoming cynicism? Probably the most effective step involves the "big fish." In a corrupt culture pummeling some small fry involved in a small-scale corruption has little effect. Getting serious means, in many settings, frying a big fish in public with accompanying announcements of policy changes.

5. *Move positively as well as negatively.* Justice Plana did not attack the Bureau of Internal Revenue without first worrying about its morale. His very first step was to redesign the performance evaluation system, which he did in concert with a team of seasoned BIR professionals. He also undertook measures to professionalize the bureau. He defined the bureau's mission in a positive way; by offering prizes, starting clubs, and instituting new promotion policies, he gave BIR staff the feeling that the bureau was a good organization for which to work. At the same time he fried big fish, broke the culture of corruption, and implemented a variety of tough, anticorruption policies.

Tackling corruption often involves harsh measures, and an organization can easily feel besieged, resulting in a decline in performance. A shrewd strategy will therefore include positive incentives as well as penalties, measures that underscore the organization's values as well as steps to crack the culture of corruption.

6. *Link anticorruption measures to the organization's main mission.* The easiest anticorruption policy to implement will be the one that is most naturally tied to the organization's everyday objectives. If a certain technique for fighting corruption means that more arrests are made, it will be easier to implement in a police force than another technique that is arrest-neutral, or that takes away resources that could be used to make arrests. Anticorruption measures will be *easier* to implement:

- The less they interfere with routine case intake, operations, and management
- The more they reduce an organization's costs and error rates in doing its usual business
- The greater the threat corruption is, or can be made to be, to the organization's autonomy
- The greater the incentives that can be provided to lower-level staff to control corruption.[6]

7. *Find Mr. Clean and support him.* It is often said that bureaucratic corruption cannot be reduced if the political leadership is itself corrupt. The Philippines case may disprove the strong version of this proposition. Justice Plana was able to make progress in cleaning up the BIR, even in a political setting that included large-scale, high-level graft and venality. Nonetheless, Justice Plana himself was recognized as a Mr. Clean, a person whose reputation was beyond reproach. The U.S. Army's solution to collusion in Korea would have never worked if the Army's negotiators had been corrupt. Governor MacLehose and Commissioner Cater in Hong Kong were (and were perceived as) cleaner than clean.

Thus, by its very example of scrupulous behavior, the top leadership of an organization sets a standard for the rest. As a corollary, recall how important it was in many cases for Mr. Clean to surround himself with a

6. This is my rewording of part of a list in John A. Gardiner, "Controlling Official Corruption and Fraud: Bureaucratic Incentives and Disincentives" (Paper presented at the International Political Science Association, Research Committee on Political Finance and Political Corruption, Oxford, England, April 1984), 14. See also John A. Gardiner and Theodore R. Lyman, *The Fraud Control Game: State Responses to Fraud and Abuse in AFDC and Medicaid Programs* (Bloomington: Indiana University Press, 1984), 61–70.

band of like-minded, equally uncorruptible colleagues. Sometimes they were brought in from outside. Often, and perhaps more importantly, they were picked from among the middle- and high-ranking officials within the organization. Recall how diligently Justice Plana searched early in the process for the Mr. Cleans within his organization—and then how he picked them for assignments of particular responsibility. Those who are chosen by new management for strategic responsibilities make a difference in two ways: the way they handle those responsibilities and the signal that their selection sends to the rest of the organization.

It seems particularly important that inspectors, those in control of investigations and informations systems, and those with high-level discretion are, and are seen to be, impeccably clean. Along with the man or woman on top.

8 | Reviewing and Extending

Two of several definitions of *corruption* in *Webster's New Collegiate Dictionary* are "inducement to wrong by bribery or other unlawful or improper means" and "impairment of integrity, virtue, or moral principle." We have been focusing on the first definition, exploring the sources and effects of, and some possible remedies for, "bribery and other . . . means." But the moral aspect is what leaps to many minds when corruption is discussed. Because a bribe is more than an inducement and involves integrity and virtue, discussions of policy here are more problematic than, say, for policies regarding interest rates, fisheries, or food prices.

If we could calculate the ratio of "importance of the problem" to "amount of practically useful research available" for a range of policy issues in developing countries, the ratio for corruption would be among the highest. This differential exists partly because of obvious difficulties in doing research on our topic. But that is only part of the reason. The moral angle of corruption, the intertwining of ethical judgments with policy choices, makes scholars shy away. In Western academic culture it is taboo to be seen as passing ethical judgments on the poor or on poor nations, as "imposing Western values," or as attributing underdevelopment to the behavior and policies of the underdeveloped countries. And besides, isn't corruption, like sin, something we all decry but about which both social science and public policy are impotent?

The few scholars who do study corruption tend to stick to general questions. "Is corruption harmful?" is the topic of a long-running debate between the so-called "moralists" and "revisionists." As we saw in Chapter 2, it is more fruitful to ask, "Which kinds of corruption under what circumstances are harmful in what ways and to whom?" When we moved away from generalities to examine our specific cases, we caught a glimpse of the variety of possible answers:

□ Sometimes corruption is a way of getting around an "unrealistic" or "unwise" regulation. The application of such adjectives is obviously a matter on which people differ, but in our cases some may think that these terms apply to Hong Kong's former prohibition of off-track gambling and Singapore's ban on importing pornography. If so, corruption to escape those rules may create little social harm–and may even have some social benefit.

□ Often corruption helps one party at the expense of another. The collusion and corruption in the Korean case may actually have benefited Korean economic development by obtaining greater amounts of foreign exchange from the U.S. Army. Some forms of corruption in the National Food Organization benefited Ruritania at the expense of the country's other provinces.

□ Extortion seems a particularly nasty form of corruption. It leads not only to inefficiencies but the alienation of citizens from their government. When a body with a monopoly on force is involved, such as the Hong Kong Police, so much the worse. But it is even grave when as in the Philippines tax officials went looking for bribes, or as in Singapore customs officers began harassing the owners of bars and tea parlors.

□ We saw examples of bribes, kickbacks, and *arreglos* leading to a 10 to 50 percent loss in public funds in procurement and in taxation (the Philippines, Korea, and Ruritania). This money does not, of course, disappear. It is redistributed: from the beneficiaries of public programs and from honest taxpayers to business firms, dishonest taxpayers, and corrupt government officials. The most nefarious effects of corruption may be the *incentives* created for nonproductive rather than productive behavior by citizens and officials. People start looking for ways to be corrupt instead of ways to be more efficient.

□ Corruption is more harmful when it creates "public bads" or "negative externalities" than when it simply reallocates a private good. Police corruption that allows the drug trade to flourish is more harmful than customs bureau corruption over who gets served first. Bribes that undermine safety or quality permits have a different effect from bribes for import permits.

Box 17 **Participatory Diagnosis**

The first step in a policy analysis of corruption is diagnostic. In a given setting what forms of corruption are present? What is their extent? Who gains and who loses? What are the apparent causes and possible cures?

In consulting work I have found it useful to involve line managers in answering these questions. A series of meetings can be held. The first meeting centers on the importance of controlling corruption; I may have the group read a case study such as the story of Justice Plana and the Philippines' Bureau of Internal Revenue. At the second session officials are invited to brainstorm about the kinds of corruption present in their domain, who is helped and who is hurt, and approximately how much money is involved in aggregate. The third meeting moves to the causes of corruption, and the group's list typically ranges from human nature to local idiosyncrasies. The framework for policy analysis of Chapter 3 can be helpful here and in the fourth session, which focuses on possible policies.

Using the results of these meetings, a smaller team of officials and the political leaders then may begin to design an anticorruption package and an implementation strategy.

As an example, here is the result of diagnostic meetings in late 1985 with officials of the municipal government of La Paz, Bolivia:

TYPES OF CORRUPTION: A FIRST CUT

Type	Value	Who Is Helped	Who Is Hurt	Causes	Cures
Tax evasion (all kinds)	$20–30m	Evaders	Recipients of city services; non-evaders; future Paceños	Hard to pay; taxes too high; low penalties; no reviews of cases	Make easier to pay; lower rates; raise penalties and enforce them; review cases
Tax "arreglos" (all kinds)	$5–10m	Corrupt taxpayers and officials	Recipients of city services; non-evaders; future Paceños	Lack of computer-ization; low effective penalties; no reviews; pay through municipality; low pay	Computerize; raise penalties; review cases; pay through banks; raise pay; raise incentives to collect

Extortion	$0.5–1m	Corrupt officials	Direct victims	Difficult rules, rates, and procedures; hard-to-report extortion; low penalties; no reviews; low pay	Simplify rules, rates, and procedures; hotline for public reports; raise penalties; review cases; pay through banks; raise pay
Speed money	$0.5–1m	Some taxpayers; corrupt city officials; substitutes for higher pay	Most taxpayers via slowdowns; reputation of city government	Difficult procedures; lack of computerization; pay through municipality; low penalties; no surveillance; low pay	Simplify procedures; computerize; pay through banks; raise penalties; surveillance and "whistle-blowing"; raise pay
Theft (city property, parts, "boot" fees by police)	$0.5–1m	Thieves; some who don't pay vehicle taxes	Recipients of city services; trust in police	Lack of inventories; poor decentralization; low penalties; no reviews or surveillance	Computerize inventories; decentralize responsibility; spot checks and surveillance
Procurement	$0.5–3m	Corrupt officials and winning suppliers	Recipients of city services	Lack of information on prices; no reviews; low penalties; low pay	Verify prices; review cases; raise effective penalties; raise pay of decision-making officials
"Fantasmas," late reporting to work	$0.1–0.2m	Malingerers	Morale and reputation of city government	No surveillance; low penalties	Surveillance; raise penalties and enforce them

Thus, the disease of corruption exhibits more and less malignant strains and outbreaks. When assessing corrupt and illicit activities, we need to consider a variety of effects, including the impacts on efficiency, the distribution of wealth and power, the incentives of citizens and officials, and politics. We may find that some instances of corruption are benign. But we can and should push beyond the academic debate over whether, in general, corruption is harmful or helpful to development. When we get down to cases, we find less disagreement than the academic debate would indicate over the effects of corrupt acts. They are, for the most part, bad. Corruption is eating away at many developing societies, condemning their people to greater poverty and political subjection. The real question about corruption becomes, "What can be done to control it?"

To address this overlooked question, Chapter 3 proposed a framework for policy analysis. At its core was the principal-agent-client model. When the agent acts corruptly, she creates "negative externalities" for the principal. (For convenience we employ the feminine pronoun for the corrupt agent – that's liberation – and the masculine pronoun for the principal.) The agent is corrupt when her benefits from acting corruptly outweigh her costs. According to the simplest principal-agent-client model, the principal's job is to structure agents' and clients' rewards and penalties so that corrupt acts will be reduced to the optimal degree – taking into account the costs of the system of rewards and penalties itself.

We have extended this simple model; our principal may consider other policy measures as well. He may choose agents on the basis of their incorruptibility as well as their competence to perform the job. He may gather information on agents or clients, so as to have a better chance of detecting corruption. Through a variety of organizational changes he may restrict his agents' discretion and try to ensure agents do not enjoy monopoly power vis-à-vis the organization's clients. He may try to change the agents' attitudes – raising what we called their "moral costs of corruption."

These steps all have direct and indirect costs. For example, the principal may strictly limit agents' discretion via decision rules, hierarchical reviews, teamwork, and so forth. Unfortunately, such policies cost something in efficiency – maybe a lot.

The dark side of corruption fighting is the additional bureaucracy that may be generated. Indeed a prime mover in the creation of bureaucratic red tape has been a desire to control corruption. One major reason for rigid civil service rules is to avoid nepotism, spoils systems, and personnel scams in the selection and promotion of agents. If government jobs often seem to lack excitement, responsibility, and any heroic element, this absence may result from severe limits on employee discretion, which in turn stem from the fear of corruption and abuse. It follows that policies to crack down on corruption have costs in terms of the organization's effective performance of its primary mission. The wise policymaker will consider these costs as well as the benefits of reduced corruption. The ideal level of anticorruption efforts will be short of the maximum; and the optimal level of corruption will not, in practice, be zero.

In the cases examined here, corruption was well above optimal levels. When these policymakers took action against corruption, their tactics were costly in money, morale, and increased bureaucracy. But all succeeded in reducing corruption—even perhaps poor Rafiq Shabir, who now mans a border outpost for his troubles.

ANALYZING ANTICORRUPTION POLICIES

How did they do it? Different situations called for a different mix of policies. In most cases policymakers moved on many fronts at once. Chapter 3's framework for policy analysis proved a useful device for analyzing the cases. It suggested five categories of anticorruption policies.

Selecting Agents

We saw several devices for choosing more honest, dependable agents. The extreme case was Hong Kong's Independent Commission Against Corruption. Given the systematic corruption in the Hong Kong Police Force, the new agency could not take its investigators from that source. Its response was to import senior police officers from Great Britain. Such an alternative would obviously be a more difficult step to take by countries that are not colonies.[1] But the idea behind that move could also be seen in

1. Zaire "imported" many Belgian advisers in the late 1970s, including the equivalent of a finance minister, not only for their competence but for their alleged incorruptibility. Alas, that effort seems to have been insufficient to stem widespread abuses. (David J. Gould, *Bureaucratic Corruption and Underdevelopment in the Third World: The Case of Zaire* [New York: Pergamon Press, 1980].)

Justice Plana's use of civilian and military intelligence officers, instead of his Bureau of Internal Revenue's corrupted Internal Security Division. He wanted people whom he could count on to be honest—and who were members of (outside) organizations with strong ways of ensuring honesty.

Another extreme case was the U.S. Army's "solution" to collusion in Korea. Contractors ("agents") would no longer be selected via competitive bidding, which the contractors could undermine. The bidding process had forced the Army to take the lowest bidder and had precluded negotiations and bargaining. Under their new system the Army selected one contractor from a list of eligibles, usually by drawing a name out of a hat. A more capable or honest contractor was not necessarily thereby selected, but this selection system did free the Army from the constraints of the supposedly "competitive" bidding system and allowed it to use its own bargaining power to get a fairer deal.

In several cases policymakers moved early to uproot corrupt agents from crucial jobs. (For doing so without garnering the necessary political support, Rafiq Shabir lost his own job.) Particularly important were jobs with discretion and monopoly power, either over clients or over the organization's own monitoring and security system.

Most policymakers face limits when selecting agents. Systematic techniques for identifying in advance honest employees and contractors—background checks, "honesty tests," and so forth—are hardly perfect. Even with such devices, many public managers simply are not empowered to hire and fire most of the agents who work for them.

Changing Rewards and Penalties

In the Philippines case both rewards and penalties were altered. A better system for measuring performance was coupled with rewards (promotions, transfers, cash prizes, praise) and punishments (dismissal, publicity about corrupt acts and their perpetrators). Singapore gave prizes to officers who refused bribes; those who accepted bribes were treated harshly by the courts. Rafiq Shabir in Ruritania and the U.S. Army in Korea blacklisted colluding contractors.

Again, however, many policymakers find it difficult to manipulate government pay scales, promotion policies, and penalties for illicit activities. Even in Hong Kong with its remarkable law that made it a crime

Box 18 **Incentive Myopia**

Other things being equal, we can expect an increase in bureaucratic corruption over the next five to ten years as public sector pay levels erode. The chronic pattern is this. Poor countries face huge debts and macroeconomic imbalances and, leveraged by the International Monetary Fund, must radically reduce public spending. But firing government workers proves politically difficult: a 10 percent cutback over several years seems the maximum. So governments instead slash public investment, maintenance, and (through inflationary erosion) real public wages. From 1980 to 1985 the real salaries of many Bolivian technocrats fell by a factor of ten, and it is literally the case there and in many African countries that the average public paycheck does not cover the minimum consumption package of an individual.

Declining wages in turn have effects. Many of the best managers and technicians leave the public service (but the worst, bereft of alternatives, stay on). Pay scales become flatter, with fewer incentives for superb performance and greater difficulty in penalizing the negligent. Absenteeism and moonlighting grow. Corruption becomes a necessity.

The quality of public policymaking and public maintenance will reach crisis proportions. The answers will involve incentives. Some public functions (data collection, quality control, certain technical jobs) can be privatized, enabling higher-than-civil-service pay and competition. Semiautonomous agencies will be created, again allowing higher and more performance-based pay scales. Within the civil service, pressures will grow for better performance measures and merit pay. In economic ministries (customs, tax collection) employees will be allowed a share of additional revenues they generate. A variety of public-private hybrids will be created to facilitate financial incentives and competition while preserving public oversight.

These possibilities have received little research; indeed the problem of public sector incentives in developing countries seems not yet to have been noticed by scholars and aid agencies. This is odd, given that the field of economic development puts such emphasis on incentives in the private sector. We need to rectify this incentive myopia.

for civil servants to have "unexplained wealth," the ICAC found it hard to get errant employees dismissed from their jobs,[2] and the stiffest penalty ever meted out in an ICAC case was seven years in prison.[3] Justice Plana had trouble getting criminal penalties to be imposed. Few policymakers have the equivalent of the Korean Hopkido Association to batter those who step out of line.

Changing the Structure of the Principal-Agent-Client Relationship

Let us skip ahead on the framework for policymakers. The cases in this book displayed various means for reducing the agent's discretion and monopoly power vis-à-vis the client. To reduce opportunities for corruption between tax assessors and taxpayers, Justice Plana simplified tax laws to reduce the assessors' discretion. The gross income tax he proposed—a version of a flat tax—was passed after he left the BIR, with further reductions in discretion. Tax cases bigger than 100,000 pesos had to be referred to the central office, taking field officers out of big-ticket cases.

Another technique was demonstrated in Singapore. Customs agents worked in pairs, reducing their ability to deal one-on-one with clients. To diminish the opportunities for buddy-buddy relationships with clients, the Philippines' BIR rotated field agents every two years.

A more radical way to reduce discretion is to change the organization's product or mission. As Singapore allowed more products to enter duty free, it simultaneously reduced the scope of the Customs and Excise Department—and ended corruption involved in importing those products. Hong Kong halted illicit payments from bookies to police officers by legalizing off-track betting. Removing subsidies is another example. After Rafiq Shabir left the National Food Organization, his country became self-sufficient in wheat. By gradually decontrolling the price of wheat, the country greatly circumscribed the procurement and distribution roles of the National Food Organization—and greatly reduced corruption. These

2. *1980 Annual Report of the Commissioner of the Independent Commission Against Corruption*, 34, 39.

3. *1981 Annual Report of the Commissioner of the Independent Commission Against Corruption*, 36.

changes are instances of fighting corruption by turning over a government agency's functions to the market. (In some cases, this change may simply legalize corrupt pricing.)

An administrator may also try to organize the clients to give them countervailing power against corrupt officials, or to provide information on extortion, speed money, and other forms of corruption that hurt the client. The ICAC's Community Relations Department was an example of the latter.

Changing Attitudes Toward Corruption

The Philippines and Hong Kong cases illustrated two approaches. Justice Plana initiated "Reorientation Seminars" to try to convince his agents that corruption was wrong. The ICAC's Community Relations Department had a much broader mandate: to convince the public. This it attempted through a remarkable array of activities, ranging from TV dramas to posters and pedagogical materials for public schools.

Collecting and Analyzing Information

Now we may move back to the third category on the checklist. Gathering information raises the likelihood that corruption is detected and punished. I found this the most interesting set of policies in the cases. We saw examples of the gathering of direct evidence of corruption. In Singapore, anticorruption agents made spot checks of customs activities. Rafiq Shabir swooped in unannounced on rural food warehouses, looking for improprieties. Undercover agents and surveillance played key roles in fighting corruption in the Korean, Philippines, and Hong Kong cases.

The organizations also gathered and analyzed indirect evidence of corruption. The Hong Kong authorities carried out what might be called "vulnerability assessments." By analyzing information on procedures, control systems, and supervision, they hoped to find areas where corruption might occur. They also reviewed data for signs that corruption had actually occurred, as in the "red flag" system for tax assessors in the Philippines. In Hong Kong and Singapore, remarkable laws made it a crime for government officials to have "unexplained assets." Such assets were considered indirect evidence of corrupt activities—unless the official could prove otherwise. In the Philippines, intelligence officers scrutinized the life-styles and bank accounts of top officials, pinpointing suspiciously rich individuals whose activities would then be followed carefully.

Using basic record keeping, information and control systems, vulnerability assessments, and undercover agents, principals were trying to solve their informational problems vis-à-vis their agents. By tying rewards and penalties to the information thus gathered, policymakers could change the incentives facing agents, making corruption too risky to undertake.

I was fascinated by these informational strategies in part because they worked—not perfectly, and not cheaply, but they worked. Moreover, these policies seem feasible. Often policymakers cannot readily choose agents or change rewards and penalties or restructure organizations or alter agents' attitudes and ethical beliefs. Yet through a variety of informational measures they can make it more likely that agents' illicit activities are uncovered.

At a broader level information may be a key theoretical variable in understanding when and why corruption occurs. Put bluntly, corruption thrives on ignorance and uncertainty. Under such conditions the principal-agent problem is exacerbated. Corruption is less prevalent when ample information is available about what agents are doing and not doing.

It is precisely a lack of information—an abundance of ignorance and uncertainty—that characterizes the environment of many developing countries. Data are scarce and inaccurate. Markets do not work well or are not allowed to, so that one cannot count on the helpful informational properties of market prices. Information processing is weak: computers are less prevalent, educational systems poorer, learning abilities measurably lower. Underdeveloped regions or countries are weak in what might be called "organized intelligence." And so, without information, even if an administrator had the best of wills, the most abundant resources, and full political support, he or she would find it difficult to reduce corruption. Agents will correctly see that their illicit activities cannot be detected, and they will continue to be corrupt. Poor information is a major source of corruption, and better information is a partial cure.

But surely not a cure-all. Even in Hong Kong, where the ICAC had such awesome powers, corruption has not been eliminated; it even shows signs of a mild comeback. Plentiful information is not by itself sufficient: witness the resurgence of some corrupt activities in information-rich industrialized nations. But information is a key variable to keep in mind when fighting corruption. We should put ourselves in the shoes of the corrupt official. What informational footprints would we leave behind when committing the corrupt act? As policymakers, what steps can we take to track that information, analyze it, and use it to raise the chances that the corrupt are caught and punished?

Such forward-looking measures are part of a proactive approach to corruption. By designing informational devices to detect illicit activities, the policymaker can deter corrupt acts. The places where such information is most needed is where other anticorruption policies are not working or cannot be made to work—where one does not have the most dependable agents, where rewards and punishments are weak, where the agents have unavoidably large degrees of discretion and monopoly power over clients, and where the moral costs of illicit activity seem to be low.

IMPLICATIONS FOR THE STUDY OF CORRUPTION

The state of research on corruption is such that we have no inductive theory or statistical generalizations about the kinds of policies that work under particular conditions. What, then, can we take away from our case studies and conceptual work? We may derive some middle-level generalizations about policies to fight corruption—perhaps more in the nature of hypotheses than findings. (The discussion about information contains several.) We also have developed and applied a tentative framework for policy analysis, which may be used heuristically to structure discussions about appropriate measures and to guide further research.

Obviously a lot more research is needed. The following are a few areas that seem particularly important and susceptible to progress.

□ *Improving the framework for policy analysis.* Theoretical analyses of the principal-agent problem are promising. Economic models will be most helpful if they combine the positive and negative actions agents can take; include the costs of information-gathering systems; include both direct (outcomes) and indirect (efforts) measures of agents' productive and illicit activities; allow the reduction of agents' discretion through

Box 19 **Information and Incentives**

Information is the foundation of a good incentive system. One level further down is a clear definition of objectives. The logic of reform moves from objectives to information to incentives.

"Incentives can be a lot more than monetary," pointed out Ira Jackson, who as Commissioner of Revenue led Massachusetts' successful campaign against tax evasion and corruption. "A public manager has to recognize that.

"Our first step in creating useful incentives was to help work teams and individuals redefine their objectives. When a tax collector, for example, thinks of his job as the civilian equivalent of the state police, he starts to see things differently. Then if you provide him with the information to realize that he's a $500 a day man in terms of the revenue he generates for the state, you provide a powerful motivator. After you develop appropriate measures of performance and generate timely data, then you can offer a variety of incentives.

"You can give prizes and recognition letters. You can install in the hierarchy special management teams with perks like a regular lunch at the Ritz or a weekend retreat. Lots of things. And it turns out that people bust their tails for these seemingly small rewards.

"What's more, information itself can be a tremendous incentive for better performance. You give info to people in a large organization and it's like giving them dough. They know something they didn't before, how well they are doing. They are enfranchised."

rules and hierarchy; and include the selection of agents as part of the principal's problems.

More so than theories, policy frameworks need custom-tailoring to the needs, habits, and training of particular policymakers. There is no one "best" framework for policy analysis – this is true for corruption or for any other policy problem. More detailed frameworks could be developed for various types of corruption (collusion in procurement, tax *arreglos*, police corruption, internal fraud, and so forth) or various kinds of agencies (welfare, military, licensing, customs, and so forth).

□ *Identifying best practices for controlling corruption.* Some firms do better than others at controlling corruption; so, presumably, do some military procurement offices, some food distribution systems, and some tax systems. It would be helpful to know much more about these "successful performers," from which so much has been learned in the education, business, and most recently, development administration.[4]

More case studies, even of failures, would be valuable.[5] Theorists, too, may profit from specific cases. As Thomas C. Schelling wrote: "In my own thinking they have never been separate. Motivation for the purer theory came almost exclusively from preoccupation with (and fascination with) 'applied' problems; and the clarification of theoretical ideas was absolutely dependent on an identification of live examples."[6] Excellent candidates for detailed research include national anticorruption efforts, such as those under way in countries like Malaysia, Zambia, Nigeria, and Mexico.

□ *Studying the trade-offs between controlling corruption and creating red tape.* Corruption is one harmful aspect of underdevelopment; red tape is another. As I have emphasized, controlling corruption is not the only thing we care about, and anticorruption efforts entail indirect as well as monetary costs. How might these generalizations be better specified? Can we offer more guidance about the types of costs that particular types of anticorruption policies have entailed?

□ *Studying the abuse of anticorruption powers.* Anticorruption campaigns have sometimes been used to clean up political opponents rather than to clean up corruption. Anticorruption agencies such as Singapore's CPIB and Hong Kong's ICAC possess powers that would frighten most civil libertarians. In the wrong hands such organizations could degenerate into secret police or nefarious sources of repression. Which powers seem most subject to abuse? What countermeasures and safeguards can policymakers employ?

4. See, for example, Robert E. Klitgaard, "Identifying Exceptional Performers," *Policy Analysis* 4 (Fall 1978): 529–47; Robert E. Klitgaard and George R. Hall, "A Statistical Search for Unusually Effective Schools," in *Statistics and Public Policy*, ed. William Fairley and Frederick Mosteller (Reading, Mass.: Addison-Wesley, 1977), 51–86; Thomas J. Peters and Robert H. Waterman, Jr., *In Search of Excellence: Lessons from America's Best-Run Companies* (New York: Harper & Row, 1982); and Samuel Paul, *Managing Development Programs: The Lessons of Success* (Boulder, Colo.: Westview, 1982).

5. Robert Wade, "The System of Administrative and Political Corruption: Canal Irrigation in India," *Journal of Development Studies* 18 (April 1982): 287–327.

6. *The Strategy of Conflict* (Cambridge, Mass.: Harvard University Press, 1980), vi.

□ *Raising the moral costs of corruption through "corporate culture."* What are the relations between the extent and severity of illicit activities and an organization's culture?[7] Given that organizational culture is in part constrained by the task environment, what can policymakers do to manipulate that culture in order to reduce corruption? Empirically, what are the effects on illicit activities of codes of conduct, training programs, participatory management, and organizational "consciousness raising"?

IMPLICATIONS FOR DEVELOPMENT ADMINISTRATION

I hope that the topic and approach of this book may have implications for research on public management in developing countries. An overlooked area in the field often called "development administration" concerns what have been disparagingly called the "maintenance" functions of government—personnel, control, administrative reform, organizational design, and the like. In recent years development administration has instead emphasized the "developmental" functions of government, those having to do with economic growth and social equity.

As with other subfields of development studies, development administration has suffered from a certain diffuseness. Many writers on development administration have felt the label "administration" to be constraining. The subject had to include policy and politics; it had to cover nongovernmental organizations and popular participation. Indeed there was little that could be left out of this subject. Words like *holistic* became commonplace. Sterile debates arose over whether one or another approach "ignored" or "neglected" one or another "dimension." Some of the most distinguished scholars in development administration began to wonder whether anything useful was being accomplished.[8]

7. See, for example, Terrence E. Deal and Allan A. Kennedy, *Corporate Cultures: The Rites and Rituals of Corporate Life* (Reading, Mass.: Addison-Wesley, 1982); Gerald Mars, *Cheats at Work: An Anthropology of Workplace Crime* (London: George Allen & Unwin, 1982); and Stanley M. Davis, *Managing Corporate Culture* (Cambridge, Mass.: Ballinger, 1984).

8. See, for example, *Education and Training for Public Sector Management in Developing Countries*, Laurence D. Stifel, Joseph E. Black, and James S. Coleman, eds. (New York: The Rockefeller Foundation, 1977); John D. Montgomery, "The Populist Front in Rural Development: Shall We Eliminate the Bureaucrats and Get On with the Job?" *Public Administration Review* 39 (Jan.–Feb. 1979); and the sources cited in Robert E. Klitgaard, "On the Emergence of Public Policy Studies and Implications for Comparative Work," KSG Discussion Paper No. 114D, Kennedy School of Government, Harvard University, May 1982.

This book's topic, if one had to place it in one category or the other, better fits "maintenance" than "development administration." (Perhaps "public management" is a better label.) Notice, too, that the book's aims are practical rather than polemical, and that it looks at what works in real cases. Its concerns are similar to those who worry about control systems, management information systems, organizational design, even personnel. I hope this book has shown that at least one area of "maintenance"—the control of corruption—is full of practical and theoretical interest.

And yet, might not many other "maintenance" topics be relevant and intellectually vibrant? For instance, consider the management of integrated rural development (IRD). Would it not be valuable to examine IRD as a question of organizational design? What system of horizontal and vertical integration of functional and geographical activities is most efficient for rural development, under what circumstances? With few exceptions, the extensive literature on IRD, which is full of polemics, politics, and "learning models," has not grabbed hold of this central managerial question.[9]

Or consider another example: personnel selection systems. Personnel is not usually a topic of strong appeal to scholars of development. But once again, this area includes important matters, abounding in political and economic implications and interesting theoretical dimensions. Surely it is vital for the developing world to select able young men and women for public universities and for the civil service. How well do existing selection systems perform? How might "well" be defined in those cases? How should policies take account of the representation of minority groups, regions, women, the poor? And how should policies take into account the incentives created by the selection systems?[10]

My intent here is not to disparage but to exhort. I wish to draw attention to imbalances in the literature on management in developing countries. "Standard" topics of management—systems of information, incentives, and control; organizational design; personnel—have been neglected. The practical has often lost out to the conceptual and the

9. Exceptions include Vernon W. Ruttan, "Integrated Rural Development Programs: A Skeptical Perspective," *International Development Review* 17 (1975); Bruce F. Johnston and William C. Clark, *Redesigning Rural Development* (Baltimore: Johns Hopkins University Press, 1982).

10. Robert Klitgaard, *Elitism and Meritocracy in Developing Countries* (Baltimore: Johns Hopkins University Press, 1986).

Box 20 **Communism and Corruption**

Interesting research questions surround corruption in the communist and hard socialist countries of the developing world. Data are scarce, but internal reports and domestic anticorruption campaigns indicate that corruption is a large and perhaps growing problem in many countries. On the eve of the 1986 anniversary of the start of the communist revolution in Cuba, Fidel Castro condemned corruption after listening to the complaints of workers and young communists. A recent report on Angola concluded: "The two-thirds of Angolans who are under the age of 25 have known nothing in life but barter and graft. There is little sign they are about to learn more." A Chinese magazine widely distributed in the Third World featured a frank article on China's "fight against corruption."

> Cases were revealed of fraud, misuse of public funds, accepting and offering bribes, searching for personal benefits, contraband, and tax evasion. It has also been observed that some youths with fathers or relatives in important positions dedicated themselves to robbery, violent attacks, and even rape, because their relatives would protect them.

Soon after assuming office, Tanzanian leader Ali Hassan Mwinyi lectured senior government officials on the "breakdown of the system" because corruption was "alarmingly present," and he promised a war against "oppression, theft, corruption, and other deeds." The leader of Vietnam's communist party told a party congress in October 1986: "Corruption is seriously eroding people's confidence in the party." He called on the people and the party to "eliminate degenerate and deviant elements who are corrupt, who steal public property, who engage in criminal collusion, who take bribes, who persecute good people and protect bad ones, and who aid speculators and smugglers." According to a recent article in the Vietnamese army daily, tens of thousands of party members have been expelled for corruption in recent years.

Western critics find corruption a natural result of communism's allocation by the state and lack of political and economic competition. Yet we might predict less corruption in communist states because of the potentially powerful tools (party, secret police) available for selecting agents, raising penalties, gathering information, and changing attitudes. "Most communist regimes make it hard for their boss to amass a Swiss bank account, but most prudent right-wing dictators like to have one for their retirement, which is one reason their subjects grow keen for them to retire."

One set of research questions, then, pertains to the extent and pattern of corruption in communist states. A second set, more in the spirit of this book, involves the prospects and problems of anticorruption initiatives there. Issues of incentives, citizen involvement, and the control of abuse in anticorruption campaigns would be particularly interesting to study.

Sources: Cuba: BBC World Service, 25 July 1986. Angola: *The Economist*, 30 August 1986, 34. China: Yi Xu, "La Corrupción: Por Qué Ocurre y Qué Se Hace para Combatirla," *China Construye* 27 (May 1986), 25, my translation. Tanzania: BBC World Service, 20 July 1986 and 3 August 1986. Vietnam: Murray Hiebert, "Soon a Crucial Congress in Vietnam," *International Herald Tribune*, 13 November 1986, 4, quoting Truong Chinh. Swiss accounts: *The Economist*, 8 November 1986, 49.

polemical. Case studies have diminished in frequency and utility. I hope the approach of this book provides a suggestive counterexample.

IMPLICATIONS FOR DEVELOPMENT STUDIES

Some of these observations are valid for development studies more generally. More case studies, more work with a practical bent, more studies of success would be welcome. I would add two other points related to the present volume.

First, I have indicated at several points my suspicion that information is a central variable in "underdevelopment." This idea has a descriptive aspect: the countries worst off on indices of "quality of life" are—I hypothesize—also the worst off in terms of the quantity and quality of data, information-processing skills, "intelligence" in the psychologist's sense, and, consequently, ignorance and uncertainty.

My suspicion may also have theoretical importance. Poor information leads to the exacerbation of the principal-agent problem, which leads not only to greater corruption but also to problems in making middle-sized and large organizations viable. Poor information can lead to "adverse selection" in markets, where poorer quality tends to drive out better quality, leading to the erosion of standards of quality and also the systematic malfunctioning of markets.[11] Poor information about individuals' past performance and future capabilities stimulates the use of group labels, like race and sex and tribe, for informational purposes; and this in turn can lead to discrimination and the reinforcement of group differences. Poor information leads to greater uncertainty, which leads to greater risk-aversion, conservatism, and unwillingness to change. These problems define some central features of "underdevelopment": ineffective large organizations; eroding standards of quality; malfunctioning markets; racial, sexual, and tribal discrimination; and resistance to change. Thus, *information* may play a central role in understanding underdevelopment and improving development policy.

My second point harkens back to the dual definitions of corruption—one of them full of moral overtones, the other more clinical. I observed that the study of corruption was itself affected by this duality. Many scholars shied away from the clinical or practical problem—how to curtail improper inducements offered to officials—for fear of accusing corruption-plagued countries of immorality or depravity, and the scholars themselves bringing accusations of ethnocentrism or worse upon themselves. At the same time the relatively rare studies of corruption could not seem to break away from grandiose, ethically loaded questions—from general issues of harm and social causes—and get down to specifics or the actual practice of corruption control. I argued that these understandable reactions left a gap in the literature: corruption was underemphasized and, when given any treatment at all, was discussed in excessively general or moralistic terms.

These points have parallels elsewhere in the study of developing countries. The plight of the world's disadvantaged nations and peoples has an inescapable moral and ethical dimension. One finds in many developing countries shocking violations of human rights; blatant racism, sexism, and tribalism; widespread exploitation; and stark injustices in the distribution of power and wealth. How do we react to these phenomena? Many students and professors avoid them altogether simply by avoiding the field itself. As with corruption, they may feel a kind of embarrassment. Subconsciously, they may suspect that studying these problems would inevitably lead to the conclusion that others are some-

11. George A. Akerlof, "The Market for 'Lemons' . . . ," *Quarterly Journal of Economics* 84 (August 1970): 488–500.

how "inferior," or in part to be "blamed" for their underdeveloped circumstances – something one would never want to say. Or they may have the nagging sense that the problems are hopeless. This may explain why remarkably few people nowadays study policy problems in developing countries.

At the same time, many people who do enter development studies tend to work and do research at a high level of abstraction. They may express a wish to "raise consciousness" about the gravity of the problems, the need for fundamental changes of various kinds, or the interconnectedness of all possible dimensions of underdevelopment. Research and teaching are thereby distorted toward polemics and stylized description. Discussions of the problems of poor countries tend to omit some of the "embarrassing" aspects, such as ethnic problems or human rights.[12] The analysis of causes of underdevelopment is skewed toward the exogenous instead of what is endogenous to a country or region, toward the misbehavior of the privileged instead of the shortcomings of the underprivileged, toward physical rather than human factors. The analysis of practical policies is shortchanged. One finds in the literature little about how to do better in human rights or to overcome ethnic inequalities or to reduce exploitation. If "policies" are mentioned, they are as general and vague as "promoting justice," "giving the issue priority," or "fomenting revolutionary change."

My point is not that these reactions are invalid, for they are not. Nor do I wish surgically to separate the moral and the clinical questions of underdevelopment. We have much to learn about how to think about and deal with moral aspects of underdevelopment, with depravity as well as deprivation. It is precisely these aspects to which I wish to turn my own attention in subsequent research and service.

But I do insist that these reactions have led to distortions and gaps in the study of developing countries. Some of the hardest questions are avoided for fear of their "moral content." If dealt with at all, they are treated at a general level, with little attention to how real policymakers might do better. And yet, as I hope this book suggests, we *can* advance understanding, and even accomplish some practical good, by bracketing

12. Interestingly, those who stress human rights often underemphasize the distribution of wealth and power and vice versa.

moral judgments about underdevelopment and thinking harder about what can be done in practice.

This bracketing process does not capture, nor does it try to capture, what one *feels* about corruption: the sense of disgust expressed at a December 1984 rally in Panama City, with signs reading "Down with Official Corruption" and "Out with the Corrupt," or the alienation expressed in this account, written to me by one of my research assistants after a trip home to study corruption:

> The all-encompassing corruption modes have created "pet" services. Those government services which directly present opportunities for cuts/bribes etc. are most preferred by fresh entrants to the civil service. An acquaintance of mine threw an engraved invitation dinner to celebrate his success in the civil service examination. After the grand dinner was over, elated by his success he said, "I shall follow my brother into the Customs group." The audience could well understand why. The brother at a basic pay of $125 per month had been able to provide two cars, a big house and all the grandeur.
>
> The widespread corruption is resulting in social repercussions of an economic phenomenon. Corruption has been accepted into the society. No longer is there any stigma attached to it. No doubt lip service is paid to extol the virtues of an Islamic Society free from all vices but the effect remains till the sound of the words.
>
> The acceptance of corruption has created an interesting situation. Everyone finds himself entrapped in a vicious circle of corruption. The word is "money." It is possible to obtain anything, it is only a matter of having enough money to pay for it. So you strive for the-other-kind-of-money. What counts socially is the type of job where you can make money. You run private (often illegal) errands for your boss and his wife; you keep your influential relatives happy; you stand a lot of nonsense from your big shot friends; all in hope of a future when you shall be in their place.

Something is *wrong* in societies where corruption takes over. And just so, something is wrong when great wealth coexists with squalor, when human rights are squashed, or when racism denies our common humanity. We should not lose this sense of moral violation. But as we reflect on questions of why, we should also do our best on questions of how. We should not yield to the temptation to escape from the hardest and most ethically loaded problems on the grounds there is nothing we can do about them. For as I hope this book shows with regard to corruption, policymakers and citizens are not helpless. There *are* things we can do about even this most difficult of problems. At least this practical and normative assumption should drive more of our work on the problems of the poorer nations.

Index

Designer: Mark Ong
Compositor: Harrison Typesetting, Inc.
Text: 10/12 Berkeley Book
Display: Berkeley Old Style

9 780520 074088